THE
JOURNEY

J.D.

Copyright © 2023 J.D.
All rights reserved
First Edition

NEWMAN SPRINGS PUBLISHING
320 Broad Street
Red Bank, NJ 07701

First originally published by Newman Springs Publishing 2023

All scripture quotations herein are from the Holy Bible, authorized King James version. The right of the University of Cambridge to print and sell the book was granted by the Honorable Henry the VIII in 1534. All such text is preexisting in the public domain.

ISBN 978-1-68498-281-3 (Paperback)
ISBN 978-1-68498-282-0 (Digital)

Printed in the United States of America

To Jesus, Daphine Matthews,
LaTonya Smith, Gene P. Kindle,
Vernon Holmes, Tony Matthews,
Pastor Robert D. McSwain,
and all JD *offspring*.

The Journey

John D. Simpson, an African-American political prisoner, was thirty four years old, gainfully employed, and born on February 28, 1942, in Fayetteville, North Carolina. While enroute to New York from Lexington, North Carolina, he was stopped several times by local law enforcement officials, then arrested and convicted—whose sentences span over four decades and counting—in the Commonwealth of Virginia, as a first time offender. Will you venture to read the journey?

Several years later, I met Robert D' L. Carlos McSwain (a.k.a. Minister Brother MC) during one of his and his wife's Essence of Love Gospel Ministry programs conducted in the chapel at Powhatan Correctional Center. Over time, Minister MC became my spiritual advisor. Upon discussing my criminal case with him, he communicated that he was not a bleeding heart soft on crime nor voting criminal behavior citizen. He told me contrary to that he and his wife raised three daughters, one son, and great-great-grandchildren that have grownup and others must yet grow up in this Commonwealth of Virginia/world, and he continued to say it is frightening to think what could happen to them. Or the effect on them being compulsorily exposed academically or socially to such, perhaps admixture of

God opposed, by in large selfish, often time violent, uncaring societal effect may have on either one or all of them.

As days elapse into spent annals of time, I started to trust Minister MC sufficient enough to send copies of my original indictment and court trial transcribed records, totaling eight hundred-plus pages of evidence. After perusing the said trial transcripts, Minister MC communicated to me that he was inspired to become involved, although he is quite the advocate of: if you do the crime, then you should do the fair required amount of time. But he also believed in justice, fairness, equity, truth, and the established principle standard of law that, in essence, states, a man, woman, teenager or child, charged with a crime in America (i.e., Commonwealth of Virginia) must be presumed innocent until proven guilty beyond a reasonable doubt, in the presence of a fair and impartial judge or jury of their peers, according to our guaranteed right to due process of law, under Amendment 14 of the United States Constitution. These are a few of the reasons why, after having met, then became spiritual pen pals with me from the eighty ties to date. Also, after receipt, and having thoroughly considered most of the above transcribed evidence, plus my forty-six-year long legal plight, pleadings, letters written, and responses received from fee paid lawyers, such as Tom Sum, Amin, Will Rob, and Lawyer Jack, license defense attorneys, who extracted my family's money, only to sit on my case or submitted out-of-time statute of limitations, time barred habeas corpus pleadings, over periods of two to five years each.

Minister MC told me that it is his belief that my original transcribed indictment and trial recorded evidence attests to the truthfulness of my maintained innocence plea and suggested that we pray and meditate about God's revealed will and the Holy Ghost affixed message in the book of Psalms 103:6, "The Lord executes righteousness and judgment for all that are oppressed." Upon completion of our meditation and prayers, we determined that you, the public tax-paying citizens, should become the fair and impartial jury that I never had in the Circuit Court of Halifax County, Virginia, as the true story emanates from this eyewitness, John David Simpson, throughout the below pages.

Chapter 1

I was born in Fayetteville, North Carolina, on February 28, 1942, to parents Mrs. Blanche E. Boone Simpson and Mr. Robert Simpson. My father's dad and mother, Robert and Mrs. Leslie Simpson, homestead on approximately two hundred-plus acres of farmland located seventeen or so miles from Fayetteville, in Saint Paul, North Carolina (Roberson County), just beyond Toko Mo. My mother's Mom, Mrs. Jannie L. Boone (husband deceased), and her mother lived several miles from Toko Mo general area on six or seven acres, surrounded by pine, maple, oak, pecan, black walnut trees, and grape orchards. My grandmother Leslie being a devout Christian/retired schoolteacher required everyone to be seated around the huge mahogany conference looking dining room table, prior to every meal and that everyone be prepared to cite a Bible verse. My mother's mom Jannie and my great-grandmother Georgia Spearman became spinster widows after their husband's death, and as I recall, at the time, when a male factor came calling, they were shown the elaborately placed wooden swing adorning their in-the-woods two-bedroom home, which had no plumbing yet! All the comforts and the best hand pumped pure well water in America.

I had five uncles and two aunts on my dad's side, namely Hobson, William, Edward, Perry, and Alton, together with Aunty

J.D.

Lillian and O'desa Simpson. Neither JD's dad or they possessed any love for working those farm fields—containing seemingly one-hundred-acre rows of tobacco, corn, cotton, green string beans, beets, squash, butter beans, pinto beans, cabbage, okra, various types of melons, potatoes, beets, apples, peaches, pecan, walnut trees, plum and grape vineyards, huge smelly hen chicken houses, hogpens, low pastures, and barn, the place they heat cured cropped tobacco. The tobacco, cotton, apples, peaches, plums, and various vegetables was transported to Raleigh, North Carolina, by mule driven wagons to be auctioned, several times per year. Such auction trips were also under taken in old model T Ford trucks, one required a hand frontal crank and the other a two- to four-inch coil round wire starter post, located inside on the driver side, to activate the motor.

On JD's mother side of the family was Uncle Theodore Spearman (i.e., brick mason) and his wife, plus one other aunt who bore the name Aunt Treva. Soon after 1949, my uncle's distaste for the farm lifestyle compelled the oldest Hobson onto becoming an undertaker at Steve Rogers Funeral Home in Fayetteville, North Carolina. My dad, the second oldest, was to become an interstate black tar topping highway construction foreman. The third oldest, Uncle William, was to become a hot rod car builder/moonshine runner until he opened Simpson's Janitorial Services, among other businesses in Philadelphia. Uncle Edward, the fourth oldest, attended college in Durham, North Carolina, then became a Christian minister teaching about life after death, plus sin, in accordance with the gospel message of his Lord Jesus Christ. Uncle Perry, the fifth oldest (my favorite), joined the United States Air Force. But after he married and moved to Fayetteville, North Carolina, he began to purchase real estate, some with houses thereon, and house trailers which he placed along Murchison road, Nicky Avenue, North Hills, and other localities to rent out. Uncle Alton, the sixth and youngest, enlisted in the Navy, married and settled in North Philadelphia, not far from Aunt Lillian who had also married and relocated in West Philadelphia.

At the turn of 1950, my father had begun laying black top from Siler City up Route 38 to Lexington, North Carolina. My mother had predetermined that my dad was not to get more than one hundred miles away from home, unless he established a home for the family in the proximity of one hundred miles in the direction the job would carry him. My father owned a five-ton dump truck and a tractor trailer rig, which he loaded the furniture and family into, to relocate the family in Lexington, North Carolina. The first month in Lexington, our family seemed to occupy one complete floor of an east side boarding house until my dad registered my older brother Robert Jr., older sister Lucile, and me in the segregated Dunbar Elementary School, with grades 1 through 8 located on North Fourth Street, Lexington, North Carolina. My baby sister Lillian was in kindergarten. At this time, my family had moved into a home on North Railroad Street within half block of the aforementioned school.

Unlike my grandparents homes in Saint Paul, North Carolina, that was located in the center of acres of land with self-sustaining food/water supply and a mile or so separating every home. My family's home on North Railroad Street was flanked by other single family homes with approximately twelve to twenty-one yards between each, with a busy railroad and trains that ran North and South affixed about one hundred yards behind our home. Also, there was a red clay with rock embankment etched in with bushes and grass, which captivated my attention after school. Soon afterward, my family settled there, a neighboring African American girl named Mamie Payne befriended me, and we developed routine after school play wherein we collected large empty discarded card board boxes to build a play tree house, as well as to slide down the grassy slope an extension of Mamie and my backyard. plus, down the steep declining railroad banks from time to time.

A note about my school teachers who possessed wooden or plastic paddles and a profound interest in their pupils' learning, reading writing, math, grammar, language, geography, French and business education. Mrs. Mosbly, my language instructor, assigned me a role in that *Romeo and Juliet* play by Shakespeare, plus, a shepherds role in the years' end story about Jesus. I also enrolled in the school glee club and learned to sing second tenor. This was a time where my ability to learn flourished and the place that my home upbringing taught me respect for my neighbors opinions, property, person, plus the importance of not lying became fortified.

The year was 1950. I was seven years old and in the second grade. While I was in class, my schoolteacher instructed me to report to Ms. Hargrave, Dunbar Elementary School principal who told me to collect my things because my mother needed me to come home. Immediately, I collected my books, adorned my coat, and exited the front doors, but took the short path that led through Ms. Moore's, my math teacher, property then through Mrs. Minnie Payn's connecting yard. Thus, within minutes, I was entering our front door. My mom was always a family stay-at-home mother for my older brother Robert Jr. (age ten), older sister Lucile (age eight), baby sister Lillian (age six), and I gathered around my mother. She interjected that my father had driven his truck home for lunch—complaining that he had a headache. My father ingested a BC powder, drank a Coca-Cola, then returned to the site on Route 38, where he and his work crew were lying black tar—far the highway just beyond Burlington, North Carolina, coming east. But not long after my father departed, one of his coforeman traveled to my mother and informed her that my dad had undergone a stroke, which ended his life. Later, Dr. Bing—the family physician—explained that my father was suffering with untreated hypertension. We wept right much. Within a day or so, my uncle Perry and William arrived at our home in Lexington made arrangements to transport my father's body and us back to Saint Paul, North Carolina.

Notwithstanding, my mother advised her in-law family members that she (we) would indeed go back to bury my father in the family burial place located in the rear of the Second New Light Church, but that she was not going to take us out of school. Instead, my father's family would remain housed in Lexington, North Carolina. As I recall, the family on both sides, assembled to put my father in the earth. It was such a grievous mourning. Only recalling those times and/or details are too painful still.

THE JOURNEY

However, worthy of noting. Before my dad fell asleep, my brother Robert Jr. had a *Lexington Dispatch News* paper route, and I had taken portions of the load of papers to help complete that days' delivery quicker. Note upon our bicycle ride home, my brother decided he would smoke a camel cigarette from a pack he retained on his person. Arriving home, we went into the basement. Meanwhile, unknown to us, Daddy's dump truck appeared in the yard, and our father practically jumped out to investigate the smoke that was emitting through one of the basement windows. Whereupon entering the basement door, he saw Junior puffing the cigarette. I bailed hastily up the staircase and ran/dive slid on my stomach upon the hardwood floor, beneath our bunk bed, while my father, with belt in hand, chased me. Thank God for my mother's intervention. With my sweet mom running interference, my dad commenced an about-face as he proceeded back to the basement with a whole carton of camel cigarettes in hand, sat them before Robert Jr. with an order for Junior to smoke every one of them before leaving his seat in that basement. The day after burying my father, my favorite Uncle Perry drove us back to Lexington. Instantly, the family that our Pop's physical presence guided, realized his absence, in that all the decision-making, plus provision responsibility, was inherited by Mother who also was our very best friend. Notwithstanding, however challenging my mom/father and friend's role was Mother never complained, and we never had known concern regarding the roof over our heads. Neither food, clothing, nor shoes for our feet, or money because of my dad's long-range vision and elaborate goal-oriented future preparation along his path for our family's well-being.

Afterward, during spring school break, my mother offered and I accepted the awesome privilege to spend the entire summer months down home that is to say at my grand/great-grandmother's modest no indoor plumbing home located in Saint Paul, North Carolina (i.e., Toko Mo), a region of Robeson County, North Carolina. This was a memorable time, too extensive to record herein. Though it will suffice to say that it proved to be an additional learning experience involving wisdom of the loving adult relative versus the finite views and the inquisitive mind of a seven year older. At the onset, I learned firsthand how to water prime/extract water from and outside the house well with a hand pump, collect eggs from beneath cackling hens, milk a cow, slop feed hogs/pigs, ride a huge mule, run in and out of hot smelly tobacco-curing barns, pick wet dew-drenched green beans, watch a mule pull a plow, eat apples from the back of a horse, build vine-riddled tree houses, and attempt to pick dew-saturated cotton, which quickly convinced me that that was not something (i.e., picking cotton) I desired to embrace as a lifetime skill.

Notwithstanding when my grandmother Jannie placed her black steel skillet over the kitchen hearth's open flame and prepared hoecakes (i.e., similar to pancakes, only better with crispy outer regions…humph!), grits with perfectly sliced fat back pork side for breakfast, and a touch of Grandma's molasses overlay just seem to make everything so deliciously all right.

That summer, I frequented going to Grandma Leslie's and my uncles' on my father's side. I equally became content with the meaningful daily chores Granny would ask me to do. Having thoroughly enjoyed doting in and out the grape vineyard, building white clay alike sand castles, walking dusty, brandishing visible waves of heat roads, and sitting at Grandma Jannie's feet as she literally preserved apples, pears, peaches, and grape jelly in clear, see-through jars that were stored in the walk, in pantry. Plus, seeing her exit the ham-curing smokehouse with huge snakes in her hands, as well as collecting walnuts from beneath the tree located in the front yard. That summer began to close, and Grandma Jannie placed numerous gallon jars filled with silver dollars, other change, and paper money into my grip, money enough to purchase all my clothes and school supplies for the year.

CHAPTER 2

Fast-forward, if memory serves, grades 1 through 7 at Dunbar Elementary School yielded As and B averages as I interacted with my older sister Lucile who was a straight-A student. She was especially helpful with homework. By 1957, Lucile had transitioned onto grade 9 and I to grade 8 at segregated Dunbar High School. My older brother Robert Jr., then sixteen, had retired from school after holding coveted position of captain in the school corridor, monitoring and street crossing patrol. He started a prosperous lawn and shrubbery grooming business, which I partook in after school, as well as all day on Saturdays, taking in extra finance. Besides, I loved to hang with Junior who taught me how to drive his on the column gear shift Henry J. Still, at that time, Lucile and I had to ride the city transit bus from East Fourth and Railroad Street to Smith Avenue to and from segregated Dunbar High School.

Upon entering Dunbar High School, I noticed that the academic curriculum I'd become accustomed to became radically altered, adding different challenges (i.e., arithmetic transitioned into algebra/calculus). Then the add-on of business education, science, biology, advance English/French, history/sociology, physical education (football, basketball, baseball, track and field, and volleyball), and the school glee club. Science and biology were required subjects, which was taught by Mr. David Moose, an eloquent and scholarly well-polished African American scholar, particularly with regard Darwin's evolution theory. A subject every student was compelled to engage, learn, and successfully pass as it dealt with one of two major position that in my respectful opinion, sets forth conjecture that claims this present world developed as a result of the big bang theory and/or the human race sprang forth from a monkey and overtime evolved into mankind, absent establish fact or evidence matter.

Moreover, I personally reason that this aforesaid evolution theory (i.e., the State of North Carolina compelled us to learn) that I was taught and accepted (at that time) unquestionably managed to breed and continues to breed selfishness with the tint of covetous practices, resulted in my learning little or nothing of value! I raise the question "What is anything without love?" Thitherto, the theory about evolving from an ape removed any possibility of that because for all intents and purposes, the ape's brain was not created with the ability to evaluate, deduce, or that in my respectful opinion sets forth conjecture that claims this present world developed as a result of the big bang theory and/or the human race sprang forth from a monkey and overtime evolved into mankind, absent establish fact or evidence matter.

Meanwhile, new friends such as Johnny (Coltrain) Watson, Billy Roman, Roslyn Transuer, Betsy Welborne, Wade Matthews, Roy Lee Holt, Daisey Black Brown, Elizabeth (Lib) Carson, Earl Kellar, Elwood Brown, Little Betty Mock, and others constituted members of my academic class and social life. Plus, my very best friend Johnny (Coltrane) Watson, Wade Matthews, Roy L. Holt, and I tried out for and earned major starting positions on the Dunbar Blue Devil Double A, segregated, four consecutive years in a row, undefeated champion football team. Also under the expert guidance/instruction/design of Coach Ingram, Wade became the Blue Devils full back, plus alternate QB. Roy Lee, who could accurately throw the pig skin (i.e., football) the length of the football field on target, was designated quarterback, while my best friend Johnny (i.e., Coltrain) became the premiere right half back. I became starting left half back and also played defensive safety position. Johnny and I became inseparable friends, notwithstanding the fact Johnny live on the outskirts of the Twin City, Winston, Salem, North Carolina, some fifteen or so miles from Lexington.

What's more important was neither Johnny nor I ever spoke a word of profanity nor used any sort of alcoholic beverage nor cigarettes. We trained religiously daily after school, yes, of course! During scheduled football practices by taking and giving football hand-offs, blocking, running designed routes, and catching passes, together with several five-mile runs uptown and across Lexington and back, both Johnny and I joined the track and field team that competed with other schools one per year in Durham, North Carolina. I maintained my after school trade of cutting folks lawns, sometimes fields all over Lexington, which, more often than not, required me to invest two days to cut and manicure Dr. Foil and Dr. Bingham's lawn/shrubbery, flowerbeds, and pick-up nonscheduled smaller lawns in route along Fairview Drive and East Center Street in Lexington, North Carolina.

In addition, my older brother Robert Jr. had begun to work at the Lexington Chair Factory located on Raleigh Road, just beyond its bridge, from 7:00 a.m. to 4:00 p.m. He also worked part time at the city's Caucasian segregated country club on Country Club Drive from about 5:00 p.m. until closing—around midnight or 2:00 a.m.

The year 1957 culminated with the Blue Devils football team going undefeated. Reminiscing, I cannot recall whether my mother took on a job at the Lexington Memorial Hospital in 1958 or 1959, but she did over the objections of the lot of her children because we could not understand the need. I joined the work force craze (at age fifteen while in the tenth grade). I applied and was hired to be the busboy/dishwasher at the newly erected Howard John Restaurant located on West Center Street Ext., adjacent to Interstate I-95 and 301 highways, which catered only to Caucasians. Note: If African Americans desired to purchase one of its fifty different-flavored ice creams or other food sustenance, they were required to stand at the back kitchen entrance to both place and pick-up said order.

J.D.

My job responsibilities at this restaurant found me sitting upon a pillow, under the steering wheel of my brother's second automobile, an A model T Ford, where the gear shift in neutral position, with my right leg and foot extended down, depressing a coil spring-loaded floor starter. Once the motor began to run, I slowly backed out onto North Railroad, and headed down West Center Street, passing by Court House Square, then the Lexington Police Station, on through a Caucasian-littered neighborhood, furniture factory just across the railroad track on the right, and a cleaner, service station, just inside the stoplight. Mind you, I had no driver's license (learner's permit only) but was well-loved and highly respected by much of the police (i.e., because, I suppose, they all supported Dunbar Blue Devils Championship football Team), who believed I was conscientious and would take necessary safety precautions, both en route to work and return therefrom. I always took the direct route there and back. My goal was to purchase an automobile.

The year 1958 found me in the tenth grade at Dunbar High School. My grades were not what they could or should've been—averaging B and C plus general math, English, history, and biology subjects. Yet I got A in business and typing execution under Mrs. Lg. Added to this, a new girl and her family moved into the neighborhood on North Railroad Street, just after my mom moved up on the hill off East Second Avenue, whose backyard ran just below the Simpson's (JD) uphill driveway. And new girl caught my attention with her South Carolina Country tone and nicely shape bow legs growing out through her ankles. I was found often at their back door attempting to befriend the young lady. But she would never formally commit, although at that time, I had become one of about fourteen Red Letterman of the Dunbar Blue Devil's undefeated squad. It did not matter because the new neighborhood girl had cast her eyes on a member of our high school basketball team. That was also well-coached by the highly esteemed Coach Ingram.

Before spring school break, I being extremely shy yet interested in spending time with the attractive true red bone who was slender and quite beautiful. Therefore, I confided in the advice of my good friend Lucile (my older sister) concerning my interests in the above mentioned young lady. Lucile advised me to personally voice my interests to the slender beauty, then wait for her response. I did so and found favor sufficient to be invited to her home located one street away from North Main and East Center Street, only three blocks from my home. That visit an a few others eventually led to the slender beauty and I going steady.

The following spring break, my older Robert Jr. has become one of the topnotch upcoming business men while adorning special tailor crafted suits, top hat, and shiny wingtip shoes had recently bought a powder-blue 1949 Eighty Eight Oldsmobile with positive traction rear end. Junior was dating one of three cream of the crop sisters (lookers). One weekend, I literally pleaded with Junior to give me a ride, along on one of his Friday night outings. It was the night he'd taken this cream of the crop sister on a date. After Junior picked her up at her mother's home, they cruised Lexington for a spell and arrived at a drive-in night spot operated by Mr. Oscar located on Raleigh Road. Junior accelerated his Olds into a fish tail, circle spin after entering the large red-dirt clay lot beside Oscar's place. A night spot where Junior and others showed off their ladies and stylist automobiles. I exhaled after hearing the roaring deep-toned echoing sound that emitted from those sweet exhaust mufflers on that seemingly—one of a kind Oldsmobile 88. I instantly fell in love with that car. After parking there, Junior said something to his girlfriend, then appear to have smote her on the cheek with his open palm. To my surprise, his girlfriend likewise uttered return verbal comments, then smote Junior upon his face with her open hand just as he exited the driver's side. After the awkward exchange, seemingly confused moment, I asked the young lady if she was okay. She replied yes. I decided to exit that sweet hollow-sounding 1949 Oldsmobile as I headed home, which was only three blocks if I cut through the small graveyard, then proceeded up Railroad Street onto Second Avenue, then up our driveway.

The day afterward, Saturday, to my dismay, I found that my evening shift at the Howard Johnson establishment was not yield-

J.D.

ing the finances I expected. It seemed the restaurant withheld more taxes (i.e., they said) than my pay yielded weekly! By midsummer, my brother, manning two jobs, managed to open several shoeshine with top hat molding/styling small businesses. One on Main Street downtown Lexington and the other at the corner of East Fourth Street and North Pine. I served two-week notice at Howard Johnson restaurant but began opening my brother's hat styling/shoeshine parlor on North Main Street, where I earned more money than I made working for the restaurant.

Mostly, I worked Saturday and Sundays after 11:00 a.m. on account that my mother mandated church for my two sisters and me. Moreover, at the First Baptist Church located between North Pugh and Pine Streets. I would tarry an hour in Bible study and afterward proceeded upstairs to partake in the main Pastor Tinsely's message. The church stood directly in the rear of my classmate's and friend's parents' home. Although I could never understand a word Minister Tinsley preached. Why? The hocking and yelling made word discernment difficult. Therewith, I went to the Sunday-compelled worship combined with Easter and Christmas rituals, which my neighbors and I performed without asking questions.

After church, I adorned in work jean and apron apparel headed uptown to my brother's hat/brim styling shoe shine parlor. Business was good with tips. Plus my academic grades promoted me to grade 11 at Dunbar High with the Blue Devils boasting yet! Another undefeated football season, as was highlighted by the Lexington, North Carolina, dispatch newspaper. Noting that sitting in the back posture for African Americans/youngsters while riding the city Trailways or Greyhound bus continued. Also, I recall that a young male African American neighbor whose name was Oscar, several pounds heavier and much taller than me, decided to bully me on our return school bus journey. In our midst came other school and neighborhood associates namely Herman, Albert, plus other by sitters etching Oscar on. Upon exiting the bus, Oscar up close walked, talking trash to me for a distance, down the hill on Railroad Street, past Albert's and Herman's houses until we reached my driveway.

THE JOURNEY

Wow! I thought. Bystanders bolstered Oscar's courage. Though I was no brawler, I knew that I would be required to reckon with my bro Junior if ever he caught wind that I chose to walk away from the bully who had inherited a huge sump saddle in the center of his long head. Then and there, I told Oscar I would return after going home to remove my school clothes, including the white turtleneck letterman pullover. I returned, sharply descending to the bottom of our driveway, where Oscar shoved me. Then it was on! After about five to eight minutes of fist exchanges, the standby children stepped in when they recognized the bully was receiving the worse end of the blows thrown in that matter. I knew not that I'd defeated the bully until the following day while seeing the bully climb aboard wearing sunglasses on the 7:30 a.m. bus ride to school. Oscar hardly looked up or glanced at me, but someone was kidding him and snatched off his large-frame sunglasses to reveal he'd sustained two black eyes from the altercation he instigated into blows with me the day before. There was never a word from Oscar to date.

Back at Dunbar High School, the year is 1959. I am an eleventh-grade junior amid a tight-knit loyal body of student peers. Johnny (Cold Train) Watson and I have grown closer as friends with our left and right half back positions safely in our grasp. Johnny had begun driving by often to pick me up in his brother William's 1957 two-door hard-top brown and gold Chevy with continental spare tire rear rack setup—a very unique and classy ride. Sometime, Johnny drove this automobile to school, which our young girlfriends piled into during lunch as we headed to the nearby snack shop, the Du Drop Inn located a couple of blocks from Dunbar High on Holt Street. There, we ordered the specialty, a famous tiny burger that was a little larger than a hamburger, plus hot dogs, dressed. Then it was back to Dunbar's grind.

I enrolled in arts and craft where I enjoyed fashioning, sanding, stain brush, blotted and oftentimes varnished the upright four- to five-foot bookshelves, coffee tables, bookends, and other woodwork that we were ordered to make throughout that course. Mine went to my beautiful mother, Blanch Simpson.

J.D.

I've put away some money in a Lexington State Bank savings account but need a little more to enable me to pay cash for the automobile I'm eyeing. To accomplish this, a nearby neighbor name James helped me secure an 11:30 p.m. to 7:00 a.m. second shift job at the Lexington Memorial Hospital as a nurse aid/orderly. There, my duties consisted of inserting enemas, emptying bed pans/urinals, taking regular pulse/rectal temperatures, also sterilizing operating and delivery room equipment, as well as maintained the coal-operated boiler room, with its two large and one small hot water supply boiler units. This required manual labor as I shovel and scoop coal from the spacious basement coal bin beneath the hospital dining area into those boilers, whose pressure gauges required consistency. Plus, the boiler's ashes had to be removed as needed with the same shovel and deposited in a makeshift drum, which I lifted/raised from the basement boiler room, then tying off/securing the raised ash barrel (i.e., a one-man operation) to allow me to dot run up the staircase pass through the emergency ambulance entrance/exit doors at the rear of the hospital onto the parking lot, where a metal shed housed the wheelbarrow that I used to carry the ashes to their designated dumping area. The entire boiler stoking/ash dumping caper process required twenty to twenty-five minutes. And yes, there was a shower in the basement, only seven or eight feet to the right of the big boiler 2 that I frequented before leaving the basement. After I proceed up to the first floor, then entered the hospital kitchen to eat breakfast before catching a ride to school. By the way, at the time head nurse employed me for the orderly job, she encouraged me to bring any assigned homework from school to work, and she would ensure that I received ample time to complete same. Plus Nurse Bates availed herself to answer any arisen questions, whether job, school or, other related puzzling suspicions I perchance encountered there.

Before long, my brother Robert Jr. turned nineteen, and his girlfriend gave birth to their first male child, and he named him Robert LeAnder Simpson. Afterward, Junior took me shopping for a car. I purchased a green 1949 four-door Pontiac. It was hardly the automobile I'd envisioned. Yet it provided the means to transport my beloved mother and I to and from work—yes, to school also.

During this time, many of my classmates and I would assemble in our cars on the paved black top inside Dunbar Elementary School, where designated school administrative personnel showed movies against a large outdoor movie screen at dusk dark until nine to ten o'clock, which we could view from the hood, top, or inside of our rides. From thence, we would drive downtown Lexington to show case our cars while cruising up and down North and South Main Street. However, before we completed the initial cruise, we were first accosted by a few Caucasians yelling abusive, hurtful, obscene phrase, such as "Nigger, get your black asses off our streets!" Some hurled stones along with said insulting outbursts. One of our youth who was behind the wheel of his hot rod, a 1937 Chevy, with exhaust emitting directly from the manifold, revved his engine as he removed a rifle from within and fired several rounds into space. Without confrontation, a State Trooper appeared. Instantly, we trailed the lead car down South Main Street, turned left at the stoplight, and headed down Highway 8 past Eanes School (all Caucasian segregated) onto Smith Avenue and eventually parked on Holt Street, out front the Du Drop Inn Cafe. We discussed the matter and spoke of future resolutions.

I truly lament, while thinking about that time, my best friend/Mom asked me to go pick-up some fresh collard greens and snap string beans from the Caucasian segregated and operated uptown Piggly Wiggly Market. Once I stepped inside that store, a Caucasian store clerk asked what was I doing. I gave my mother's shopping list. That clerk received the list but instantly escorted me out the front door with instructions to go around to the back entrance to pick up my order. Rage mounted in me as my first thoughts prompted me to walk off and leave the clerk with the greens and beans in-hand, but my mother was expecting those items, so I anxiously retained mixed thoughts with emotions that ran off the charts. That was the time that I would've given anything to be down home at my grandparents place, where no such racial antics exist in their mile long farm fields.

Lucile, my oldest sister, now seventeen years old, played the guard position on the girls' varsity basketball team at Dunbar High School. During basketball season, although I was unable to qualify for a spot on the male squad, Coach Ingram handed me the clipboard and issued statistician instructions. In this same period of time, my beautiful slender girlfriend was not athletically inclined yet popular. Therefore, she was assigned the position of statistician with the girls' basketball team. This arrangement permitted her and I, for the most part, to travel on the same bus when both girls and guys played at the same school, Asheboro, North Carolina, for example. Those were pure days of learning without expecting anything. Newsflash! The Blue Devils for the third year went undefeated with practically all Lexington male residence, both people of color and Caucasian folk supported Coach Ingram's winning tactics. This rendered the all-Caucasian segregated Hope Moffett baseball field (then located on South Main and Fifth Avenue) accessible to the Dunbar Blue Devils home game exhibitions.

At this stage, my shiny green 1949 Pontiac began to destroy timing gears/chains. Seems almost every week, it was docked at Clark's garage being worked on. For this reason, I discovered myself catching a ride or the city bus to school often! The champion Blue Devils only became more proficient with Roy Lee Holt at the quarterback helm. I'm spending a lot of time at my girlfriend's parents' newly erected home on Smith Avenue, two doors from the highly esteemed African American dentist. One night, for the first time, I learned she had reached out to solicit the assistance of a math tutor. Namely, a bookworm, who is with her seems like every time I visit with her. Yes, apparently, the old yellow head of jealous/covetous spirit arose in me, but she quickly allayed it at the onset.

At that time, James, a coworker at the hospital, have persuaded Bishop and I to travel with him over the weekend to Kannapolis, North Carolina, whose football team the Dunbar Blue Devils had severely beaten and smashed their hope year after year. However, during said time, some of their sophomore, junior, and senior young ladies/girls became attracted to the fellows from Lexington. I admit that was a distraction I could ill afford. Nevertheless, I still made several visits there to the night club owned by Mr. Moon, the gentleman that had taken to task to mentor Johnny Mae, a young lady friend I carried to dinner and to a couple of dances through-out that entire spring; but the slender beauty in Lexington, remained my decided squeeze.

Johnny Watson and I still hang tight, especially throughout high school, plus evening exercise and football practices. Why? The midnight hospital job, plus the weekend lawn work that I inherited from Junior made any accessible leisure time rare. By now, I have gotten a driver's license and stopped by Oscar place on Raleigh to get a snack. Inside it was equipped with dining tables surrounded by booths. A young lady, conveyed my cheeseburger or french fry order to the table where I was seated. I can say she was very cute, with a pleasing brown skin tone, in a word stacked! The establishment had an adjoining pool hall. Wherefore, between walking to and from there, I communicated with Pat, which revealed that she was the daughter of the establishment's owner. Pat and I became movie-watching friends from my parked automobile at the Thursday evening dust dawn pictures shown at the Dunbar Elementary School's administration building yard. This was the place my firstborn son Gene was conceived, according to Pat who brought him forth mid-1960, my senior year. Pat was the woman that I wanted to and should've asked for her hand in marriage. Notwithstanding, both Pat and I felt like at her age with a full life ahead and me turning seventeen at the turn of the year believed we were too young to marry. Therewith, I set out to provide weekly/monthly sustenance, food, and clothing for my son.

I was certain my slender beautiful girlfriend across town had learned about my outside activity with Pat. Still she remained by my side. This year, my senior graduating class took a week field trip that began at the Morehead Planetarium and Science Center in Chapel Hill, North Carolina, onto explore the lost Caravans (Caves) in the Commonwealth of Virginia. Then we were bus transported to the Washington, DC, Hotel Complex. There, we were assigned two guys to a room, and so were the girls with their business education teacher Mrs. Long designated hotel corridor/room chaperon, while Mr. Roach chaperoned the guys. During the course of the 1960 Dunbar High School graduating class brief stay in Washington, we made group tours to the Library of Congress and also visited inside the Halls of Justice and actually entered the Rotunda located in the House of Congress. Plus, we ventured into the Supreme Court of the United States, wherein I saw pictures of Caucasian men adorning white- or gray-colored wigs. In the Rotunda's half-moon seating arrangement were plush grayish seats with a phone and/or headset in place. Johnny and I with the others desired to go inside the Statute of Liberty, where we found elevators that would rapidly ascend and descend with an upward and extremely narrow spiral staircase, which structural ascent gave those patrons that didn't particularly care for the fast-paced elevator the sensation of climbing inside a large hollow cylinder. I took the stairs due to my apprehension of heights. In spite of the said fear of heights, I accompanied my best friend Johnny and a few others into the eye of the marvel or cement structure's face. I exhaled, attempting to properly describe that adrenalin rush.

Thereafter, my classmates and I were transported across the Arlington Memorial Bridge onto the Arlington Military Burial Grounds' parking surfaces, then paid tribute at the Lincoln Memorial Statute. The trip proved to be very educational, refreshing, plus enlightening and at the same time, provided the opportunity for the class of 1960 to preserve notes to queries posed and corresponding answers for personal archive creation(s), as well as opportunities for the class members to be on their character building and best behavior. Naturally, Johnny, my slender beauty, Betssy, and Inez enjoyed breakfast on occasion and visited the other's suite. The buses pulled up at Dunbar High School Thursday evening at approximately 4:30 to 5:00 p.m., with parents and loved ones eagerly awaiting the class's safe return.

My girl's home was less than a block up Smith Avenue, so I walked her home, kissed, and told her that I would see her tomorrow. Then I climbed into my Pontiac and drove home. My mother was as happy to see me as I was to see and hug her always calm demeanor.

THE JOURNEY

I began to discuss how I had set my focus on attending A&T University, a segregated agriculture school located in Greensboro, North Carolina. Thus, I rehearsed in my mom's ears that early-on I'd not taken to heart Mr. Callough (math teacher) and other teachers' candid admonishments regard doing my very best to absorb those instructions they'd provided everyone as they instructed our classes, which had left me unprepared to achieve adequate SAT scores for acceptance at A&T. Without a critical word, Mother admonished me to patiently solicit additional knowledge to help prepare to be accepted during the upcoming summer months.

Friday came with several of us anticipating going to the dance slated to take place at the Du Drop Inn Cafe on Holt Street. I was looking to be had in honor. Therefore, after checking out those in attendance at said dance, I proceeded to walk next door to play a game of eight-ball pool. But while waiting for the crowd to thin out; there was a gorgeous girl there who appeared unattached. I approached her and discovered she was looking for a ride to Thomasville, which was located approximately ten miles or so north of Lexington, North Carolina. The young lady was brown skin with black straight hair and a looker. I agreed to take her home after the eight ball game was finished.

Upon seating said girl and had gotten behind the steering wheel, I turned the radio on, which was dial to pick-up Randy Record Mart broadcasting live out of Nashville, Tennessee. Her favorite song "When a Man Loves a Woman" authored by Percy Sledge was playing. I started the car's engine and asked if she had a boyfriend. She replied, "No, why?" At that time, I explained that I was in a relationship, but up to this point, my steady was saving herself for marriage. Her head turned as she gazed intently toward me and at the same time slid her hand onto my upper thigh and moved in near unto me. I pulled into James's driveway and parked.

The young lady and I began petting with exchanges of french tongue kisses, plus we got busy, so much so until one of her pubic hairs manage to cut the uncircumcised skin that joined the tip of my manhood. Blood squirted out all over her beautiful white dress. I was so green I believed she had injured me. For that reason, I asked her to leave. She asked why. I was holding myself trying to staunch the flowing blood, asking her again to leave. Then I drove home to commit the seemingly urgent matter into my brother's expert hands. Junior explained that the girl did nothing wrong. The cut of my manhood developed on account I had never been circumcised but had just received one for free. I made diligent attempts to find her, so I could personally apologize for my adolescent behavior without success. It turned out that another invaluable lesson was given, and I learned to be informed, get understanding, and make certain the path of my feet was sure. Yet this was insufficient.

Afterward, prom preparation was rapidly approaching, and I had to rely on Lucile, my older sister to teach me to waltz. My fellow letter man Johnny and I traveled to Winston, Salem, North Carolina, to rent a couple of tuxedos. Prom night, we drove to Smith Avenue to pick-up my main lady at home. The prom went very well, so did the after party located some five or so miles away down Highway 8 in South Mount at Lexi (Dunbar High School's band drum major) home. There was a huge turnout there. Together with my main lady's two uninvited nuisance brothers. Alcoholic beverages were on-hand, but neither Johnny, my squeeze, or I drank. My gorgeous slender eloquent lady and I seemed like a match made in heaven, there slow dancing in each other's arms. Both she and I desired more, so we kissed, gently joined hands together while heading through the front door onto the outside where Johnny's 1957 Chevy was parked. Turns out that there were cars that came after us jam in front and back, so much as to wedge Johnny's car hopelessly between them. Still we got in, turned the radio on, but before my lady and I engaged in a much-needed kiss, we heard banging noise on the closed windows. To her and my amazement, said bangs were coming from the palms of her two brothers. They were unbelievable, ragging my lady 'til she got out of the car, then left South Mount with them.

I returned to the flowing party, engaged Lexi in a slow dance with some small talk. Leaving the party, Johnny's first cousin—a smart lady and great basketball player—accompanied us up the road to Johnny's home near Winston. When we stopped at the end of Johnny's driveway, a joint of weed showed up. Though skeptical, Johnny, Robbin, and I took turns sampling it. Around 2:00 a.m., Johnny said good night and told me to come in when ready. Instead, I asked Robbin if it would be all right if I joined her in the back to chat a little. She nodded that it would be all right. So I got out and entered the back but didn't know that she, one of Dunbar's star girl basketball players, had ever noticed me, let alone wanted to get with me. Robbin and I began to touch finger-hand play as we communicated of future college plans (i.e., over a musical backdrop). We began to kiss pet and engaged in passion filled slow-motion gyrating love intercourse until day dawned. An eye exchange confirmed the pleasure and contentment which Robbin and I achieved throughout the course of this not planed event. We got dressed, and I walked Robbin home that was a block or so from Johnny's home. Robbin's parents were obviously well blessed, given the appearance of their lavishly decorated home that was surrounded by huge well-groomed landscape. We partook of breakfast, then chatted for a spell. In parting, I thanked her for the kindness shown with a fond hand-finger touch. Johnny Coltrane and I returned the rented Tuxedos, plus drove back to Lexington.

There was always needless racial tension, especially when African Americans sought to utilize drug store counters/seats therein, restaurants, buses/stations, trains, schools, and even downtown main street. In fact, I knew another man named Johnny who worked at the ice plant across the railroad tracks in back of our former house on North Railroad Street. Mr. Johnny also worked from time to time in the plant's Caucasian proprietor's home located about fifty yards from said plant. Word circulated that Johnny's employer's wife had a thing for Mr. Johnny, and one day her husband made an nonscheduled stop at home where he allegedly found his wife and Johnny active in sexual intercourse. The Lexington Dispatch in 1957–'58 reported that Johnny was tried for rape. Then the State of North Carolina sentenced him to die in the gas chamber.

Chapter 3

By mid-1960, not only was I undecided about college, but also my older sister Lucile's best friend Mae and I were working on my other child. I was currently working at the Thomas Ford motor car dealership located up Route 38. Also, I opted to buy a solid black V-8 two-door with overdrive 1949 Ford, equipped with fender skirts and wide oval white wall tires. I was seventeen and had grown more popular so much so! Until during one Sunday, while out cruising Highway 8 and Holt Street, three to five girls flagged me to stop. Ann, one of them, was so beautiful. She approached the lowered window, asked for a ride to Parker and Wall Town. She seemed to make it a mission to raise the passenger's side seat to permit three of her friends enter the back seat so she could get in the front, where she scooted over close to me so that the fifth girl could get in front beside her. Yes, conversation ensued as I proceeded to Wall Town and began to let the others out upon request. After arrival at Ann's Mom's home, I found out that her mother not only knew my mom but also worked at the same hospital with her. I asked Ann if I could see her again. She replied yes, smiling.

My best friend/mother had to receive physician care. I was giving serious thought about joining the army, particularly after understanding that Uncle Sam will pay its soldiers to secure an education

THE JOURNEY

and even for attending college. I remember thinking how rapidly the year was passing with Johnny Coltrane, being a scholar, was accepted to Fayetteville State College, others to Greensboro Agriculture University and Chapel Hill. I feel as though I'm spending my wheels.

Meanwhile, the extremely attractive girl Ann and I have been doing more than just riding, talking, and eating ice cream Sundays. I've began to park and engage with her for gratification. I'm contemplating marriage with Ann except that Mae with them bow legs emanating out from her ankles as noticed upon her visits with my sister. Plus, found operating one of her mother's after hour spots I begin stopping at. Mae has a friend from Thomasville, North Carolina, who she confirms is not in her good grace any longer. Therefore, I made a move toward her home around 11:00 p.m. where we collectively found compatibility. The year is well into 1961.

I went to communicate with the army recruiter on South Main street next door to segregated Carolina Theater. That day, unbeknownst to anyone, I voluntarily signed up for the US Army. Also unexpectantly my best friend (my mother) Blanche instantly became ill enough to require hospitalizing in the Lexington Memorial Hospital on its first floor segregated ICU. All supervisory personal gave way to my presence there at all hours, for they remember the labor I'd put in there over the years. Upon one of my late 10:00 or 11:00 p.m. arrival at my mother's bedside, she was already rendered incapable to respond, an occasion that brought and now again brings my soul much sadness, so much so until I refuse to permit the pen to legislate it.

About the same time, Mae, my sister's good friend, informed me that she was pregnant with our child. During Mae's pregnancy, Ann from Wall Town and I have been doing more than just seeing each other. All at once, the army commands me to report to Charlotte, North Carolina, Army Induction Center—the place where a host of all day tests, such as psychological, aptitude, medical/eye exams, too many shots and the issuing of military garb occurred. This center caused approximately forty new inductees, including me to be bus transported to Fort Jackson South Carolina, where all inductees learned to answer "Yes, Sergeant" or "No, Sergeant." I was assigned to a platoon with four eighteen-man squads, whose domiciling existed in well-kept wooden buildings until their basic training concluded. And 95 percent of each awakening day began with a shout from the platoon sergeant or designated troop—around 4:00 a.m., crown with roll call, then a progressive one- to two-mile run and back to the pull-up bars erected just beyond steps leading to breakfast, dinner, and supper in the mess hall/dining room. I became part of a closely knit team of well discipline men who diligently work toward having all things in common to accomplish the very best the A-1 assault weapon and .45 five pistol in briefest time spans; as well as hit a 50-cent coin a mile away with said A-1 assault weapon. The platoon crawl beneath barb wire obstacles with chaser weapon rounds passing overhead, as we proceeded on into a gas chamber and upon command to retrieved the gas mass attached to our utility waist belts, cleared gas therein, then adorn same with tearstained burning eyes.

    I recall that everything including sets of push-ups, training movies, marching/running, and platoon tactical field exercises was accomplished by the number. At the completion of basic training while awaiting permanent assignment orders, I went back to Lexington, North Carolina, on seven-day leave for a brief reunite with remaining family. Plus, went to Wall Town to check up on Ann who I'd impregnated. Ann was in good spirit and carrying our baby quite well. My older brother Robert allowed me to drive his powder-blue 1956 Buick back to Fort Jackson accompanied by Mae, we traveled back to the Fort with one final assembly before I was transported to Germany. During the p.m. drive, I momentarily fell asleep behind the wheel, and narrowly encountered a head-on collision with an oncoming car traveling above fifty miles per hour. But I awoke at that instance the car seem to have moved to the right, out of the oncoming car's path, barely scraping the oncoming automobile put Mae and my unborn child, my brother and I at significant risk for harm. Much, much later in life, I acknowledged that that intervention was wrought by the providential love, mercy, and tender care of the ONLY TRUE LIVING GOD, whom I knew not at the time.

THE JOURNEY

  The day after, Mae and my brother Robert Jr. watched from a distance. Me and others boarded a four-prop cargo air plane in route to the Fort Dix, New Jersey, over sea processing company. But just prior to that plane's arrival—one of its motors on the side I was seated went out—that is, stopped running. Yet the plane landed safely at McGuire Air Force base directly across the street from Fort Dix. My fellow comrades and I were picked up and truck transported, baggage and all to the Fort Dix Army base. There we were placed in a two-story wooden barracks with community showers, heads, and toilet. Plus, assigned a single bunk in a fairly relaxed surroundings while awaiting transportation, several comrades convinced me to walk to a nearby recruit beer selling club where I sipped on a 3.5 percent mug of Budweiser beer and did not care for its foam or bitter taste. My first sample of alcohol.

  Within three weeks, I was summoned and instructed to board a huge jet-propelled airplane in route to Stuttgart, Germany. But the recent experience I'd had on the cargo plane, where I personally saw one of its prop motors cease to work proved sufficient to convince me—that flying was not part of my pedigree. Therewith, I declined to board that plane. Instead, I elected to board a ship several weeks after at Fort Hamilton, New York, whose voyage required approximately nine days, plus negotiating the Suez Canal, which requires another book. But briefly herein, the Suez Canal is a sea-level waterway in Egypt, connecting the Mediterranean sea, I'm told through the Isthmus of Suez constructed by the Suez Canal Company between 1859 and 1869. It was officially opened on November 17, 1869. The canal offers water craft a more direct route between the North Atlantic and Northern Indian Oceans via the Mediterranean and Red Seas, thus avoiding the South Atlantic and Southern Indian Oceans and thereby reducing the journey distance from the Arabian Sea to, for example, London by approximately 8,900 kilometers (5,500 miles). It is alleged to extend from the Northern terminus of Port said to the Southern terminus of Port Tewfik at the City of Suez. Its length is 193.30 kilometers (120.11 miles), including its Northern and Southern access channels.

Moreover, the ship I boarded, contained sleep accommodations three flights below deck (i.e., triple stack close hammocks) with fellow comrades abode five and six abreast with cigarette smoke billowing throughout the steel quarters, with accompanying occasional sea sickness, also the common practice of holding on to your food trays and frequent on deck wet and breezy outings, sweetened by an occasional movie shown in the mess area.

Without significant incident, the ship docked in Stuttgart, Germany, on the eighth and a half day. The other half day was occupied with me and about two hundred other soldiers being processed off the ship. The lot of them were conducted to a train in route to various concerns. Myself and twenty or so others to the train station located in the City of Heilbronn, Germany, where a military deuce and a quarter picked us up and transported some to the Walton Barracks, Company A, First Battalion, Fourth Infantry Division USA R SEVEN, still in Heilbronn a mile or so from Bad Kitchen. Although physical training and strict military drills, long walks with full back packs and M-14 semi-automatic weapons in route to various live rounds firing ranges continued the landscape with tree alignment "dress right dress" was a marvelous work of art to behold.

I reiterate being assigned to Company A, in a three-story marvel-type structure. I was blessed to have one soldier who shared a large four-man room sleeping quarters. The shower room was spaciously equip with several individual sinks, mirrors, latrines, and stalls. The marvel-type structured chow hall was elaborately sanitized and its operational staff was German, thus eliminated kitchen patrol (KP) duty. The armory was located in company A-basement. I was selected to be a member of the special missile unit, and the compound was fully equipped with medical dispensary, PX, enlisted and commission officers clubs. The soldiers reported to the old man's office/captain/commander monthly to be paid cash American wages (i.e., hardly no money). The American dollar valued at 1.25, 25 cents more than the German/Dutch mark. Plus, the cost of living there and downtown was surprisingly cheaper than in the US of America.

THE JOURNEY

Leave in Copenhagen, Denmark, proved equally economic, where breakfast with two to three eggs, sausage and/or side dish, with juice/fluid cost .25 to .35 cent American (converted to kroner). Plus there were no penitentiaries, and the crime rate was supper low 2–4 percent said a Fraulein. I was primarily assigned TDY-SP (special police) duty at the main front gate, attired in blows razor pressed fatigues, spit shiny black leather/white shoe laced boots with starched long-sleeve shirt an adorned silver tailor made steel pot and was often times posted in the midsection of the street, directing in and out traffic while checking identification cards of those entering or exiting the base. My eighteen-month tour of duty was nearly completed, and I wanted to reenlist, having met the seemingly one of a kind Fraulein who graciously returned the love I shared. Notwithstanding, I had left Sallie in Lexington, North Carolina, my potential behind the scene bride state side, with not made-up mind. Plus, Germany's frigid year around temperatures became the deciding factors, especially during bivouac.

I left reluctantly and arrived by ship at Fort Hamilton, New York, with the expectancy to temporarily lodge with my older sister Lucile and her husband Tommy Loppe, at their one family home located in Jamaica Long Island, New York, but upon my arrival there, Lucile informed me that Sallie had married an under taker at the King's County Hospital in Brooklyn, New York. The year was 1963. Also that Sallie had given birth to one child. Plus one was on board. My soul sank, and although I had low-alcohol consumption tolerance, I purchased a bottle of vodka, became drunk that night, and had sexual intercourse with Carole, a telephone operator an associate of Lucile. Thereafter, on November 29, 1963, I reenlisted in the army. In time, I became promoted to specialist five and was assigned to a transportation unit motor pool at Fort Dix, New Jersey. I had learned to work well with others in a discipline manner. But regretfully, I did not finish my educational college vision pursuit.

Long story shortened, in 1969, I received news that my baby sister Lillian had been killed in a car to telephone pole accident on Highway 8 in Lexington, North Carolina. She left four children—

the oldest a male child named Robert Jr., age five; Angie, four; Kim, three; and Henry, one. Her spouse Robert, plus the Simpson, Loppe, and Payne families mourning.

I returned to Lexington, North Carolina, leaving house trailer and a 1959 Ford two-door Galaxy 500 (collector's item) in Pemberton, New Jersey, to attend my friend/baby sister's funeral. There I determined to remain—to aid my old sister care for the children—and discovered that Ann had given birth to my son Vernon, who was age nine already. Yes! My older sister Lucile and her husband Tommy had previously returned to Lexington. I secured a job at Midstate Tile Plant, but the take-home pay was hardly worth getting out of bed for. Thereafter, I proceeded to get hired at the box plant corrugating and shipping boxes, with fork lift duties from 3:00 to 11:00 p.m. A great job with advancement opportunity, yet I simply wasn't satisfied with my take home pay and that with three different children to provide support for.

Meanwhile, Lucile have convinced our grandmother Jannie to come live with her, and her son Larenzo because our Great-Great-Grandmother Georgia had fallen asleep. Plus Lucile's husband Tommy had also fallen to sleep. There being no necessity for our Grandmother Jannie to remain in Saint Paul, North Carolina, alone in their modest in the woods home. I never knew Tommy's cause of death but incurred shock as a result thereof. Lucile had begun dating a young man name willy who I had gotten wind that he'd starting an abusive attitude toward her on a number occasions. One suitable day while checking up on Lucile, my nieces and nephews at her home, I thought it necessary to address willy and advised him not to strike or abuse Lucile ever again. If he couldn't live peaceful with Lucile (i.e., a very meek, yet high standard set woman), then he should pack up and leave. Not long afterward, while James and I drove up Talbert Boulevard, I spotted Lucile's Plymouth sitting on the shoulder of Talbert boulevard adjacent to the lot where Grubb motor company park its tractor trailer. Upon James's and my inspection of Lucile's car, we determined no mechanical failure existed. We split up and searched as we walked looking for Lucile among the park trailers.

THE JOURNEY

Suddenly, James and I heard pounding on the pavement as if someone was running. Lucile appeared with Willy in pursuit. By this time, I had picked up the overt cursing habit, therewith lit in on Willy with intent to persuade him not to abuse my sister. But Lucile intervened attempting to convince both James and I that Willy had not struck her. Not long after, I stopped at Lucile's house. Only to learn from my nephew Robert Jr. that Willy had been fighting Lucile earlier. I immediately stepped to Willy, and Willy came after me with a butcher knife. I ducked beneath his lung and cold cocked him in his private region, sending Willy and his genitals to Rowan General Hospital, located in Salisbury, North Carolina. Willy recovered, and my sister Lucile stopped dating him. Nothing followed. During the period of 1974, I began work on a four-man maintenance engineer crew at the Lexington Memorial Hospital from 7:00 a.m. to 3:00 p.m. off East Center Street, repairing air-conditioners, commodes, painting/refurbishing rooms, and general maintenance duties. Daphine and I have been cohabiting in a three-bedroom house on Salisbury Street, with one African American family on our right, and to our left were several middle-aged Caucasian family members, very quiet, laidback neighborhood. Daphine have, a few years earlier, given birth to my third son whose name is Tony at the onset of 1972. Several homeowner husbands invited us to take an active part in their social motorcycle club, wherein on weekends we assembled to socialize, then collectively rode our bikes to neighboring city's motorcycle programs (i.e., that was sometime conducted in Charlotte, North Carolina, approximately sixty miles from Lexington).

There, the South Carolina Holy Davis Motor Cycle Organization and the huge Caucasian Outlaw Bike Club came together to put on quite an acrobatic display of motor bike skills consisting of jumping, wheelies, barbing apples, tree/pole hanging fruit, riding feats which I made no attempt to duplicate while consuming alcoholic beverages. At this point in time, Pat, Mae and Ann have moved on and settled into homes with honorable husbands, all very gorgeous special women of integrity, having provided me every opportunity to do the right thing.

J.D.

It appears that I'm beginning to find my place too while learning the electrical, plumbing, plaster, and painting trades, as well as making hospital cash bank drops in the hospital pharmacy transportation. Note that after 3:00 p.m., I became a Red Bird taxi hustler driver until business slows. Daphine worked at one of the factories a mile or so toward Linwood from our place on Salisbury Street. Therefore, at the turn of 1975, I transported Daphine to Denton's Ford Motors, where she chose a yellow two-door 1975 sports Mustang and drove it home that day.

During the month of August 1975, while at work removing the radiation x-ray apparatus's bubble for the purpose of transporting same to Charlotte, North Carolina, to be refilled, a seemingly healthy blond Caucasian lady, by appointment or happenstance, came into the emergency room of the hospital with one of Daphine's mother's neighbors. Mr. Shop and I commented that she was a looker. I had half hour before noon lunch break, so I asked the two of them out to have a brunch at a nearby drive-in-window fast-food sandwich spot near the hospital. Later, Daphine got information that I may have been devoting more than lunch time with the girl whose name turned out to be Wonda. Daphine confronted me. A significant disagreement between us developed, and Daphine leaned toward one of her sister's suggestions and decided to take a trip to New York to visit a spell with her.

Meanwhile I was always mentally and physically active in the civil rights movement that had begun extending its action roots into North Carolina State government. In this, part of my duty was to supply automobiles, encourage nonvoters to vote, and to transport registered voters to the poll machine booths. I convinced Wonda, my Caucasian friend, plus sister Lucile to drive, assist voters with completing ballots, and drive such to their district poll designation in Daphine's Mustang. Subsequently, I verbally and physically supported African American Reverend Betts rather than for Doc, which drastically diminished the relationship I had had with Doc, during those periods my slender friend girl and I visited with Doc and his misses. Doc had been my family doctor.

THE JOURNEY

After several weeks passed, Daphine's mother advised me that Daphine wanted me to send her airplane fare so she could return home. I deposited the money into her mother's hands. But a few weeks went by without Daphine appearing…So I requested the lead supervisor at work for a couple of days' vacation time for the purpose of driving to New York to find out why Daphine had not come back to Lexington.

Chapter 4

Thereafter, on or about November 10, 1975, I neatly placed several pairs of dress pants, shirts, socks, under garments into the rear seat of our yellow 1975 Ford Mustang along with my pistol on the front seat. I drove to my coworker JD's home around 7:45 p.m. to let him know I was gonna go to New York. I left there not desiring to go alone due to my habit of falling asleep while driving. So I went to Sallie's mother's home located on Maple Avenue, in Lexington, North Carolina, to ask Mayhew, her brother, to ride with me. It was around 8:20 or 8:40 p.m. I discovered Mayhew was already out on one of his over the road tractor trailer runs. Therefore, I left there and stopped by the bike club on Salisbury Street to ask George to go. George said his money was a little low and declined. At about 9:00 p.m., I proceeded to go by this spot to get a few no-doze upper brown and clear pills to help me stay awake. Plus, I stopped at the ABC store and bought a pint of vodka, then pulled up at the service station located on the corner of North Main and Raleigh Road and filled the car with gas. Afterward, I negotiated the stoplight and drove straight out onto Highway 29/30. Today, it's called I-85 to Greensboro onto Danville, Virginia, unto Route 58. It must've been around 11:30 or 11:45 p.m. when I came through a town because the speed limit dropped to thirty-five or forty-five miles an hour. Not long afterward, a red-and-blue light began to flash in my rearview mirror. I sense it was law enforcement, so I pulled over. I ingested a brown and clear no-doze pill, rolled down my window, and asked the officer what the problem was. The said officer asked where I was going and whether or not I'd seen a light sports car in my travels, and he asked for my driver's license as well. I informed said officer that I was enroute to New York, and no I had not seen much traffic or light sports car. The officer leaned in, shined a flash light into the back seat, then opened the door and reached in and stirred the clothes around, which I had placed on my car back seat. The officer closed the door, returned my driver's license, then told me to have a safe trip, but not drink any more if I was going to be driving.

As I continued on Route 58, hoping to reconnect with 29/301, flashing lights appeared again in my rearview mirror. I slowed down in search of a place to pull to the shoulder of the highway where I stopped. A different officer looked like a town cop, approached my car, asked for my driver's license and registration, which I placed in his hands. Then said officer told me to get out of the car. Upon doing so, the officer placed handcuffs on my wrists and said he was holding me for further investigation. I asked, "For what?" The officer walked me to the front of his cruiser, then went back, opened the driver's side door, reached into my car, then into the back seat, then walked to the passenger's side, opened that door, and appeared to be searching around. Then he picked up what appeared to have been my pistol that had been laying on the front seat unloaded. When said officer came back to me, he placed me in his cruiser and drove to a lock-up or police station. He escorted me into a room, where he was joined by other law enforcement officers who accused me of being a three-time loser and now rape assault. The arresting officer told the State Trooper who came in that little room he'd found a gun and was about to charge me with carrying a concealed weapon. I made a telephone call to Lexington, North Carolina, seeking someone to put up bail money. Then the Trooper handed me over to two brown-skinned sheriffs that looked just alike who transported me back to the rear end of my car that was still there on the shoulder of the road, where many Caucasian officers were inside and on the outside searching the car. One of the African American sheriff officers got out the car I sat in and went to talk with a Caucasian officer, then returned and transported me to the front of a house/home, stopped, then turned the inside cruiser's lights on me.

I knew nothing about legal or illegal searches or necessity of having Miranda right warnings administered. Still, I immediately asked the brown officers for their names when I saw that the Caucasian officer was walking toward the cruiser where I sat, accompanied by several mature-looking Caucasian folk and a Caucasian youngster. One of the lookalike officers replied, "Why do you need to know our name?" I interjected, "Can't you see they are trying to railroad me with a one-man targeted lineup?" I attempted to duck my head into my lap. Afterward, one Caucasian official came and told the brown-complexioned officers to take me around to the jail. Later, I discovered it was the Halifax County Jail.

At the jail, my clothing, identification cards (i.e., social security and driver's license), and money was taken. I was escorted to a one man jail cell. After half hour or so passed, a Caucasian who identified himself by the name George brought me a Gideon's small King James revised New Testament Bible. Believe it or not, for the first time in life, I began reading the book entitled Revelation. The no-doze brown and clear upper I'd ingested early on would not permit sleep to adorn my eyes so I read and read until fear enveloped my mind while reading: "I saw the dead, small and great, stand before God; and the books was opened; and another book was opened, which is the book of life; and the dead were judged out of those things which were written in the books, according to their works." (See King James Version Bible, New Testament book entitled Revelation 20:12.)

The following morning, one of the jailers escorted me out front, where I was fingerprinted, with various pictures taken, then sent back to that cell. Just minutes before 11:00 a.m., the same Caucasian trustee inmate who had delivered that little Gideon New Testament Bible to me approached the cell and informed me that Sheriff Edmon or Edmonson (i.e., one of the Caucasian jailers) was heard communicating to his fellow officials that his Aunt Joyce was related to the alleged victims, and they were gonna hang this nigger, because she was going to be one of my jurors. Inmate George strongly suggested that I hire a good lawyer. That evening, I was again escorted out front where three civilian-clad Caucasian men hustled me into a room, gave me a cotton swab with instruction that I put the swabs (i.e., three swabs) in my mouth and wet them. I refused and requested to see a lawyer. Two of those officers took hold of me while the other forced inserted fingers up my nostrils and proceeded to force my head backward and mouth open. He inserted the unsanitary swabs and scrub my tongue and inner side of my mouth. Was I furious!

Also, on the morning of December 12, 1975, a lawyer named, McLau summoned me up front and into a room. There, he talked with me for approximately ten to fifteen minutes, concerning using a weapon in commission of two counts of abduction, one count of rape of a female considered to a minor, my whereabouts on November 10, 1975. Plus, whether or not I had witnesseses that could confirm my whereabouts on November 10, 1975, and whether or not I committed the crimes that I was being charged.

I communicated to McLau that I did not kidnap or rape anyone ever, as well as being driven to the front of someone's home while sitting handcuffed in the back seat of the two black sheriffs' cruiser with its inside dome light spotlighting me during the course where a Caucasian law enforcement officer with others and a Caucasian youngster approached this cruiser where I sat for possible one man targeted/profiled identification purpose, en route to railroad me. Also about the probability of the alleged victims Aunt Joyce sitting on my jury should the matter go to trial. I communicated compelled McLau to demand a lineup be had, so the alleged victims could see that I was not their perpetrator.

Thereafter, on or about December 12, 1975, at approximately 10:30 a.m. or so, a sheriff walked, escorted me into what appear to be a court room, where approximately five to six different African American men was paraded one at a time into another room. There sat what appeared to be the youngster that came down that sidewalk while the black sheriffs had me parked in front of the abovesaid home, surrounded by other Caucasian adults and a State Trooper. Upon entering this room, I was handed a paper with a phrase written thereon, which I was told to verbally read out loud. When the five jail detainees and I were finished, I was told that the alleged male victim did not identify me as their assailant, and neither did the alleged female victim.

At that instant, I informed McLau that I was attempting to hire Ms. Ruth Harvey, a young African American female lawyer from Danville, Virginia. McLau's reply was, "Why? I'm going to defend you the same as if you paid me!" Of course, at that juncture, I possessed not the knowledge to discern McLau's speech, which turned out to be part of his collusion antics. I had not beforehand been a felon and knew nothing about the court system or procedural due process rights. Therefore, I was at a loss to separate integrity from McLau, one possessed with scam skills. After all, I had personally toured the United States Supreme Court, plus House of Congress, where its walls were covered with photographs of Caucasian men adorned with graying wigs (i.e., men who allegedly frame the constitutional due process liberty laws, which governs the American citizen) during my 1960 senior high school year. Thus, I was fairly confident that the United States Constitution's structure words, plus evidence and facts, would exonerate me since I had broken no written or posted law.

During my December 12, 1975, grand jury indictment hearing conducted in the Juvenile Domestic Court located in Halifax County, Virginia, the commonwealth's attorney asked the state's primary witness State Trooper Fow, "Were any saliva test taken of the defendant?" Fow's answer was, "Yes, sir." Defense objected, interjected, that "the affidavit was invalid, the search warrant. I made that motion in the [preserved on December 12, 1975, Juv. Tr. Ex. 55, p. 140] original motion. The affidavit states conclusions of law which do not satisfy the requirements."

The Court interjected, "Looks like they might have to go into a hearing on the validity of the search." Defense interjected, "Your

Honor, this is a question that requires no evidence. It resolves strictly upon the affidavit under the law you cannot go outside the confines of that instrument." The Court interjected, "I haven't seen the affidavit." Defense's reply was, "Well, I think the statute requires that it be filed in the Circuit Court." Commonwealth's attorney's response was. "I wonder if Mr. McLau could take this matter in the other court, the circuit court if he deem it necessary?" (id. Tr. Ex. 55-B, p. 141). Then commonwealth's attorney emphatically interjected, "I wrote the Affidavit. I thought it was proper, so that is my argument right here, sir" (id. Juv. Tr. Ex. 55-c, p. 143).

Now the following are those statements embodied in said deficiently vague erroneous sworn affidavit:

1. Material evidence was found in the automobile. Doesn't say whom.
2. It does not say who found the evidence of the alleged foot print because the identity of the footprint as being the same one could not have been averred by the affiant (i.e., Fow), for he do not appear to have been an expert (we cannot go outside the four corners to determine that) (id. Juv. Tr. Ex. 55-c, p. 143).

The Court asked Fow, "Let me ask you a question. It is alleged in the affidavit for the search warrant that the victim had positively identified the automobile used in the abduction and rape." Fow's response was, "He asked me if I knew whether they had or not, and I told him not to my knowledge they had not!" The court interjected, "Then when was the positive identification made?" Fowler's reply was, "I don't know if there was a positive identification made" (December 12, 1975, Tr. Ex. 55-F, p. 169, 170). Defense reiterated, "Your Honor, please, I want to renew my motion to exclude this evidence in view of the Trooper's evidence" (id. Juv. Tr. Ex. 55-E, p. 146). The Court ruling that commonwealth's attorney had established probable cause was improper misconduct, as tending to intimate the bias of the Court with respect to the character of the weight of commonwealth's attorney's structured false probable cause identification affidavit's information and unverified trooper's statements without authority. The said ruling could not be lawfully adopted as being founded upon material facts in that same is outside the perimeters required by State Statute Virginia Code Title 19.2-54, which provides in pertinent part that "no search warrant shall be issued until there if filed, material facts constituting probable cause for the issuance of such warrant."

Upon the bases of the above, the affidavit failed to set forth any facts establishing a connection between the affiant and the information averred therein the invalid affidavit. See the Supreme Court of the United States decision in the case of *Riggan v. Virginia*. See the Supreme Court of Virginia determination in the case of *Morris v. Commonwealth*. The evidence obtained as a result of a search warrant issued upon insufficient affidavit was inadmissible, says the Supreme Court of Virginia in the case of *Wiles v. Commonwealth*.

The aforementioned juvenile indictment court's probable cause saliva search warrant ruling presents a conflict of opinion between different panels of the Supreme Court of Virginia and United States Supreme Court; therefore, said ruling violates clear precedent of the courts constitutes extrinsic fraud and denied me the due process of law, in violation of Amendment 14, US Constitution.

The facts above evince a legitimate inference that not only was the saliva search warrant not supported by Fourth Amendment probable cause or a valid affidavit as required by Statute, Code of Virginia Title 19.2-54 (i.e., state procedure requirements). Those facts illustrates that the commonwealth's attorney alluded to his own personal integrity and/or oath of office (i.e., by saying I wrote the affidavit, so that's my argument right there, sir, preserved in December 12, 1975, Juv. Tr. Ex. 55-c, p. 143) to bolster the government's case, tantamount to vouching for the credibility of state star witness Fow was improper misconduct, says the Supreme Court of the United States in the case of *US v. Young*, which held, "The prosecutor's vouching for the credibility of witnesses…carries with it the imprimatur of the government and may induce the jury [grand jury] to trust the government's judgment rather than Its own view of the evidence," constituting extrinsic fraud; and a due process violation;

That was compounded when grand jury indictment hearing court, after astutely noting the affidavit for the search warrant—erroneously claim the victims had positively identified the automobile used in the abduction and rape, but the affidavit affiant Trooper's reply was, "He didn't know if there was a positive identification made (preserved in id. December 12, 1975, Juv. Tr. Ex. 55-F, pp. 169–170). Notwithstanding the false, tainted stench, the facts indicate the commonwealth's attorney knowingly used said false positive identification and presented it to the grand jury to secure that indictment was improper misconduct in contravention of those court officials' duty to seek justice in all criminal cases. (See Supreme Court of the United States' decision in the case of *Berger v. US*). This amounts to extrinsic fraud that was double compounded by the court overruling defense motion to suppress saliva seized evidence violated the statute code of Virginia, as well as violated my constitutionally guaranteed right to due process of law under Amendment 14 of the US Constitution. The Supreme Court of Virginia in the case of *Wiles v. Commonwealth* establishes that "the evidence obtained as a result of a search warrant issued upon insufficient affidavit was inadmissible."

Bottom line, the commonwealth's attorney, indictment judge, and appointed trial attorney may not use or knowingly present false testimony to the jury, and have a duty to correct testimony that he or she know to be false, says the Supreme Court of the United States in its established 1959 and 1935 decision in the case of *Nape v. Illinois*. See also the case of *Mooney v. Holohan*. The Fifth Circuit Court of Appeals in the case of *US v. Mason* held, "Prosecutor's failure to correct government witnesses' statement regarding plea agreement, was improper and violated due process."

The reader is encouraged to visit their local law library or go online to review the case law cited herein and, in so doing, key up the *Richmond Times* dispatch archives to review the issue about the commonwealth's attorney's invalid false identification structured affidavit that was considered by the Supreme Court of Virginia Justice

J.D.

Judge Bradley B. Cavedo in a similar matter as above penned. You can find it in the dispatch February 4, 2016, edition, which stated that "at least eight Circuit Court Judges had already void convictions against prisoners whose cases were investigated with that single issue—involving tainted search warrants obtained by former Richmond detective Jason."

Chapter 5

After the above John Gotti roughshod probable cause indictment court ruling, of the commonwealth's attorney had called Sheriff Deputies C. J. and C. W. (African American twins), the initial officers to respond to the missing persons call from Mrs. Barbra—the alleged victim's home. The sheriff would have testified, "They were dispatched to the [alleged] victim's home around 9:25 p.m. because he wrote it in his log book." Moreover, at the end of the day, the court clerk claimed she/he don't know what happened to the tape because it contained Deputy Taylor's testimony (i.e., probable cause testimony evidence, helpful alibi defense fact). I personally reviewed the December 12, 1975, Juvenile Court record and discovered that the aforesaid helpful defense alibi testimony was not recorded. And the twin African American sheriffs are referred to numerous times through the testimony of the alleged male victim, their mother, Trooper Fow, indictment and trial court judges, and other commonwealth's witnesses throughout both grand jury indictment hearing and extended trial proceedings, raising significant questions, such as, Why did said clerk not alert the court, commonwealth's attorney or defense attorney early on? And why did not my appointed trial attorney make a motion for mistrial or cause a subpoena to issue summoning the twin sheriffs as defense witnesses? In

J.D.

that the twin sheriffs' 9:25 to 9:55 p.m. arrival at the alleged victim's home correlates with the alleged female victim's going to the little orange market around 9:30 or 10:00 p.m. time frame (preserved on May 26, 1976, Tr. Ex. 15-A, p. 27).

Without ensuring a ruling be had by the indictment court, for determination as to the degree of prejudice caused to my procedural due process right to present the twin African American sheriffs' aforesaid loss time factor testimony, in my defense to a fair and impartial judge and jury or for appellate purposes.

My indictment hearing proceeded with the commonwealth's attorney calling Deputy Mor, who on direct exam, testified that he received radio message from the dispatch to be on lookout (BOL) for a light two-door sports car. Afterward, around 11:23 to 11:50 p.m., he and another deputy sheriff pulled me over. Mor noticed an open bottle of alcoholic beverage in the car and also noticed clothes in the back seat. Mor said he lifted those clothes to see if someone was beneath them (although no one could hardly be concealed beneath two pairs of dress pants, two folded dress shirts, several pair of socks, and a three-quarters top coat that was also folded). Mor testified he had no reason to hold me, then interjected, "If you are going to drive to New York, you probably shouldn't drink anymore of this stuff. Have a safe trip" (preserved on December 12, 1975, Juv. Tr. Ex. 50, p. 60). Mor still testifying, said about five minutes after he got the first call, he got another call from the dispatcher saying it was a Mustang II with a dark top and the girl and boy had been located. He then called South Hill Police Department and told Officer Tay what he'd been told and gave the license plate number and description of the man (i.e., me) (preserved in March 3, 1976, Tr. Ex. 44-H, p. 110; id. Tr. Ex. 44-I, p. 111). On cross exam, Mor further testified that Mecklenburg gave him information about yellow Mustang II and North Carolina tags (preserved on December 12, 1975, Juv. Tr. Ex. 51-E, p. 85).

Thereafter, during my grand jury indictment hearing, upon commonwealth's attorney's direct examination of state primary witness State Trooper Fow who testified again under sworn oath that deputies (African American twin sheriffs) picked up the male victim at RN's house on

THE JOURNEY

Route 58; that he saw the alleged male victim in said twin sheriff's car in Riverdale; that Michael, the alleged male victim, and female victim was in his automobile, where he talked with her on the way back to the hospital, and she gave him the abductor's car description in route, plus said there was trash and things in the front floor board, papers, and so forth on passenger side, and there was a lot of clothing on the back seat; and that it was a yellow Mustang II (preserved in Juv. Tr. Ex. 54-C, Tr. Ex. 54-D, pp. 122–123 respectively). Both alleged male and female told him practically the same thing, and this gave him probable cause.

Almost four months have passed, where I've been found daily reading, studying and learning about how God created the heavens, earth, sun three hundred thousand times larger than this earth, moon, innumerable stars and everything that exist, as well as man from the dirt and breath into him—that is, into Adam the breath of life. I suspected I'd be released during the March 3, 1976, salty aged (one token grain of pepper) jury trial, having gained godly favor with one of the Halifax County Jail keepers. In the middle of the day, my older sister Lucile and my friend Wonda, a blond Caucasian well-figured (looker) woman, came to the jail to visit. I was informed that Wonda would be seriously injured if she ever returned to the jail. Thereafter, I sent Wonda away with grief, although she would've been a viable alibi defense witness. After which, I heard that Wonda and her baby girl seemly vanish from Lexington, North Carolina, then off the face of God's green earth. I unsuccessfully committed to find her with much prayer, trusting each of them to God's providential protection and care.

Back in the court's atmosphere, during the appointed defense attorney McLau's March 3, 1976, cross-examination of state's alleged male victim witness (i.e., from which the above alleged source of probable cause information emanated). Defense asked Mic, "How many times did you talk to Trooper Fow the night this thing happened?" Mic's answer was, "Once."

> Q: About how long after were you let out of the abductor's car? Did you first speak to Trooper Fowler?

A: It was after they had found my sister.
Q: Where did this conversation take place?
A: At my house.
Q: Have you talked to anyone prior to that?
A: Yes.
Q: Who was that?
A: The two policemen that came up there first.
Q: Do you know who those police man were?
A: No. They looked like twins.
Q: Were they white or black?
A: Black.
Q: Now they were wearing brown uniforms, weren't they?
A: Yes.
Q: Did you talk to anyone else before you talked to those police man?
A. No.

In addition, the record shows after about five to ten minutes elapsed, the alleged male victim was let out his abductor's car, first according to his own testimony…The alleged male victim under commonwealth's attorney's direct exam, "Were you able to see any license plate?" Mic's answer was no. The lawyer asked, "Do you remember the top of the car?" Mic answered, "No. It was a black stripe at the bottom of it, on the side." This is preserved on May 26, 1976, Tr. Ex. 33, p. 8. Further, Defense asked Mic about the nature of the information he gave Mr. Per and the two twin black officers (i.e., who he said that he first talked with on the night after the alleged crime) that came to him first (March 3, 1976, Tr. Ex. 27 & Tr. Ex. 28, p. 20, 22, respectively).

The aforementioned interjected testimony offered by the alleged male and female victim in my court proceeding appeared to be information sufficient to raise reasonable doubt, plus evidence that would impeach and refute the aforesaid testimony given against me by Officer Mor and Trooper Fow, which was deliberately suppressed by commonwealth's attorney, trial court, and appointed defense attorney who appeared to have knowingly used said alleged impeach asserted yellow Mustang II, with black top and North Carolina tags (i.e., probable cause testimony) to fraudulently obtain my conviction.

At the time, the appointed defense attorney raised question regard the description information state's alleged male victim gave the first officers (i.e., twin black sheriff), the commonwealth's attorney objected and interjected, "I feel I must object to this testimony. His feelings or his emotions or what he told this officer and the evidence that he is going into may or may not be relevant in this trial unless he is going to bring these people in, and I am not aware of any assumption" (March 3, 1976, Tr. Ex. 28, p. 22). Then the trial court intervened and in essence ruled that "defense was not allowed to question Mic about anything he might have told anyone other than Trooper Fow" (Tr. Ex. 54-J, p. 25);

This is causally connected with defense attorney asking Fow "to describe the conversation he'd had with [i.e., twin black sheriffs]." Before Trooper Fow could answer, the trial court and commonwealth's attorney Ben again unduly prevented my (i.e., attorney) confrontation cross-examination probes by the trial court ruling that interjected, "What kind of difference does the conversation make? Well, ask him any relevant things. You are just imposing on the Court's time with a matter that I cannot believe had anything to do with this thing. Just tell me what difference does it make," was improper misconduct, as tending to intimate the bias of the trial court with respect to the character of weight of the defense impeachment evidence, plus carried with it the official approval of the government and may have influenced the jury to trust the court's judgment rather than its own view of the testimony evidence, to my prejudice, constituted extrinsic fraud, compounded by trial court's improper relief of the commonwealth's attorney's duty to prove every element of my charged offenses beyond a reasonable doubt, thereby arbitrarily denying my constitutionally guaranteed right to due process.

In case you, the reader, don't know, just as I didn't at the pretrial rehearsed 1975 and 1976 mock trial, the Supreme Court of Virginia, in its 1970 established law, in the case of *Powers v. Commonwealth* determined, "It is elementary that the burden is on the commonwealth to prove every essential element of the offense beyond a reasonable doubt," supported by its 1985 decision in the case of *Hankerson v. Moody*, quoted in *Commonwealth v. Flaneary*.

Neither did I know that relevant to my constitutionally protected Sixth Amendment rights that was drawn into my juror's above evaluation regard the alleged probable caused information given to the twin black sheriffs by the alleged male victim, connected with the conversation information state's primary witness, Trooper Fow had with those twin black sheriffs' value:

The Sixth Amendment to the United States Constitution in pertinent part provides the following:

> **In all criminal prosecutions, the accused shall enjoy the right to a speedy and public trial by an impartial jury of the State and District wherein the crime shall have been committed; to be confronted with the witnesses against him, to have compulsory process for obtaining witnesses in his favor, and to have the assistance of counsel for his defense.**

At the same time, reader, you may find it interesting to know that a year or so prior to my 1976 Circuit Court of Halifax County State Court trial—the highest Court in America in the 1974 case of a man named *Davis v. Alaska* first determined the following:

> **The jurors were entitled to have the benefit of the defense theory before them so that they could make an informed judgment as to the weight to place on [their] testimony.**

Second, the *Davis* Court at p. 318, said,

> **If the right to effective cross-examination, embodied in the Sixth Amendment, is denied, constitutional error exists without the need to show actual prejudice.**

The aforesaid Supreme Court of the United States establish law Ruling, instantly became applicable to the State Circuit and Supreme Courts throughout America by means of Article VII, Section 1 of Amendment 14, which provides,

> **All persons born or naturalized in the United States, and subject to the jurisdiction thereof, are citizens Of the United States and of the State wherein they reside. No State shall make or enforce any law which Shall abridge the privileges or immunities of citizens of the United States; Nor shall any State deprive any person of life, liberty or property, without Due Process of law; Nor deny to any person within Its jurisdiction the equal protection of the laws.**

Notwithstanding this aforestated governing applicable laws, not once did my court-appointed attorney McLau, or trial court refer thereto or take any action to subpoena the twin black sheriffs who were obviously the first law enforcement officials to arrive at the alleged victim's home to investigate the mother's missing persons call at 9:25 to 9:55 p.m. on November 10, 1975. Plus, according to the testimony of the alleged male victim, who interjected the twin black sheriffs were the first law enforcement officials he talked with after being let out his abductor's car who first receive the alleged description of the alleged victim's perpetrator's car (i.e., being a light sports car) that said sheriffs caused to be (BOL) put out over the radio airways the night of November 10, 1975 and required defense attorney to make motion to produce the misplaced transcript of the December 12, 1975, grand jury indictment proceeding allegedly recorded on Tape No. A 4, by the court reporter (i.e., sheriff deputies) that court reporter claim was missing from December 12, 1975, Juvenile Domestic Court Indictment transcribed record, p. 87 (i.e., defense relevant time factor material evidence). Due to error in indictment court's case management system, to my prejudice, to be made part of the record in the Circuit Court of Halifax County and a copy of the Halifax County Sheriff Department on November 10, 1975, officially maintained 9:25 to 9:55 p.m. Dispatch time log (i.e., and protocol/procedure) noting twin black sheriff deputies departure to investigate a missing persons call at the alleged victim's home on the night of alleged crime (November 10, 1975). Information relevant to the preparation on my alibi defense appeared to have been intentionally suppressed by prosecuting court officials' acts in concert with appointed defense attorney McLau's collusion as inferred by defense's inaction, except to note his objection.

Noteworthy here: The above action/inaction is the direct affront taken by the trial court, commonwealth's attorney, and appointed defense attorney to outright abridge my Sixth Amendment right to both cross-examine states witnesses against me and/or compulsory process to obtain twin black sheriffs with Halifax County sheriff's 9:25 to 9:55 p.m. dispatch log book notations attendance, thereby prejudice my defense and violated my due process rights under Constitutional Amendment 14.

May the writer further explain (thank you, I'll be delighted to) above where the principal issue appear to surround information that allegedly provided the State witnesses Sheriff Mor, then Trooper Fow's asserted probable cause justification to warrantless search and arrest me, the night/morning of November 10, 1975, information allegedly garnered from the alleged male victim (i.e., although Deputy Mor alleged dispatch information source was unknown and left my jury to speculate, which cannot be legally regarded as fact information evidence), whose testimony together with that of the initial contact twin black sheriff deputies above, sharply conflicts with that of Deputy Mor and Trooper Fow. The same became especially significant. There in my 1975–1976 prosecution, where the commonwealth of Virginia's case being all of a sudden wrestled out of the care of the initial twin black sheriff, who the record reveals talked to the missing person caller first, also who face-to-face contacted and received information from the alleged male victim concerning the description of his alleged abductor and his car. At that time, it was almost entirely dependent on the testimony of Trooper Fow (Caucasian), which, without it, there may have been no indictment and no evidence to carry the case to the grand jury. Therefore, both Mor, Fow and Sheriff Tay's credibility as a witness was an important issue in my March 3, 1976, through May 26, 1976, trial. And any evidence of any understanding as to the nature of the information that state alleged male victim (i.e., and/or alleged female victim) communicated to the two twin black sheriffs that came to the alleged male victim first prior to his talking with Fow (preserved in March 3, 1976, Tr. Ex. 26, 27, pp. 19–20 respectively), as well as the nature of Fow's alleged conversation had with said twin black sheriffs, is relevant, and the jury should've been entitled to know of it. Yet the trial court vehemently made improper comments about the weight of the aforesaid conversations to impair the said testimony from entering the jurors hearing ears.

    The defense was questioning both the alleged male victim about the description he gave the first officials (i.e., twin black deputy sheriffs) and also Trooper Fow about the conversation he had had with same regard to information he allegedly sent out on the police network radio may have disclosed or lead to the disclosure of the material information that comprised the alleged probable cause requisites and prejudice, which was materially relevant to the question of the validity of those several warrantless searches and may well have impeached the credibility of the state testimony given against me said the Supreme Court of the United States in the case of *Davis* cited above.

    That is to say my jurors' determination of credibility was the critical aspect of my trial versus the trial court's numerous comments about the weight of the commonwealth's witnesses testimony evidence, which improperly resolved material issues in dispute, thus interfered with this determination. In that the trial court's ruling that defense was not allowed to question the alleged male victim about anything he might have told anyone other than Fow causally connected with the trial court's disdain demeanor and emphatic opinion interjection of, "What kind of difference does the conversation make? Well, ask him any relevant thing. You are just imposing on the Court's time with a matter that I cannot believe had anything to do with this thing. Just tell me what difference does it make" (preserved in March 3, 1976, Tr. Ex. 54-O, p. 77), whereafter Defense asked the state star witness Fow to describe the conversation he'd had with the twin black sheriffs indicates that the trial court was vouching for the credibility of the conclusion of state witnesses (Mor, Tay) and Fow's asserted probable cause description testimony evidence that was allegedly received from the alleged male and female victims, which said he never spoke with nor laid eyes on Fow until the officials found his sister at their home around 2:00 a.m. This may have influenced the jury to adopt the trial court's views as improper misconduct, as tending to intimate the bias of the court with respect to the character of weight of said testimony, constituted extrinsic fraud. In that the Supreme Court of Virginia during the year of 1999 while deciding a similar issue in a Mr. Barksdale's case determined that "credibility of the witnesses, weight accorded testimony, and inferences to be drawn from proven facts are matters to be determined by the fact finding juror." Also, in 1960, the *Diggs* Supreme Court took the matter a step farther by holding: "It is reversible error not to so instruct the jury." There was no evidence of that!

As pertaining to the aforementioned issue, in 1986 in a similar issue, in *Henshaw v. Commonwealth*, citing the Supreme Court of Virginia established law in the case of *Mazer v. Commonwealth* held,

The Courts and the legislature of this State have been extremely jealous of any expression of opinion by the trial judge upon the weight

of the evidence or the credibility of witnesses. Such expressions have been uniformly held to constitute reversible error.

Hence, the abovesaid trial court's extrinsic fraud errors became compounded by the court's failure to instruct my jury regarding the principles of law in evaluating facts surrounding noncontradicted evidence of impeached witness credibility, thereby prejudiced and discriminated against me by arbitrarily and capriciously depriving me of a fundamentally fair trial before an impartial judge and jury of my peers, in violation of my constitutionally guaranteed right to equal protection and the due process of law under Article VII, Section 1 of Amendment 14 of the US Constitution.

The scribe herein is convinced that you, the reader, have not remotely considered or given any serious contemplation about the above Appeals Courts of proper jurisdiction have long ago determined about such matters, which implicates serious misconduct on the part of a Trial Court Judge who uses his /her oath of judicially appointed authority to bolster a state's case by making rulings to curtail my—an indigent person on trial (i.e., literally for his life)—lawful right to cross-examine the commonwealth or State witnesses against him or prevent such defendant from submitting his evidence to the jury. Well, it may shock you to know that the *Davis* case alluded to above is properly cited by the Supreme Court of the United States as *Davis v. Alaska*, a decision that was had several years before my November, 1975–1976 farce mock trial, which all of the above name trial court officials, including McLau my court-appointed attorney knew or should have had knowledge thereof with fingertip access to yet choose to ignore at the crucial time my constitutional rights beckon, practically pleaded for their attention.

I'm speaking about the *Davis* Court decision that is command applicable to all State Supreme and circuit Courts, which holds in pertinent part the Sixth Amendment right of confrontation of witnesses require that a defendant in a State criminal case be allowed to impeach the credibility of a prosecution witness by cross-examination directed toward revealing possible biases, prejudices, or ulterior motives of the witness as they may relate directly to issues or personalities in the case in hand. The Court noted that one way to discredit a witness is to introduce evidence of a prior criminal conviction of that witness to afford the jury a basis to infer that the witness's character is such that he would be less likely than the average trustworthy citizen to be truthful in his testimony. The partiality of a witness is subject to exploration at trial and is "always relevant as discrediting the witness and affecting the weight of his testimony." (The Supreme Court cites 3 A. J. Wigmore Evidence Section 940, p. 775)

Therefore, it is appropriate to write that as a result of the trial court making rulings it could not legally make, together with my court-appointed defense attorney's gross negligence and/or collusion covenant with commonwealth's attorney and trial court. I was foreclosed from any inquiry with regard to the essence of the materially relevant information that state's alleged male victim communicated to the twin black sheriffs, who initially responded to the missing persons call at the alleged victim's home: who the alleged male victim testified he first talked with after being first let out of his alleged abductor's car, where the trial judge prohibited defense's probe efforts to cross-examine both the alleged male victim about the description he gave the first officials as well as defense probe to cross-examine state's star witness Trooper Fow about the nature of the conversation he had had with the twin black sheriffs with regard to the information garnered that he allegedly sent out on the police network radio, which allegedly formed probable cause basis to warrantless arrest and search me and my car, thereby severely prejudiced my defense by unduly impeding my right to cross-examine, confront, and offer the testimony (or refute) of witnesses, and/or compel their attendance if necessary. In plain terms, it is the right to present my defense and present my version of the facts as did the commonwealth's attorney present matter to allow the jury to speculate upon so it could decide where the truth lies. It was improper misconduct, which prevented me from receiving the benefit of my defense before a fair and an impartial judge and jury constituted extrinsic fraud in violation of my constitutionally protected due process rights under Article VII Section 1 of Amendment 14 of the US Constitution.

If the aforementioned cross-examination been allowed State Trooper Fow might not have answered truthfully, given the previous testimony under sworn oath regard having gotten his asserted probable cause description information from the alleged male victim, who said he never spoke with Fow until the officials found his sister, which was around 2:00 a.m. at his home.

At the same time reader, it would be negligent of this book scribe not to provide you with the discretionary perimeters etched in stone by both the Supreme Court of Virginia and United States Supreme Court to guide the lower Circuit Court judges integrity, demeanor, and the above trial courts' conduct during its criminal adjudication of cases brought before its jurisdiction as my case was. For instance, with respect to the liberty, life, and my property being at stake, the Supreme Court ruled on a similar issue in the case of an individual whose last name is *Mazer*, determined that

> The high official position of the trial judge in a criminal case gives great weight with the jury [i.e., Means: the Judge's position of authoritative ruler ship can easily sway the jurors view of testimony/evidence during trial] to his words and conduct, and it is incumbent upon Him to guard against any manifestation of his opinion either upon the weight of the evidence or the credibility of the witnesses. All expressions of opinion, or comments or remarks upon the evidence which have a tendency to intimate the bias of the Court with respect to the character or weight of the testimony, particularly in criminal cases, are watched with extreme jealousy, and generally considered as invasions of the Province of the jury.

J.D.

The *Mazer* case is cited *Mazer v. Commonwealth*. If you desire to visit your local law library to ascertain the truthfulness of the above opinion, then it will benefit you to know that the 142 prefix number directly after the printed title commonwealth of Virginia is the volume number you must ask the librarian for. Also, the suffix number 649, 653–654 directly after letters Virginia signifies the precise page in volume 142 the court's opinion appears.

May we proceed to review the decision had by the Supreme Court of the United States rendering a similar judge's guidance of opinion, cited in the Supreme Court of Virginia case of *Powell v. Commonwealth*, citing *United States v. Throckmorton*, defining judges conduct and fraud extrinsic or collateral, held in pertinent part that:

> Keeping the adversary's witness from court; secreting or purloining his testimony; or any conduct of the kind mentioned [which[+] would tend to prevent a fair trial on the merits, and thus to deprive the innocent party of his rights. So if a judge sits when disqualified from interest or consanguinity; if the litigation be collusive; if the parties be fictitious; if real parties affected are falsely stated to be before the court; "this definition is in substance approved by the holding of the Supreme Court in the case, as set forth in the learned and instructive opinion delivered by Mr. Justice Miller. It would seem, however that the doctrine of intrinsic and extrinsic fraud is, after all, not much, if at all, [page 755] different from the rule of policy. Above referred to, which refuses a new trial on the ground of after discovered evidence, where the evidence is of the character mentioned above as falling within the condemnation of the fifth rule on the Subject of granting of new trials on the ground of after discovered evidence,

other than proof of perjury or mistake, where such proof has come into existence after the former trial. The latter character of proof tends to show that no fair trial on the merits has been had. It is a matter not suspected to have existed, and so impossible to have been considered or to have been "matter tried by the first court" which the courts have in mind which adhere to the intrinsic and extrinsic fraud doctrine. [See opinions of Chief Justice Shaw in the leading case on the latter subject of *Green v. Greene*, 2 Gray, Mass., 361, 61 Am Dec. 454]. Hence, the granting of a new trial on the ground of proof of perjury or mistake, where the evidence of it has come into existence since the former trial, and appears to be true, not to be collusive, and ought, if true, to produce a different verdict on a new trial, does not violate the doctrine just mentioned.

Much to my surprise, the Supreme Court of Virginia decision in aforementioned *Mazer* case, together with the United States Supreme Court controlling decision in abovementioned *Throckmorton* case is all established governing law before I was born and was certainly known or should've been well known, plus easily accessible to my court-appointed defense attorney, commonwealth's attorney Ben and circuit court trial judge yet! Neither sworn-oath court official made any attempt to summon/call to remembrance these applicable established principles of law to guide their conduct in the exercise of its oath and/or sworn duty to safeguard the federal constitutional rights owed you and I. See the Supreme Court of the United States 1945 established law in the case cited *Hawk v. Olson*. "In the exercise of the duty which lies on us as well as the Nebraska Courts to safe guard the federal constitutional right of petitioners" in its adjudication of my 1975–1976 extended trial.

Moreover, the above-stated scenario necessarily raises other significant questions, such as What nationality, financial cultural or political group did defendant *Mazer* and *Throckmorton* belong? If the answer is Caucasian, McDonald, or Republican, Greek or Polish descent, it becomes clear why I wasn't accorded the benefit of said governing precedent or due process of law principles embodied in the United States Constitution. Thitherto, the pages herein reveals another shocking/A-typical example of the long time standing disparity in fair adjudication and/or failed application of established federal/state statute, rules of law and US constitutional provisions to people of African origin. In direct departure from the ONLY TRUE LIVING GOD's detail command to court and law enforcement officials, over two thousand years ago, saying:

> You shall do no unrighteousness in judgment: you shall not respect the person of the poor, nor honor the person of the mighty: but in righteousness shall you judge your neighbor.

See the Old Testament King James Version of the Bible book entitled *Leviticus* 19:15. Also *Deuteronomy* 1:17.

Chapter 6

The above pretrial rehearsed commonwealth's attorney, trial court, and appointed defense attorney McLau's psyche (i.e., taught at an early age to look down upon and to hate people of African descent, hatred buried deep, deep within the throes of every fabric and fiber of their being) collusion/covenant scam to unlawfully convict me that is finally being pulled up out of the eight-hundred-plus indictment/trial transcribed tomb pages into public view. This triggers memories regard the Jim Crow/Kangaroo court system that Caucasian slave traders/owners, businessmen, Ku Klux Klan—man, law men, governors, and corrupt dishonest judges devised to deny people of African descent/color its guaranteed constitutional rights, rights which were ratified in 1868, after the abolishing of physical slaver in 1865. (See US Constitution Amendment 13, Section 1).

As set forth early on herein this book, being of the age seven, I had begun vividly to experience the oppression of the just us Jim Crow segregated school and housing system. I remember being forbidden to utilize public rest rooms, water fountains, public transportation system, where seats were designated for African Americans above the die set engine or tires at the rear of said bus, hangings of black men for returning cordial speech, in reply to a Caucasian female's greeting, generally was met by unlearned, shallow-minded Caucasian folk with face mask, adorned in white cloth bag or sheet draped over their brainwashed mindset. African American property/homes and livestock was systematically set ablaze. Also, in the case of being accused of breaking a written/unwritten law, such as defending oneself from an act of aggression initiated by the Caucasian counterpart, more often than not, the courts were stacked with racist dishonest judges and jurors who sentenced the African to hard time to be served at a chain gang, with genocidal intent, attired in black and white coveralls, leg irons, and transported to work gangs, where they were daily put to work on railroads, sewer drains, located mostly in Caucasian populated regions, highway landscape, bridges, etc. This history would require additional books. That trend of things prevailed through 1975. There, the acts of bigotry to a few onlookers have gone under cover, plus transformed into democratic, Republican and Tea Party politics, and even there the US government by and for the people have cunningly reserved a back plush seat within its contrived Trojan Horse electoral college vote determining system that is/was established by Caucasian millionaire/billionaire folk to control the governing law-making body in the US of A. This Jim Crow nature promises to become more and more apparent herein. as this book proceeds. To wit, its transparent corrupt activity.

    Only if you can imagine, reader, the multitude of black lives maimed, homes riddled to shreds, children left orphans during the occasions when many of us boycotted the public bus and rail transportation systems in exercise of attempting to acquire our constitutionally guaranteed liberty travel interest. Also to achieve the constitutionally protected right to vote and voice in the manner we the US citizen will be governed. Surely you recall the Rosa Parks, Frederic Douglas, Martin Luther King's prophetic movements, and his barbarous, needless, thoughtless assassination in April 3, 1968 that the ONLY TRUE LIVING GOD via Jesus Christ risen merits utilized to draw light to the fact that people who pay taxes in the US of America maintain the right to have a say in who would represent them (i.e., taxation for representation), in both federal, state, and local governing authorities.

For this cause, black America endured a tremendous battle in 1960–1968, 1970s (my army military days) attempting to access its right to register and to cast a vote, which was determined by the US Constitution Amendment 15, which says, "The right of citizens of the United States to vote shall not be denied or abridged by the US or by any state on account of race, color, or previous condition of servitude." Section 2 provides, "The congress shall have power to enforce this Article by appropriate legislation."

However, many conscious citizens clearly recognize the various ploys orchestrated by covetous, insecure, power-struggling men, some women, who attempt to further discourage the black and poor Caucasian vote by redistricting heavily populated African American communities, particularly in the case of the aged uneducated who must totally depend on others to be kept abreast of such said activity, wickedness personified, satanic, if you will. To momentarily stir your memory, earlier herein you may recall that just prior to my November 10, 1975, vacation travel through Virginia, I actively provided several of my automobiles with at least two of my associates to effect transportation to and from the governors, senatorial, and city councilman polls, then being conducted in the Piedmont that is located in Davidson County, Lexington, North Carolina. My automobiles gave free rides to the polls for anyone requesting it, especially the elderly and/or home ridden people so targeted, when they expressed their interest to vote. My associates would sit in the back seat with the potential voter with a practice ballet in hand to instruct and assist with any questions with respect to properly selecting a particular candidate of their choosing and also explain the nature of such candidates' objective and platform ideology and core values as pertains to the voter and their family well-being.

Perhaps we ought to reconnect with the existing theatrics being professionally portrayed (roleplayed) in my once thriving life, plus the lives of my children, the oldest male being fifteen, by the Halifax Circuit Court judge, its commonwealth attorneys Ben and Bled and prominent defense attorney McLau's collusion who said court assigned as defense attorney at my November 12, 1975, grand jury indictment hearing, plus extended March 3 through May 26, 1976 Jim Crow trial to ensure that my constitutionally guaranteed right to due process was buried deep beneath trial court, the commonwealth's attorney and trial counselor's eight-hundred-plus transcribed records of theatrical roleplay.

Reader, if you do not know or understand what the United States Constitutional Amendment 14, due process rights guarantee you (us) and all other citizens in the respective state where you reside, then the following definition declaration offered by the justices at the Supreme Court of Virginia should help, where the court interjected that

> All authorities agree that due process of law requires that a person shall have reasonable notice and reasonable opportunity to be heard before an impartial tribunal, before any binding decree can be passed Affecting his/her right to liberty, or property.

You can review this case law at your city's law library cited as *Ward Lumber Co. v. Henderson—White Mfg. Co.*, volume 107, Va. 626, 59 S. E. 476 (1907). This equally guarantees you, the citizen, and me the right to present any claim or defense, which are embodied in the term procedural due process. (See *In Re Nelson*, volume 78, N. M. 39, 437 P. 2d. 1008). Aside from all else, due process means you are legally entitled to fundamental fairness during any court proceeding. See West Virginia Supreme Court decision in the case of *Pinkerton v. Farr*, W. Va. 220 S. E. 2d. 682, p. 687.

Just as important or more! At the onset of my November 10, 1975, trials, the ONLY TRUE LIVING GOD OFFERED me the pause spoken of early on in this chapter. This timeout provided me blessings with an opportunity to both study the whole recorded story of the God who is a jealous God, refusing to share His glory with anyone, thing, or idol. At this point in time, I could learn and put to practice the role I played in God's plan but also to know that said role is informed by what has gone on before, what is happening right now, and what will someday occur, or come to pass. Inside my studies, I instantly came under conviction after reading the entire book of Revelation, although I could not at the time, understand the various symbols represented therein. Revelation 20:12 stood out like a huge neon warning sign that read,

> I saw the dead, small and great, stand before God; and the books were opened: and another book was opened, which is the book of life: and the dead were judged out of those things, which were written in the books, according to their works; and the sea gave up the dead which were in it; and death and hell delivered up the dead which were in them; and they were judged every man [and woman] according to their works.

After attentively reading the entire book of Revelation, I came under conviction and I acknowledged that along life's path, I'd sin—transgressed the Ten Commandments of God—in various ways by my sometimes covetous action. I instantly repented while upon my knees, asking God to cleanse me from every sin, both those that had been revealed, as well as them I was unaware of in my heart and soul on the risen merits of Jesus Christ God's son. Whom the King James Version (KJV, hereinafter) of the Bible in the Old Testament book entitled Isaiah 53:5 declares,

> [Jesus] was wounded for out transgressions, and bruised for our iniquities: the chastisement of our peace was upon him; and with his stripes we are healed.

J.D.

Together with the New Testament book entitled 1 John 1:9 proclamation which purports,

> If we confess our sins, he is faithful and just to forgive us our sins, and to cleanse us from all unrighteousness.

Webster defines the term "sin" as "the act of breaking a religious or moral law." I define sin as the willful disobedience to the ONLY TRUE LIVING GOD's revealed will. Most of God's revealed will is encompassed in the Ten Commandments as reviewed in the Old Testament book entitled Exodus 20:1–17, paralleled in the New Testament book entitled Matthew 19:17–21.

Thereafter, I became addicted to reading, absorbing, daily studying, plus inserting God's word of wisdom and instructions into the way I ordered my path in my association with others. Because, as I read, I became more and more persuaded that "all scripture is given by inspiration of God, and is profitable for doctrine, for reproof, for correction, for instruction in righteousness." (See KJV New Testament book entitled 2 Timothy 3:16, buttressed by book entitled 2 Peter 1:20–21.)

Interestingly, without any struggle, God's Word totally diminished the foul language I had gotten into daily practice employing during my six-year army stint until November 10, 1975. At this station in time, I began to adopt terms such as *yes*, *no*, or *should look into it* and ask God to help us select the right course of action. Also, I discovered that that tiny small voice I'd heard many times from my youth up was not my conscience (as I'd previously supposed) rather the faint voice was the voice of the HOLY SPIRIT (see New Testament book entitled Acts 1:8, 2:2–4 KJV), which God had assigned to lead me in the way that pleases Him—a way that would promote firm faith in God's word that began to transform my temporal, carnal understanding and knowledge into a right standing spiritual life or surrender with blessings to influence not only my destiny, but everyone God would place within the circle of my influence.

That is to say in the very midst of March 3 and May 26, 1976 trial persecution, I was receiving the beginning of the Holy Spirit's instructions on how to study and learn what God require of me from the Holy inspired words uttered, then penned by Jesus's initial disciples, disclosed in the New Testament book entitled Matthew 13:8 saying, "Every scribe which is instructed unto the kingdom of heaven is like unto a man that is an householder, which brings forth out of his treasure things new and old." These instructions aptly applied to me in that I having already determined in my heart that God's expressed words concerning my once sinful nature, together with its declaration that this same Holy God had, in fact, created both the heavens, sun, moon, stars innumerable, gravity, oxygen, atmosphere, celestial and terrestrial bodies, plus the earth and all that is therein, as well as mankind, to be invaluable treasures I now possess by the grace and good pleasure of the only TRUE LIVING GOD via Jesus Christ's risen merits. That great patriot prophet Elijah at Horeb heard the aforesaid still small voice of god in the Old Testament book entitled 1 Kings 19:12 (KJV). He received godly understanding with instructions and much, much more. I am by no means comparing myself to Father Elijah, for I consider myself unworthy to bear a cup of water for him!

Additionally, God put into service the Holy Spirit to prompt the ancient prophet Isaiah (approximately 722–721 BC) to interject:

> Whom shall He teach knowledge? And who shall he make to understand doctrine? Them that are weaned from the milk and drawn from the breasts. For precept must be upon precept, precept upon precept; line upon line, line upon line, here a little, and there a little

God left nothing to chances for how I would learn about His holiness, mercy, grace, and being abundant in TRUTH.

During this time, unlike what I was taught and learned in high school this world's academic hall of instructions, I discovered anew that neither mankind nor I evolved from a monkey nor did this earth emanate from Darwin's theory of biological evolution. To this, the Holy Spirit inspired utterances of Father Moses the prophet, as it is written in the Old Testament book entitled Genesis 1:1–31, but specifically verses 26–27 (KJV). In the beginning God created. I vividly put on the reality check that I was/am still father to Gene, Pete, LaTonya, and Tony—with the oldest at age fifteen and youngest age four—and a full-time physical exercise participant, exercising approximately two hours daily in cell, as well as out in the solarium of the six-man cell unit there in the Halifax County Jail. Between appearances in the Circuit Court of Halifax County, Virginia. My faith and trust is being grounded in the WORDS I absorb daily from the pages of my little and full-size King James (versions) Bibles. Somehow, by faith I suppose, I believe that God was at work in the affairs of them I'd been so abruptly taken away from. Also at work on my behalf in the Halifax Circuit Court's persecution. Also, I was moved to write my older sister Lucile, Gene my firstborn, and the Liberty Baptist College, expounding my newly professed faith in Jesus Christ's risen merits. Plus, I launched queries as to what specific day father Moses writing, by Godly inspiration in the Old Testament book entitled Exodus 20:8–15. Am I commanded to observe as holy? Verse 10 specifically says,

> **But the seventh day is the Sabbath of the LORD your God; in it you shall not do any work, you nor your cattle, nor your stranger that is within your gates, says because in six days the LORD made heaven and earth, the sea, and all that in them is, and rested the seventh day; wherefore the LORD blessed the Sabbath day, and Hallowed it.**

Now I'm back in the Circuit Court of Halifax County where Judge Merid presides over the critical issues of the credibility of State law enforcement officials where the principal issue surrounds information that is alleged to have emanated from Deputy Mor to Deputy Tay which allegedly provided Tay's probable cause. Although Tay never said he had probable cause, neither did appointed defense attorney asked him whether or not he had probable cause to warrantless stop, handcuff, search my car, and arrest me while I was on vacation and in route to New York City from Lexington, North Carolina, back on November 10, 1975.

First, perhaps it would throw additional knowledge into the above reference probable cause matter, if we examined the initial source of the information that allegedly caused the very first be on the lookout (BOL hereinafter) to issue over the radio air way from the local Halifax sheriff's dispatch, which the record evinces began with the alleged victim's mother telephoning the local Halifax County Sheriff Department to report what she believe to be a missing persons caper on November 10, 1975, around 10:00 p.m. The said mother after first testifying that upon getting home from work, she'd received a long distance phone call after her children left to go to the little orange market. She talked about seven to ten minutes. She then called the store clerk Ms. Jen who informed her the children was in the store only a few minutes and had left (preserved on May 26, 1976, Tr. Ex. 38, p. 194). The above 10:00 p.m. time correlates with the time testimony of the alleged female victim, who testified that on the night of the alleged offense, she and her brother went to the little orange market somewhere around 9:30 or 10:00 p.m. (preserved on May 26, 1976, Tr. Ex. 15; Tr. Ex. 15-A, pp. 41–42, respectively). "Mama get home about 9:30 p.m. that about ten minutes after Mother was home. We left to go the store" (preserved May 26, 1976, Tr. Ex. 16 and Tr. Ex. 17, p. 42, 43). This testimony is the only uncontradicted state witness testimony.

In the above May 26, 1976, transcribed court record, the alleged male victim testified that it took about five minutes to get from his house to the little orange market, that it only took a minute or so in there, then started back toward home. In just two or three minutes, this car picked him and his sister up (Tr. Ex. 36, p. 21). The alleged male victim allegedly first to be let out of the alleged perpetrator's car and source of the information given to the two policeman that came up to Mr. Per's house, where Mr. Ken, the first civilian person that picked him, carried him. Same allowed them to call the local sheriff's office (preserved on March 3, 1976, Tr. Ex. 27, p. 22 and Tr. Ex. 28, p. 32) there first (preserved in id. March 3, 1976, Tr. Ex. 26, p. 20). They looked like black twins and wore brown uniforms, that he talked to no one else before he talked to the two black policeman the night of the November 10, 1975, offense. Except to Ken, the man that first picked him up (id. March 3, 1976, Tr. Ex. 27, p. 22).

The above recorded testimony agree with the alleged victims mother's testimony, who, in essence, testified that after the store clerk Ms. Jen told her that her children was only in the store a few minutes and left. The said mother claimed she sensed something was wrong, then called the sheriff (i.e., local implied) department (preserved on May 26, 1976, Tr. Ex. 38-A, p. 195). The sheriff said, "They had just had a report that they had found a boy at Grasey Creek and had sent an officer to investigate" (id. May 26, 1976, Tr. Ex. 38-B, p. 198). Reasonable inference had to indicate the sheriff department sent the twin African American sheriffs who the alleged male victim said came up to the Jen's house first to pick him up.

The above facts provides a reasonable inference existed to further indicate that the alleged male victim told the twin sheriffs that he and his sister had been abducted by a person of color (i.e., be it Mexican, Latino, Black, African, Indian, etc.) driving a light sports car. This information was obviously reported to the sheriff department by the twin black sheriffs, then put out over the radio airways to BOL for a light sports car that was responded to by aforementioned official, Deputy Mor, the officer who initially stopped me on routine license check, who physically examined my car and its content, then advised me to have a safe trip (preserved in December 12, 1975, Juv. Tr. Ex. 51, p. 60), suggesting that prior to Deputy Mor's alleged second BOL information that allegedly issued from his dispatcher said, "The car involved was a yellow Mustang II with a dark top and the girl had been located; which Mor allegedly transmitted to officer Tay via call to South Hill Police Department, and gave the license plate

THE JOURNEY

number and description of the man" (preserved in March 3, 1976, Tr. Ex. 44-H and Tr. Ex. 44-I, pp. 110–111). Car information and alleged assailant description that could not have emanated from the African American twin sheriffs, the initial law enforcement officials who got the BOL information description from the alleged male victim, as attested to by alleged male victim in the March 3, 1976, trial session (preserved in id. Tr. Ex. 26 and Tr. Ex. 27, pp. 20–22).

The record also reveals that the alleged male victim further testified "he did not see no license plate, neither the top of his assailant's car" (preserved in May 26, 1976, Tr. Ex. 33, p. 8) evinces a legitimate inference exist to show that Deputy Mor's aforesaid dispatch reception information was in fact commonwealth's attorney, trial court, and appointed defense attorney's pretrial rehearsed collusion/covenant theatrical description supplied by Officer Mor of me, my car's top, and license plate number, which Mor noted/observed during his alleged routine license check stop, constituted acts of committing fraud on the court (i.e., extrinsic fraud misconduct) to bolster commonwealth's case against me.

In addition, the aforesaid contrived erroneous sworn testimony evidence purported by commonwealth's witness Deputy Mor of Mustang II with dark top, license plate number, and description of the man in this car indicates a definitive description of said yellow Mustang II, plus description of me, was paraded as fact before my jury, tended toward testimony which suggests to the jury that they may be allowed to link this said fraudulent, erroneous evidence by speculation with commonwealth's claimed probable cause—me, my car, and the alleged victims crime, if they wish, which was highly prejudicial to my defense and constituted extrinsic fraud misconduct: in that my juror was not entitled to hear commonwealth's extraneous pretrial rehearsed erroneous probable cause, matter.

Note that appointed defense attorney McLau never tendered any objection. Neither did he preserve or bring the said extrinsic fraud matter forward to my first appeal as of right: therewith, prevented me from obtaining the benefit of my defense before a fair and impartial judge and jury of my peers, in violation of my constitutionally guaranteed right to due process of law embodied in Amendment 14 USC, as well as violated section 11 of the Constitution of Virginia.

The aforementioned bold line drawn by the embolden detail facts, regard the description information the alleged male victim gave the twin African American sheriffs. Plus the information the twin black sheriffs allegedly communicated to Trooper Fow makes abundantly clear—the reason why the trial court and commonwealth's attorney refused to permit defense cross-examination probes of Trooper Fow and/or the alleged male victim—regard this vital probable cause information issue (preserved in March 3, 1976, Tr. Ex. 28, p. 22 and Tr. Ex. 54-J, p. 25). For they—the commonwealth's attorney and trial court—vehemently suppressed the above detail probable cause fact answers, which would've rendered said court officials' entire mock trial to be an affront to the judicial system without credible witnesses or reliable evidence of fact.

Other significant unfavorable defense factor, is the failure of appointed trial attorney McLau to request a subpoena be issued to compel the twin black Sheriffs appearance at trial, also motion to compel the production of the sheriff department's November 10, 1975 at 9:00 to 11:00 p.m. dispatch time log, together with BOL messages, plus failure to mount defense argument to trial court's out right suppression of the alleged male victim's description information statement given to said twin black sheriff, together with its suppression of the communication state Trooper Fow intimated he had had with the said twin black Sheriffs, regard description information said sheriffs allegedly obtained from the alleged male victim the night of November 10, 1975, which violated the federal constitutional guarantee of due process under US Constitution Amendment 14. The exclusions as set forth above, rendered it impossible for the jury to reach a fair and an impartial conclusion as the validity of the state claim probable cause issue.

Directly after Deputy Mor's abovesaid radio transmission containing commonwealth's attorney, trial court, defense attorney, and his contrived pretrial rehearsed theatrical description of me, my automobile, and North Carolina (North Carolina hereinafter) license plate

THE JOURNEY

number to South Hill Officer Tay. Officer Tay, during cross-examination by court-appointed defense attorney, testified, "He was told by officer Mor to stop and hold the black man and a yellow Mustang with dark top" (preserved in March 3, 1976, Tr. Ex. 45, p. 134), and "Mor gave him the license plate number" (preserved id. Tr. Ex. 45-A, p. 135). Further, Officer Tay testified he acknowledged the message to hold me, then got out of his cruiser and told me he was going to hold me for further investigation—then put handcuffs on me (id. Tr. Ex. 45-B, p. 143) and placed me in front of the police car and went back to secure my car; and in the midst thereof. "Tay, warrantless, reached in the driver's side and is alleged to have found a bullet in the seat; closed that door to lock it, went to the passenger side _ opened that door (id. Tr. Ex. 45-C, p. 144), looked inside, and there saw a bulge on the passenger side mat" (Tr. Ex. 45-D, p. 145). When Defense asked Tay whether there was any trash on the passenger side (March 3, 1976, Tr. Ex. 31, p. 36). Tay interjected testimony said, "There was no trash or anything to obscure his view of the bulge" (March 3, 1976, Tr. Ex. 45-E, p. 146). Afterward, Officer Tay testified that "he wanted to see if he could find a gun" (Tr. Ex. 46-B-2, p. 147). Then Tay said, "He transported me to South Hill Jail and secured me in a room. I was not free to leave" (id. Tr. Ex. 46, p., 149). At this stage, state Trooper Fow (i.e., was recruited) entered into the court officials cleverly devised drama at South Hill where Tay testified that he told Fow—before Fow arrested me or charged me with abduction and rape—that he had me under a charge for carrying a concealed weapon, a pistol he allegedly found under the passenger side floor mat of my car.

Perhaps you, the reader, is somewhat confused about the posture of what the governing state of the laws or what it offers—regarding arrests, search and seizure of US citizens traveling the interstate highways or local streets of a given city, right? If so, the Fourth Amendment to the United States Constitution, after ratification in 1791, provides,

> The right of the people to be secure in
> their persons, houses, papers, and effects, against

unreasonable searches and seizures, shall not be violated, and no warrants shall issue, but upon probable cause, supported by oath or affirmation, and particularly, describing the place to be searched, and the persons or things to be seized.

Importantly, Officer Tay disclosed reasons for stopping, handcuffing, the warrantless search and seizure of me, my car, and an alleged unloaded pistol did not purport any evidence into the trial record or file in the Circuit Court of Halifax County to support any mandate requirement necessity to search (i.e., where the evidence above showed that the alleged probable cause description information transmitted and received by Officer Tay from Deputy Mor was the fruit of the commonwealth's attorney, trial court, defense attorney, and Mor's contrived pretrial rehearsed theatrical tree that was never purged of its extraneous illegal taint), absent my consent or viable search warrant because Tay did not possess a search warrant and neither of the two historical rationales for the authority to search incident to arrest existed, such as (1) the need to disarm me in order to take me into custody and (2) the need to preserve evidence for later use at trial. In that once I was stopped on the bases of the aforementioned tainted radio transmission—that is, contrived dark top, North Carolina license plate number, yellow Mustang II—description provided by Deputy Mor and put into handcuffs. All the alleged evidence to prosecute was secured.

The facts above clearly shows that where Deputy Mor conducted a routine license check of me, even reached into the back seat of my car and moved clothing around. Then said he had no reasonable basis for suspecting I or my car to have been involved in any criminal activity. Mor did not see a gun or anything that looked like a gun. There was no evidence that I appeared nervous or behaved in a threatening manner, so Mor told me to have a safe trip (preserved on December 12, 1975, Juv. Tr. Ex. 51-C, p. 64), indicating "no essence of probable cause exists where the facts and circumstances would warrant a person of reasonable caution to believe that an offense was, or is being committed." Meanwhile, the same night and prior to December 12, 1975, indictment and March 3, 1976, trial, Mor, Tay, Fow, alleged victims, commonwealth's attorney, appointed defense attorney, investigators and others go to inspected my impounded car. Thus, birth was given to court officials and Mor's pretrial rehearsed collusion/covenant theatrical supplied description of me, my car, and North Carolina license plate number, which could not be legally employed to create viable, proven fact or probable cause to support Officer Tay's warrantless search, seizure, and my arrest, therewith amounted to extrinsic fraud misconduct and violated my Fourth Amendment rights, as applied to the state via Section 1, Amendment 14.

Reader, may I respectfully suggest that you take a bird's-eye view of the principles of law governing the Fourth Amendment protection against illegal searches and seizures, as interpreted and established by the Highest Court in the Nation, in a 1968 decision in the case of *Terry v. Ohio*. Your local law library will be willing to assist you or go online.

Also, reader, it may interest you to know the law-making authority in the commonwealth of Virginia generated Section 19.2-54 of the Virginia Code standard to govern law enforcement officials and its court's judiciary conduct perimeters, which provides,

> **No officer of the law or any other person shall search any place, thing or person, except by virtue of and under a warrant issued by a proper officer (i.e., Judge or Magistrate judge). Any officer or other person searching any place, thing or person otherwise than by virtue of and under a search warrant, shall be guilty of malfeasance in office. Any officer or person violating the provisions of this Section shall be liable to any person aggrieved thereby in both compensatory and punitive damages. Any officer found guilty of a second offense under this**

Section shall, upon conviction thereof, immediately forfeit his office, and such finding shall be deemed to create a vacancy in such office to be filled according to law.

What do you think? Pretty disappointing picture of the American Judicial Justice System at work in the commonwealth of Virginia's Circuit Court of Halifax County during the course of adjudicating my criminal case, huh! I was a lone black man traveling through Virginia on vacation, en route to New York City, actual destination, Bronx.

Therewith, upon additional defense cross examination of state witness, Deputy Sheriff Tay regarding possible impeachment testimony responses to defense queries about the legality of Tay's (i.e., alleged unspoken probable cause assertion/assumption) initial warrantless searches (preserved in March 3, 1976, Tr. Ex. 45, p. 134, Tr. Ex. 45-A, p. 135, Tr. Ex. 45-B, p. 143, Tr. Ex. 45-C, p. 144 and Tr. Ex. 45-D, p. 145) to ascertain the accuracy/validity of his interjected testimony evidence, regarding the manner he entered and searched my car after he'd secured me in handcuffs (preserved in Tr. Ex. 45-D, 145).

Note: Below are direct quotes from my March 3 and May 26, 1976, transcribed court extended documents, as well as quotes from Justices deciding similar issues in the Supreme Court of Virginia, Virginia Court of Appeals and United States Supreme Court:

Defense asked Tay, "When you looked on the passenger side of the car, down on the floor, you didn't see the gun then, did you? You saw a hump?" Tay's answer (A hereinafter) was, "A hump on the floor. Yes, sir."

> Q: Was there any trash on the passenger side?
> A: I'm not too sure about the trash, but wasn't anything over the hump.
> Q: Do you remember testifying previously that there was no trash at all on the passenger side of the car?

> A: I might have. I'm not sure.
> Q: Has anyone told you since then that it might create some problems in the prosecution?

> Commonwealth's attorney objected. The court sustained (preserved on March 3, 1976, Tr. Ex. 45-D, p. 145). Thereafter, defense questioned Tay during my May 26, 1976, trial, as shown in Tr. Ex. 59, p. 115.

> Q: Do you remember testifying [see Tr. Ex. 59-B, p. 116] about this matter on March 3, 1976?
> A: Yes, sir.

> Defense is reading from the aforesaid March 3, 1976, transcribed queries.

> Q: Was this your testimony on March 3, this year? Was there any trash on top of the floor on the passenger side?
> A: No, sir, no trash at all." (March 3, 1976, Tr. Ex. 45-E, p. 146]).

Those defense-Tay exchanges occurred on May 26, 1976, Tr. Ex. 59-C, p. 117. Defense questioning continues

> Q: Is that your testimony on March 3?
> A: Yes, sir.
> Q: Is that correct testimony?
> A: Yes, sir.

Commonwealth's attorney interjected, "He answered the question." Defense questioned Tay's answer. It is critical for the jury's determining the credibility of Tay's prior testimony which tended to discredit Tay's alleged (i.e., unspoken) probable cause inferences.

Particularly in light of the fact that the alleged victims testified, "Their abductor's car was littered with trash on the front passenger floor side" (May 26, 1976, Tr. Ex. 18 and tr. Ex. 18-A, pp. 26–27). Also see, alleged male victim's testimony preserved on March 3, 1976, Tr. Ex. 31, p. 36.

Notwithstanding its relevancy, the trial court Judge Dor intervened, then interjected, "Yes, don't argue with the witness. He said exactly what he knows about it." Defense asked Tay again: "Do you remember seeing any trash at all on the floor of the passenger side?" (preserved in id. May 26, 1976, Tr. Ex. 59-C, p. 117). Thereafter, the Court intervened by interjecting in pertinent part, "He said he can't remember particularly, and he knows there wasn't anything over the bulge. You can't make him say anything. So I don't see any point in pursuing it." (See Court's vouching remark preserved in id. May 26, 1976, Tr. Ex. 59-D, p. 118.)

The trial court's forbidding defense cross examination of state witness, Sheriff Tay, regarding possible impeachment trash no trash testimony responses to defense queries about the legality of Tay's initial warrantless searches is contrary to the Supreme Court of Virginia determination in the case of *McGhee,* having similar impeachment issues, the *McGhee* Court, held the following:

>The fact that his present testimony is inconsistent with his prior statement justifies the showing of the inconsistency, provided he is given an opportunity of correcting the present testimony by directing his attention to the time, place and circumstances of the prior utterances. He cannot escape the consequences by saying he does not recall what he said on the prior occasion.

Above where the aforesaid Ruling was pronounced, is cited *McGhee v. Perkins.* The same holding was cited in 2007 by the justices in the Virginia Court of Appeals, in the case of *Garnett v. Com.*

THE JOURNEY

Reader, if defense cross-examination had been allowed, Tay, might have continued to reply contrary to his prior March 3, 1976, conflicting testimony, and presented my jury a reason to infer that Tay's character may be such that he would be less likely than the average trust worthy citizen to be truthful in his testimony, which is relevant to the question of the validity of the searches, where Tay allegedly found a bullet, secondly a gun, and may well have impeached the credibility of the State bullet and gun testimony given against me. Plus, he may have disclosed possible bias or Tay's incentive to support the commonwealth's attorney's case because the jurors was entitled to have the benefit of defense theories before them as well as the commonwealth's attorneys so they could make an informed judgment as to the weight to place on Tay's testimony. This above rationale is supported by the land mark decision cited by the United States Supreme Court in id. The *Davis* case, cited *Davis v. Alaska*.

Furthermore, the facts and evidence show that the jury's determination of credibility of the witnesses was the critical aspect at my trial and that the trial court's several comments on the weight of commonwealth's attorney witness Tay's testimony improperly interfered with this credibility determination. For reader's clarity here, the Court's improper interference and remarks on the weight of commonwealth's testimony evidence is worth repeating. First, the judge prohibited the defense from attacking Deputy Sheriff Tay's credibility. Secondly, the judge's interjection ruling of (extraneous matter): "Yes, he said exactly what he knows about it, he said [he can't remember particularly], and [he knows there wasn't anything over the bulged] you can't make him say anything, so I don't see any point in pursuing it" (id. Preserved on May 26, 1976, Tr. Ex. 59-D, p. 118), evinces a legitimate inference, which indicated prosecutor and court officials' deliberate suppressing evidence that might've impeached Tay's credibility. Also, a possible knowing use of perjured testimony to support commonwealth's case. The Supreme Court of the United States favorably addressed a similar impeachment issue in the *Napue* and *Mooney* cases, cited as *Napue v. Illinois* and *Mooney v. Holohand*. Decisions that are viable today.

Also, the judge's improper comments on the weight of Tay's impeachment testimony presents a reasonable inference sufficient to indicate that the judge was using its oath of office to vouch for the credibility of state witness Tay's perjured testimony, which may've influence the jurors to trust the court's judgment instead of its own views of the evidence. The Virginia Court of Appeals in the *Henshaw* case—that had similar improper comment issues—issued an opinion that supports the above reasoning. If you the reader desire to view its decision, the case is cited in *Henshaw v. Commonwealth* citing the Supreme Court of Virginia holding in the case of *Mazer v. Commonwealth*, when it was the Jury's duty to determine witnesses credibility, weight accorded testimony and any inferences to be drawn from proven facts, says the Supreme Court of Virginia, in the *Diggs* case, cited *Diggs v. Lail*, whose opinion was buttressed by the Virginia Court of Appeals in the case cited *Barsdale v. Commonwealth* and the United States Supreme Court in the case cited *Giglio v. United States*. All established controlling law in place before my mock 1975–1976 persecution.

The trial court abovesaid improper remarks, together with appointed defense attorney's refusal to defend, tended toward allowing my jury to link by speculation—possibly perjured testimony evidence to me. Plus, this may've conveyed the impression that Tay and the commonwealth's attorney were in a special position to influence the judge, was improper misconduct as tending to intimate the bias of the trial court with respect to the character of the weight of Tay's testimony, constituted extrinsic fraud, as determined by the Virginia Court of Appeals in the above stated *Henshaw* case, citing above Supreme Court of Virginia's decision in *Mazer* that held the following:

> The Courts and the legislature of this State have been extremely jealous of any expression of opinion by the trial Judge upon the weight of the evidence or the credibility or witnesses. Such expression have been uniformly held to constitute reversible error.

THE JOURNEY

Causally connected with the trial court's above underlined "improper remarks" upon the weight of commonwealth's attorney witness's testimony evidence; is its failure to exercise its discretionary duty to safeguard my federal constitutional rights, as determined by Its sworn oath and the Supreme Court of the United States in the case cited *Hawks v. Olson*. Subsequently, the aforementioned extrinsic fraud misconduct was compounded by the trial court's failure to instruct my jurors regarding the principles of law in evaluating facts surrounding non contradicted evidence of impeached witness credibility, as was decided by the Supreme Court of Virginia. In the *Hankerson* case, cited as *Hankerson v. Moody* quoted by the Virginia Court of Appeals decision in *Commonwealth v. Flanery*.

As a matter of fact, I was foreclosed from any inquiry regard. State witness Tay's prior March 3, 1976, conflicting no trash at all testimony, credibility of state bullet and gun testimony that was introduced at trial against me, and/or whether there existed possibly bias or Tay's incentive to support commonwealth's attorney's case—when the judge vehemently prohibited defense from cross-examining Tay's credibility, thereby prejudiced and discriminated against me by unduly impairing my constitutional right to cross-examine, confront, and offer the defense theories, is, in plain terms, the right to present a defense, the right to present my version of the facts as well as the commonwealth's to the jury, so it might decide where the truth lies, constituted extrinsic fraud misconduct that amounted to arbitrary and capricious deprivation of a fundamentally fair trial before an impartial judge and jury of my peers, in violation my due process rights under Section 1 of the US Constitution Amendment 14.

It may interest the reader to know the Supreme Court of Virginia decision involving the defense not being allowed the benefit of his defense, similar above stated legal issues in the case of *State Farm Mutual Auto INS. Co. v. Remley*, citing *Owens-Corning Fiberglas Corp. v. Watson*,

> Courts have long-held that the judgment of
> a Court, procured by extrinsic fraud, [i.e., "by

conduct which prevents a fair submission of the controversy to the Court is void and subject to attack, direct or collateral at any time"].

My court-appointed lawyer made no further attempt to question State witness Tay or discover whether or not Tay had secured a search warrant after he'd handcuffed me or prior to commencing a warrantless search of my car—after he received commonwealth's attorney, trial court, appointed attorney, and Deputy Mor's pretrial rehearsed collusion/covenant's theatrical description of me, my car, and license plate number, which Mor obviously made notes of during his initial alleged routine license check stop (i.e., profiling) on November 10, 1975.

At this juncture, a more complete analogy of the foregone beckons our attention beginning with Deputy Mor's conflicting accounts of his alleged dispatcher's BOL radio transmissions (i.e., as reported in December 12, 1975 Juv. Tr. Ex. 51, p. 60). Radio dispatcher said BOL for a yellow two-door Mustang. Then on March 3, 1976 (Tr. Ex. 44-H and Tr. Ex. 44-I, pp. 110–111) dispatcher said the car involved was a yellow Mustang II with a dark top, North Carolina, license plate, and probable cause description of me).

Together with the twin black sheriffs being the first and only law enforcement officials the alleged male victim communicated a description of their alleged abductor and his car too before his sister the alleged female victim was found by commonwealth's truck driver witness, Charlie, the night of the alleged offense—around 10:15 or 10:30 p.m. (preserved in May 26, 1976, Tr. Ex. 41, p. 60) and the 10:30 time factor ending the alleged abduction i.e., corresponds with the alleged female's 9:30 or 10:00 p.m. story (preserved in id. May 26, 1976, Tr. Ex. 15-A, p. 27) chain of evidence, evinces a legitimate inference exist to show the commonwealth's attorney, trial court, and my appointed attorney McLau, realized the state's case lack fact bases to establish probable cause to stop, arrest, and warrantless search my car traveling through South Hill sometime after 11:00 p.m. the night of the alleged offense.

Therefore, commonwealth's attorney acting in concert with trial court and my court-appointed attorney on bases of Deputy Mor and Court official's above mentioned pretrial rehearsed theatrical covenant/collusion description of me, my car, and license plate number (preserved in December 12, 1975, Juv Tr. Ex. 51-E, p. 85), decided to bring in twenty-year veteran State Trooper Fow, and at the same time prior to indictment or trial: secretly rehearsed the hands-on physical description provided by Deputy Mor above and my corralled automobile; plus inserted the 11:30 p.m. (thereabout) time factor of crime ending into said pretrial rehearsal attempting to match my 11:00 p.m. travel through the general Virginia region (i.e., said official even transported alleged male victim to view my impounded car, prior to indictment or trial) to ensure that Deputy Mor, the alleged victim's mom, the alleged male victim (i.e., alleged first victim that was let out the alleged abductor's car who obviously communicated with the alleged female victim). Also the above named truck driver Charlie and Trooper Fow's testimonies align. The aforementioned matters together with those forth coming ones are matters which the *Throckmorton*, US Supreme Court Justices determined to be extraneous matter "not suspected to have existed, and so impossible to have been considered or to have been matter tried by the first Court," which the courts have in mind which adhere to the intrinsic and extrinsic fraud doctrine, cited in *Powell v. Commonwealth*.

Alleged male victim testified that he went to look at my impounded car (accompanied by State Police Investigator Jac, his dad, and first cousin) at the state police station in Centerville, the same night the alleged crime occurred, about 3:00 a.m. (preserved in December 12, 1975, Juv. Tr. Ex. 37, p. 211). They attempted to access my car that night with a uniform officer (preserved on March 3, 1976, Tr. Ex. 54-V-5, p. 17) as attested to by his mother who interjected that about 3:00 a.m. the male victim left home that night with his father (preserved on May 26, 1976, Tr. Ex. 39, p. 198). Also wrecker driver Jerry testified he saw a little boy approximately twelve years old come in the Halifax Jail with two men while waiting for Trooper Fow (preserved in id. Tr. Ex. 42, p. 15). Alleged victim's mother testified that the children left home about 10:25 p.m. (preserved id. Tr. Ex. 38-A, p. 194), which conflicted with one of the two commonwealth's witnesses—that court officials could not persuade to commit fraud on the court, namely the alleged female victim who testified, "Mama get home about 9:30 p.m. and about ten minutes after mother was home, we left to go to the store" (preserved id. Tr. Ex. 16, p. 42 and Tr. Ex. 17, p. 43). commonwealth's attorney attempted to change alleged female victim's 9:30 time departure, but alleged female victim went on to say, she (mother) gets off at 9:15 p.m. and gets there (home) at 9:30 p.m., and we left going to the store about ten minutes after for the second time again. The alleged victim's mother testified that Trooper Fow came to her house that night around 2:00 or 2:30 a.m., and as she went out on the walk, she saw them take a man out of one car and put him in another car. Defense asked her what the police wanted at that time. The response was they wanted the children to see if they could recognize him (preserved on December 12, 1975, Juv. Tr. Ex. 52-D, and Tr. Ex. 52-E, p. 45 and 46, respectively). And in the March 3, 1976, Tr. Ex. 54-V-4, p. 11, the alleged male victim testified they wanted us to go down there and look at this car, and I went down there to see if it was it—evinces a reasonable inference that Deputy Mor, Fow, with other law enforcement/court officials and alleged male victim got firsthand run through pretrial rehearse instructions.

In addition, alleged victim's mother testified that it was about quarter or close to eleven o'clock p.m. when she telephoned the sheriff department, they had already found her son (preserved on December 12, 1975, Juv. Tr. Ex. 52-F, p. 43) and told her to come pick him up. But when she arrived, they (i.e., the sheriff) had taken him home. That is when she got the report that they had found her daughter (the alleged female victim) and taken her to the hospital (preserved in id. Juv. Tr. Ex. 52-G, p. 44);

Commonwealth's truck driver witness, testified that at approximately 10:15 to 10:30 p.m., as he top a rise at Hyco Landing Bridge, he noticed a car in the medium. The car made a left turn and headed east. As he started down the hill, there was a youngster

THE JOURNEY

walking on the side of the road (preserved on May 26, 1976, Tr. Ex. 41, p. 59). He kept going five or six miles, and at the time the CB, radio announced that something was going on with some youngsters (Preserved in id. Tr. Ex. 41-B, p. 60). So he turned around and went back, by the time he got back the girl was standing directly opposite Hyco Landing Store (preserved in id. Tr. Ex. 41-C, p. 61). Truck driver's 10:15 or 10:30 p.m. interjection time factor changed, when plugged by commonwealth's attorney to 11:30 p.m. time of sighting the alleged female victim. Note, truck driver's initial 10:15 or 10:30 p.m. time factor correlated with alleged female victim's above testimony interjection "Mama gets off at 9:15 and gets home around 9:30 and about ten minutes after we went to the store" testimony. Plus this indicates the approximate time the alleged abduction began and ended at 10:15 to 10:30 p.m. It also shows that the victim's mother's 10:45 to 11:00 p.m. testimony to have been embolden and/or pretrial rehearsed. Also the March 3, 1976, Tr. Ex. 57, p. 75 and May 26, 1976, Tr. Ex. 54-V-6, p. 148 shows commonwealth's star witness Trooper Fow initially fixed the time for the alleged abduction at 10:30 p.m., compared to Fow's apparent pretrial rehearsed time factor testimony (practice) out of jurors' presence, but in commonwealth's attorney, appointed defense attorney, and trial judge's presence, Fow interjected that "he got alleged male victim in Riverdale from Deputy Twins, two African American brothers" (i.e., radically conflicts with alleged male victim's March 3, 1976, Tr. Ex. 25, p. 18 testimony that "he talked to Fowler one time that night at home around 2:00 a.m., after they found his sister," shows a reasonable doubt) that are deputy sheriffs (preserved in id. May 26, 1976, Tr. Ex. 44-F, p. 89). He got the first call from alleged male victim at 11:23 p.m. and a few minutes after, he put out the second BOL for a yellow Mustang II, black stripe at the bottom, headed east of 58 (preserved in id. Tr. Ex. 44-G, p. 90), causally connected with Trooper Fow's sworn testimony evidence reported by the December 12, 1975, Juv. Tr. Ex. 44-D, p. 59-Fow interjected that "he put out the original report [BOL] for a yellow Mustang II and that the sheriff's office and he apparently received the call" (i.e., alleged abduction information) about the same time between 10:30 and 11:00 p.m. (preserved in id. Juv tr. Ex. 54-F, p. 159), which was apparently adjusted again by the said pretrial rehearsed theatrical testimony evidence as reported by the preserved May 26, 1976, Tr. Ex. 54-G, p. 91, where Fow gave substantially different time factor testimony upon the same matter, Fow stated that "he first received the call at approximately 11:23 p.m. and about seven to ten minutes later after talking to alleged male victim, the APB (i.e., all-points bulletin) was put out immediately thereafter 11:30 to 11:35 p.m." (preserved in May 26, 1976, Tr. Ex. 44-G, p. 90). On defense cross-examination, Fow was asked, "You said you first received the call at 11:23 p.m., what time did you first speak to alleged male victim?" Fow's answer was, "I would say approximately seven to ten minutes later."

> Q: Something like 11:30?
> A: 11:30 to 11:35 p.m., and the APB was put out immediately thereafter.
> Q: And your APB was put out entirely on information given you by the alleged male victim?
> A: Yes, it was (preserved in id. Tr. Ex. 54-G, p. 91)

Thereby, this completely destroyed Fow's asserted probable cause justification and created reasonable doubt in the jurors' mind, in my favor.

Notwithstanding the above conflicting materially relevant time factor testimony, favorable to my defense, instead of appointed defense attorney developing the alternative defense, that the law enforcement officials were either mistaken or had erroneously embolden key facts surrounding the time the alleged crime began around 9:55 to 10:00 p.m., according to alleged female victim's interjection that "mama get home about 9:30, and about ten minutes after mother was home, we left to go to the store, testimony" (preserved in May 26, 1976, Tr. Ex. 16 and Tr. Ex. 17, p. 42, 43 respectively) and/or ended at 10:15 or 10:30 p.m. according to Charlie—Commonwealth's witness tes-

THE JOURNEY

timony that purported "found the alleged female victim standing directly opposite Hyco Landing Store around 10:15 or 10:30 p.m." (preserved in May 26, 1976, Tr. Ex. 41-C, p. 61) or falsified key facts surrounding commonwealth's attorney's probable cause description information which allegedly emanated from alleged male victim that he obviously communicated to the African American Twin Sheriff, who picked him up at Mr. Per's home, still appointed counsel adopted the strategy of least resistance, perhaps to keep astride with the pretrial rehearsed collusion/covenant the trial court, commonwealth's attorney, and he agreed on as shown above, also by his questioning commonwealth's witnesses perfunctorily, and haphazardly offered available alibi defense or other evidence at indictment hearing and throughout my extended trial, sentencing or court official's secret suppression hearing, and/or first appeal as of right to advance my best defense against all charged offenses. To wit, appointed trial counsel McLau (trial court and commonwealth's attorney) in the aforementioned sequences of the commonwealth's witnesses conflicting time factor and probable cause description testimony also failed to ascertain the validity and accuracy of the commonwealth's attorney's theory as to my actual physical whereabouts at the time of the 1975 alleged offense, failed to investigate and/or obtain a transcript copy of the local sheriff department dispatch initial all-points bulletin (APB/BOL) broadcast on the night of the alleged crime, failed to subpoena sheriff's department log that maintained the initial law enforcement officials direct contact with the alleged male victim: that is Halifax County twin black sheriff deputies to ascertain whether the description given to them of the alleged abductor or his vehicle matched or did not match the profile of me or my car:

- Failed to use discovery to compel the December 12, 1975, Juvenile Domestic Court grand jury indictment hearing court to correct clerical/court reporter mistake by producing misplaced transcript of my December 12, 1975, pre grand jury indictment recorded proceeding allegedly on tape No. A4 by court reporter (preserved on December 12,

J.D.

1975, Juv. Tr. Ex. 43, p. 87) of Deputy Tay said the clerk, but I say it was the twin black sheriffs who testified. They were the officers dispatched to check out a missing persons call at the alleged victim's home around 9:25 to 9:55 p.m., which court reporter claim was missing (relevant time factor evidence) due to trial court's case management system, to my prejudice, which improperly relieved commonwealth's attorney's duty to prove every element of my charged offenses beyond a reasonable doubt.

- Refused to utilize discovery to compel commonwealth's attorney to produce a copy of all interdepartmental memorandum protocol procedure, all rules regulations and policy protocol/practices at the Halifax County Sheriff Department related to proper dispatch in/out over the air radio BOL transmission time logging ledger in-place on November 10, 1975—the night the alleged crime circumstances evolved—helpful defense preparation fact evidence to establish the truth with respect to my specific whereabouts, comparable to the time the alleged victims claim said crime occurred central to probable cause ruling, which appear to have been deliberately suppressed by pretrial rehearsed court officials' collusion/covenant.
- Also failed to utilize discovery to compel commonwealth's attorney to produce a copy of all interdepartmental memorandum, all rules, regulations, policy/practices and protocol's substantive directives in-place at the State Trooper's barracks in Centerville and/or Appomattox State Trooper headquarters related to proper dispatched in or out over the air BOL transmission. Plus, the November 10, 1975 at around 11:23 to 11:50 p.m. time logging for the night the alleged crime involving me supposedly evolved helpful alibi defense fact materially relevant fact evidence central to trial court's favorable commonwealth's attorney probable cause rulings, with respect to the alleged purported initial (BOL) description information given by the alleged victim(s) to

State Trooper Fow, law enforcement official beneficial alibi defense evidence which the pretrial rehearsed collusion/covenant court officials appear to knowingly suppressed.

Therewith, appointed trial counselor's objection, interjection that "the crucial question that may develop in this case is whether or not described by male victim in his testimony is the same car as that which was apprehended in South Hill, after having been seen in Boydton. Now in the testimony on the suppression, it was established that the car, which was seen in Boydton was the same car as apprehended in South Hill because the license plate was the same" (preserved on May 26, 1976, Tr. Ex. 54-G, p. 9). This vividly illustrates appointed defense counselor McLau's pretrial rehearsed collusion/covenant intent to assist the commonwealth's attorney to wrongfully convict me. Thereby, rebirth in the jurors' mind/(i.e., memory evaluation) Deputy Mor's fraudulent (i.e., although the jury nor I during said trial knew nor was aware that Mor was a party in said pretrial rehearsed sham) pretrial rehearsed second alleged BOL radio transmission to officer Tay in South Hill that supposedly gave Officer Tay my car license number and general description of me after reading, rereading, and making notes of the seven hundred to eight hundred plus transcribed pages of both the December 12, 1975, Juvenile Domestic Court grand jury indictment hearing, coupled with the (convoluted) March 3 and May 26, 1976 extended trial records. Those records shows Mor's North Carolina license plate and black top BOL description information to Deputy Tay could not have come from the African American Twin Deputy Sheriffs or from Mic the alleged male victim (or from the alleged female victim) who was said to have been let out his abductor's car first because Mic's nonrefuted testimony, purported that "he did not see no license plate or the top of his assailant's car" (preserved in May 26, 1976, Tr. Ex. 33, p. 8). This conflicts with Deputy Mor's (i.e., appointed defense attorney's above license plate was the same as described by Mic, about South Hill) earlier under appointed defense counselor's cross-examination when asked, "Was the vehicle that you stopped in Boydton the same as the one you stopped in South Hill?" Mor's answer was, "Yes, sir." Then he was asked, "Same car?" He answered, "Yes, sir, I had the license number of the vehicle I had stopped on routine license stop" (preserved on December 12, 1975, Juv. Tr. Ex. 51-E, p. 85). This definitively identifies the individual the pretrial rehearsed North Carolina license plate number and dark top probable cause description information originated.

The aforementioned fact exchanges shows several legal fraud no-no scenarios. First, it shows that Deputy Mor is the person the pretrial rehearsed license plate number and dark top (alleged) probable cause description BOL information originated (i.e., but not from either alleged victim or African American twin sheriffs). Second, it shows that Deputy Mor, willfully committed fraud on the court because it was Deputy Tay, not Mor who stopped me without probable cause or arrest/search warrant in South Hill (preserved in March 3, 1976, Tr. Ex. 45-B, p. 143). Thirdly, it shows appointed defense attorney McLau's cross-examination suborned Mor to commit fraud on the Court, because appointed defense attorney knew it was Deputy Tay, not Mor who stopped me in South Hill (preserved in March 3, 1976, Tr. Ex. 45-B, p. 143). Fourthly, it shows that both Deputy Mor and appointed defense attorney's pretrial rehearsed covenant/collusion plan was to vividly connect the jurors' mindset! To me and my car as being the alleged victims abductor. Fifthly, it shows, the trial court, commonwealth's attorney and appointed defense attorney, breach their duty, when they failed to correct Deputy Mor's sworn false (i.e., fraud on the court) testimony evidence evinces improper misconduct, as tending toward showing the trial court, commonwealth's attorney and appointed defense attorney's favor toward the weight of the fraudulent probable cause testimony evidence's description information to my prejudice, constituted extrinsic fraud, thereby suggested to the jury that they may be allowed to link Deputy Mor and defense appointed attorney's pretrial rehearsed testimony interjection, saying, "petitioner's vehicle was the same Deputy Mor stopped in Boydton as the same one he'd stopped in South Hill, because he had the license number," fraud on the court testimony evidence by speculation to me, my car and the alleged rape, if they wish, thus, improperly relieved the commonwealth's attorney of its duty to prove every element of my charged offenses beyond a reasonable doubt. (Reader, if you desire to check the governing law, it can be viewed in the Supreme Court of Virginia's decision in the case of *Powers v. Commonwealth*: "It is elementary that the burden is on the commonwealth to prove every essential element of the offenses beyond a reasonable doubt.") Therewith, improperly shifted the burden of proof to me and arbitrarily prevented me from receiving a fair submission of my defense to a fair and impartial judge and jury of my peers—compounded extrinsic fraud misconduct in violation of my constitutionally protected due process rights.

Although appointed attorney objected above, he did not seek a continuance for the purpose to submit a motion for discovery, as well as an order for the production of the aforementioned failed to compel production of documented information and to obtain a subpoena to compel the African American Twin Sheriffs, to present themselves to testify or submit a notarized affidavit, stating the precise time they were dispatch to answer the missing persons—call at the alleged victim's home. Plus, what information they rec'd from the alleged male victim regarding his alleged November 10, 1975 abductor, as well as what information comprised their BOL radio message, and the time it was transmitted even over the airway. The night of alleged offense comparable to the above set forth conflicting 11:23 to 11:50 pretrial rehearsed embolden time factor probable cause testimony and evidence of fact, which would have given the jury—a plausible alternative—that the law enforcement and court officials (i.e., pretrial rehearsed collusion conclusions) were mistaken about key facts surrounding my whereabouts, time factor, and the lack of factual probable cause evidence to arrest me. Moreover, at that 1975/1976 time, I did not know or understand any of the above or the below. Nor did I know the right to call for evidence in my favor was/is guaranteed by both the Sixth Amendment of the US Constitution as well the constitution of Virginia under Article 1 Section 8. The Supreme Court of Virginia Justices in the case of *Massey v. Commonwealth* held, "A defendant is entitled to present his version of the facts along with that of the prosecution so the jury may decide where the truth lies." But the Supreme Court of the United States established decision in the case of *Davis v. Alaska* said, "The jurors were entitled to have the benefit of the defense theory before them so that they could make an informed judgment as to the weight to place on [their] testimony."

Food for thought, in spite of court-appointed attorney McLau's lawful duty to make inquiry when facts known as in my case, and available or are within minimal diligence accessible to defense counsel, which in a significant way, raise a reasonable doubt as to a defendant's guilt. The Fourth Circuit Court of Appeals for the Fourth Circuit in the case of *Wood v. Zahradnick*. This duty applies equally to factual and legal investigations to determine if certain defenses can be used, said the United States District Court justices in the matter of prisoner *Walker v. Mitchell.*

Listen, my appointed attorney McLau, came to the jail one time—the day before my grand jury indictment hearing and spoke with me about fifteen to twenty minutes but never discussed any plan of defense with me. I informed McLau that I did not rape the alleged victim and never kidnapped anyone and that George a jail trustee worker, had informed me that Sheriff Edmond or Edmon, a jailer at Halifax County jail, told his fellow jailers that the alleged victims Aunt Joyce, was a selected juror in my imminent upcoming trial, who expressed desire to hang convict me. I suggested to appointed attorney McLau that he should check the jury list to refute or confirm this claim and also for McLau to contact the witnesses who I went to see before departing Lexington, North Carolina, witnesses I'd ask to make that trip to New York with me, as well as advised McLau that I had consumed one of the three brown and clear no dose/upper pills that I purchased to prevent me from falling asleep behind the wheel. A pill that literally deadens mankind's sex drive and prevents an erection for twelve to twenty-four hours, which made it impossible for me to form an erection plus inhibits any/all sex drives. Notwithstanding, the record clearly demonstrates that McLau adhered to the pretrial rehearsed covenant/collusion he made

THE JOURNEY

with commonwealth's attorneys Ben and Bled, and the honorable trial court, Judge Merid by not discussing any plan of defense with me and never once informed me of any fact pertinent to my case and never summoned or offered the above mentioned twin black sheriffs' time frame account of their response to the missing persons call at the alleged victim's home, and/or of the probable cause description information provided them by the alleged victim Mic, since they were the first law enforcement officials the alleged victim testified he talk with the night of the alleged offense (preserved in March 3, 1976, Tr. Ex. 26, also Tr. Ex. 27, pp. 19–20) or make any sustainable effort to pursue my alibi defense.

Appointed defense attorney in failing: to present the jury any testimony from the African American Twin Sheriff Deputies, the initial law enforcement officials to interact with the alleged victim Mic to ascertain the accuracy and validity of the commonwealth's attorney's theory as to my actual physical whereabouts at the time of the alleged 1975 offense, from my alibi named witnesses below investigate and obtain the transcript of the initial all-points bulletin (APB/BOL) put on the radio air by the African American Twin Sheriffs via Halifax Sheriff department dispatcher, compel the Juvenile Domestic Court jury indictment Court Judge Carm to correct alleged clerical mistake by producing alleged misplaced transcript record on tape No. A4, compel commonwealth's attorney to produce a copy of all interdepartmental memorandum, procedures, and all rules, regulations, and policy protocol at both the Halifax County Sheriff department/South Hill, and the State Trooper Station located in Centerville/Appomattox State Trooper Headquarters and Halifax County related to proper in/out dispatch over the air BOL transmission time logging in place on November 10, 1975, the night the alleged crime occurred, with said aforementioned failures.

The appointed defense counselor denied me opportunities to strengthen the question of the (i.e., pretrial rehearsed) embolden 11:23 to 11:50 p.m. time and the state's embellished BOL for a yellow Mustang II, with a black top and North Carolina license plate number probable cause information offered against me by the commonwealth. Had appointed defense attorney conducted a bare bones discussion with my alibi witnesses and vigorously argued the evidence of the alleged female victim who testified she and her brother Mic left her mother's house at approximately 9:30 p.m. in route to the little orange market about a few minutes away on the night of the alleged offense (preserved on May 26, 1976, Tr. Ex. 16, p. 42, and id. Tr. Ex. 17, p. 43), which was not contradicted.

There was a failure to utilize discovery to compel commonwealth's attorney to produce a copy of all evidence the alleged male victim Mic averred that it took about five minutes or so in there, then started back toward home, and after just a couple of minutes this car picked him and his sister up (preserved in id. Tr. Ex. 36, p. 17).

The evidence of truck driver Charlie (preserved in id. Tr. Ex. 41, p. 59) testified that he saw a small girl that evening on the highway as he was heading west at approximately 10:15 or 10:30 p.m. (preserved id. Tr. Ex. 41-B, p. 60).

The evidence of my alibi witness Sallie Haley that she was at her mother's home in Lexington, North Carolina, at approximately 8:30 p.m. on the night of the alleged offense when I came by to see her brother Mayhew (preserved in id. Tr. Ex. 9, p. 246).

The evidence of my alibi witness George Fortune that he live in Lexington, North Carolina, and on the night of the alleged offense, I came by his house around 9:00 p.m. and asked him to go with me to New York, but his finances wouldn't let him. At approximately ten minutes after 9:00 p.m., I left (preserved in id. Tr. Ex. 10 and id. Tr. Ex. 10-A, pp. 248–249).

Also my alibi witness and (Caucasian) coworker JD Shf on the crew at the Lexington Memorial Hospital, who testified that he lives about ten miles on the other side of Lexington, North Carolina that it took him two and one half hours to drive to the Halifax County Circuit Court's parking lot, (preserved in id. Tr. Ex. 14, p. 245): establishes the factual time factor concerning me and the alleged victim's whereabouts on the night of the alleged offenses, which provided appointed defense attorney McLau, sufficient fact evidence information to mount the defense that it is virtually impossible that I could be departing from Lexington, North Carolina, at 9:10 p.m. and be committing said crime in Halifax, Virginia, at 10:00, 10:30, or 11:00 p.m. as the alleged victims aforesaid time factor testimony averred.

Notwithstanding, appointed defense attorney McLau's pretrial rehearsed collusion/covenant with the trial court, commonwealth's attorney and other State witnesses outweighed my constitutional right to call for evidence in my favor, counsel opted not to so defend my time factor alibi defense theory to the jury, which evinces a reasonable inference that show the trial court, commonwealth's attorney, and appointed defense attorney became acutely aware that the aforesaid alibi time factors regarding me and the alleged victims whereabouts on the night of the alleged November 10, 1975, crime would be a commonwealth's attorney probable cause problem. Therefore, said Court officials acted in concert to veil (deliberately suppress) the twin black sheriffs being dispatched at 9:30 to investigate a missing persons complaint at the alleged victim's home, also alleged male/female victims 9:30 p.m. in route to little orange market, plus state truck driver witnesses 10:15 to 10:30 spotting alleged female victim and my alibi witnesses 9:10 p.m. noting my departure from Lexington, North Carolina, time factor shows my and the alleged victim's whereabouts was materially relevant facts.

And at the same time, it was determined that it was important to establish before the jury, the trial court, commonwealth's attorney, appointed defense attorney and State Trooper Fow and Deputy Mor's 11:23 to 11:50 p.m. time factor (extraneous matter) (preserved on May 26, 1976, Tr. Ex. 44-G. p. 90, id. Tr. Ex. 54-G, p. 91, and Mor's preserved on December 12, 1975, Juv. Tr. Ex. 51, p. 60, respectively) suited to equal my passage through the Halifax County region that was employed to establish commonwealth's attorney and state's primary witness Trooper Fow's asserted probable cause theory. After having testified in the March 3, 1976, trial session that he put out his BOL message that the time the crime happened was 10:30 p.m. (id. Tr. Ex. 57, p. 75), violated section 8 of the Virginia Constitution—

discussed by the Supreme Court of Virginia, in the case of *Massey v. Com*. Likewise, the Supreme Court of the US addressing defendant *Davis* constitutional right under the Sixth Amendment for evidence in his favor, held, "The Sixth Amendment right of confrontation of witnesses requires that a defendant in a State criminal case be allowed to impeach the credibility of a prosecution witness," case is cited as *Davis v. Alaska*, outweighed, even trumped! McLau's nondiscretionary duty prescribed under Part 6, Section 2, Canon 6, Rules of Supreme Court of Virginia, Disciplinary Rule 6-101(A)(1) and (D), which in pertinent part, provides, "A lawyer shall inform his client of facts pertinent to the matter and of communications from another party that may significantly affect resolution of the matter," as determined by the Supreme Court of Virginia in the case of Pickus *v. Virginia State Bar*, decided under former DR 6-100 (neglect of matters entrusted to attorney).

Also the Virginia Code of Professional Responsibility, provides guidance as to types of situations that raise the specter of actual or potential conflicts of interests. For instance, Ethical Conduct. (EC) 2-39 in part states, "A lawyer should decline employment if the intensity of his personal feelings, as distinguished from a community attitude, may impair his effective representation of a prospective client." See Part 6, Section 2, Rule of the Supreme Court of Virginia Ethical Conduct, Rule EC 2-39.

Although the United States Supreme Court in the case of *Strickland v. Washington* avoided a specific guideline for attorney conduct, it affirmed that reasonably effective assistance of counsel require undivided respect for the "duty of loyalty, a duty to avoid conflict of interest, which are perhaps the most basis of Counsel's duties."

Reader, what do you think of counsel's duty as he applied to my interests herein set forth? From my prospective, so far the facts evinces that counselor McLau failed extremely short of his duties owed me, as McLau made no adequate effort to interview those above set forth important witnesses, plus failed or refused to conduct appropriate investigation, both factual and legal discoveries in accordance with the United States District Court for the Eastern District, Richmond Division, determined in the case of *Walker v. Mitchell.*

Including McLau's refusal to interview or summon Caucasian (convicted murderer) trustee inmate Geor, who informed me that he'd overheard Deputy Sheriff Edmon communicate to his fellow jailers that his wife (i.e., also a relative of the alleged victims) Joyce was going to be one of the jurors in my trial. He further expressed sentiments of "hanging me." Information that I made known to appointed defense counselor prior to trial. McLau's pretrial rehearsed collusion/covenant with commonwealth's attorney and the trial court was affective because neither did McLau summon Geor, nor did he utilize peremptory challenge to contest Mrs. Joyce presence on my jury. Please see the case cited *Bennett v. Commonwealth*, sitting en banc, the Supreme Court of Virginia, held the following:

> The trial court abused its discretion by refusing to dismiss for cause a juror who was the brother of one of the law enforcement witnesses for the commonwealth. The Court held that the juror must be dismissed to maintain public confidence in the integrity of the system even if the juror states that he can be impartial in the case.

Chapter 7

Reader, are you ministering questions in your mind as to what part of my wrongful conviction does the commonwealth's witnesses' pretrial rehearsed time factor probable cause description information of my automobile color, color of top and North Carolina license plate number, play in my actual jury conviction?

The following explanation is plausible. First, the transcribed recorded facts, plainly illustrates that Deputy Mor's initial BOL for light sports car alleged dispatch information changed after he routine stopped me for license check and told me to proceed and not drink anymore, and have a safe journey. At this point, Mor had written down my license plate number, color of my car and description of me, then communicated said information to Deputy Tay, State Trooper Fow, commonwealth's attorney, trial court and appointed defense attorney during their pretrial rehearsal. Therefore, Mor's testimony, amounts to extraneous evidence, which was derived from a contrived outside the eye-witness source.

Second, same as was Mic's yellow Mustang II with black stripe at the bottom description (preserved in March 3, 1976, Tr. Ex. 20, p. 6), was pretrial rehearsed testimony (i.e., extraneous matter), which derived also from his personal same night inventory of my automobile at the State Trooper's station impound lot (preserved in December 12, 1975, Juv. Tr. Ex. 37, p. 211), accompanied by investigator Jack (i.e., and Trooper Fow, inferred), his father and cousin with flashlights but said testimony did not come from Mic's memory after being first let go from his alleged abductor's car. Also said contrived extraneous matter description could not retroactively validate commonwealth's attorney's pretrial rehearsed 11:23 to 11:50 p.m. embolden time factor BOL for yellow Mustang II, with black top and North Carolina license plate probable cause rhetoric. Had aforesaid description emanated from Mic's memory, deputy Mor's first BOL would not have been, for a light sports car; thus, appointed defense attorney's aforesaid failures or pretrial rehearsed collusion refusal to defend tended toward relieving the commonwealth's attorney duty to prove every element of my charged offenses beyond a reasonable doubt, as well as suggesting to my jury that they may be allowed to link the above mentioned extraneous pretrial rehearsed 11:23 to 11:50 p.m. time factor BOL for a yellow Mustang II, with black top and North Carolina license plate probable cause description testimony information evidence by speculation to me, my car, and the alleged victims, if they wish, which was highly prejudicial to my constitutionally guaranteed right to present his version of the facts to a fair and an impartial Judge and jury of my peers, constituted extrinsic fraud, effectively denied my due process rights, in violation of Section 1 Amendment 14 of the US Constitution.

To this end, the Supreme Court of the United States in a similar matter in the case of *Turner*, determined the following:

> The requirements that a jury's verdict must be based upon the evidence developed at the trial goes to the fundamental integrity of all that is embraced in the constitutional concept of trial by the jury.

In the constitutional sense, trial by jury in a criminal case necessarily implies at the very least that the evidence developed against a defendant shall come from the witness stand in a public court room where there is full judicial protection of the defendant's right of confrontation of cross-examination, and of counsel, cited as *Turner v. Louisiana*. Plus, the Fourth Circuit Court of Appeals for the Fourth Circuit in the Aston case held the following:

> The impartiality of the jury must exist at the outset of the trial and it must be preserved throughout the entire trial. The device of voir dire and the right to strike prospective jurors, both peremptorily and for cause, are the means by which an impartial jury is seated in the box. Thereafter, the law guarantees that every defendant may have his case decided strictly according to the evidence presented, not by extraneous matters or by the predilections of individual jurors. The law has developed an elaborate body of the law of evidence, the overall purpose of which is to restrict "the deliberation of jurors to that which is trust—worthy, probative and relevant, where evidence is relevant but also prejudicial, the law requires that it not be received until it has been demonstrated that its relevance and probative value outweigh its collateral prejudicial effect." (*Aston v. Warden*)

The above pretrial rehearsed testimony evidence and established law evinces: The trial court employed modes of procedural rulings it could not lawfully adopt as demonstrated, after appointed defense attorney raised question about the probable cause description information Mic, the alleged male victim gave the first law enforcement officials (i.e., twin black sheriffs), and commonwealth's attorneys Benn/Bled objected. Then the trial court intervening interjected, "Defense was not allowed to question the alleged male victim about anything he might have told anyone other than Trooper Fow" (preserved on March 3, 1976, Tr. Ex. 54-J, p. 25).

After the appointed defense attorney raised second question directed to state's star witness Trooper Fow to describe the probable cause conversation he had had with (twin black) sheriffs. The initial officers dispatched to investigate a missing persons call at the alleged victims home around 9:25 to 9:55 p.m. on November 10, 1975—the first law enforcement officials the alleged male victim said he communicated with after being first let out his alleged abductors car, commonwealth's attorney objected, "What kind of difference does the conversation make?" Defense answered, "The question is whether or not this officer had probable cause to arrest this defendant, and I'm probing to see what information he had to base the arrest on." At that point, the judge interjected, "Well, ask him any relevant things. You are just imposing on the court time with a matter that I cannot believe had anything to do with this thing. Just tell me what difference does it make?" (preserved id. Tr. Ex. 54-0, p. 77). This was improper, as tending to intimate the bias of the trial court with respect to the character of the weight of the twin black sheriff's suppressed probable cause testimony evidence, constituted extrinsic fraud that was compounded by the trial court's improper remarks ruling, regard the character of the weight of the court/Commonwealth's attorney's suppressed probable cause description (i.e., inferred) information that both the alleged male victim gave the first contact officers (i.e., twin black sheriffs) and the conversation Fow had with the said (twin black sheriffs) law enforcement officials, amounted to extrinsic fraud misconduct, which may have influence the jury to trust the trial court's judgment rather than its own views of the testimony evidence, thereby virtually denied my due process required benefit of my defense to my prejudice, in violation of Section 1 Amendment 14 as well as improperly relieved the duty of the commonwealth's attorney to prove every element of my charged offenses.

Listen, we will continue to layout more of the aforementioned materially relevant issues, but before that, may I share with you the Virginia Court of Appeals addressing such an issue in the case of *Henshaw v. Commonwealth*, citing the Supreme Court of Virginia established 1925 precedent law in *Mazer v. Commonwealth*, which held the following:

> The courts and the legislature of this state have been extremely jealous of any expression of opinion by the Trial Judge upon the weight of the evidence or the credibility of witnesses, such expressions have been uniformly held to constitute reversible error.

But checkout, the Supreme Court of Virginia decision in the case of *State Farm Mutual INS. Co. v. Remely* citing Its 1992 holding in *Owen-Corning Fiberglass Corp. v. Watson* at 638-stated that courts have long-held that the judgment of a court, procured by extrinsic fraud (i.e., "by conduct which prevents a fair submission of the controversy to the Court is void and subject to attack, direct or collateral at any time").

Also, I believe it is important to note the existing probability that based on Deputy Mor's alleged first dispatch message to BOL for a light sports car (preserved in December 12, 1975, Juv. Tr. Ex. 59) presents a plausible or "reasonable inference," suggesting that said aforesaid BOL description information was initiated by the aforesaid (i.e., twin black sheriffs) as a result of the description information Mic, the alleged male victim, gave them (preserved in March 3, 1976, Tr. Ex. 26, 27, pp. 19–20) about the alleged abductor's car that had picked him and his sister up, causally connected with the aforesaid conversation state's primary witness Trooper Fow had had with said (i.e., twin black sheriffs) the night said alleged offense occurred (preserved in December 12, 1975, Juv. Tr. Ex. 54-D, p. 123). That was deliberately suppressed by commonwealth's attorney, trial court, and appointed defense attorney's pretrial rehearsed theatrics was improper misconduct.

Reader, please first consider here where the principal issue appear to surround information that allegedly provided state witnesses Deputy Sheriff Mor, Tay, then Trooper Fow's asserted probable cause to warrantless search and arrest me. Information allegedly garnered from the alleged male victim whose testimony conflicts with theirs (preserved in May 26, 1976, Tr. Ex. 33) that said he never saw the license plate or top of his assailants car. He talked to Fow one time at his home after officers had found his sister (preserved in March 3, 1976, Tr. Ex. 25, p. 18), especially where the state's case being dependent almost entirely on the testimony of Trooper Fow, which without it there may have been no indictment and no evidence to carry the case to the grand jury. Therefore, Fow's (and Mor) credibility became an important issue in my trial, and, any evidence of any understanding as to the nature of the information that State alleged male victim communicated to the two black twin sheriffs that came to him first (preserved id. Tr. Ex. 26, 27, pp. 19–20), prior to talking to Fow, as well as the nature of Fow's conversation he'd had with twin black sheriffs is relevant and the jury was entitled to know it said the United States Supreme Court in the case of *Davis v. Alaska* and *Giglio v. United States.*

The defense questioned both the alleged male victim about the description he gave the first officials (i.e., twin black deputy sheriffs] and also Trooper Fow about the conversation he had with them regard to BOL information Fow allegedly sent out on the police network radio may have disclosed or lead to the disclosure of the material information that comprised the alleged probable cause requisites and prejudices, which is materially relevant to the question of the validity of the several warrantless searches, and may have impeached the credibility of the state's testimony given against me. The above 1974 Supreme Court of the United States' established precedent in *Davis* confirms this conclusion. The jurors' verdict would've been different.

For all intents and purposes, the jury's determination of credibility was obviously the critical aspect in my trial and the court's above and below several comments, improperly resolved material issues in dispute and interfered with this determination. The Virginia Appeals Court in the case of *Barksdale v. Commonwealth* held that "credibility of the witnesses, weight accorded testimony, and inferences to be drawn from proven facts are matters to be determined by the fact finder" (i.e., jury). It is reversible error not to so instruct the jury, said the Supreme Court of Virginia in the case of *Diggs v. Lail*. There is no evidence of that! this prerogative of the jury is so jealously guarded that it is usually held to be reversible error for judge to comment on the weight of the evidence or the credibility of the witnesses, said the Virginia Court of Appeals in the above cited case of *Henshaw v. Commonwealth* (citing cases), thereby deprived me of the benefit of my defense and constituted extrinsic fraud misconduct to my prejudice and foreclosed any inquiry with regard to the essence of the materially relevant information State alleged male victim communicated to the first twin black Sheriffs, who initially responded to a missing persons call at the alleged victim's home.

When the trial prohibited defense's probe cross-examination of both the alleged male victim about the description he gave the first officials and also my appointed attorney's probe cross-examination of state's witness Fow about the nature of the conversation he had with the said twin black sheriffs, regarding information he allegedly sent out on the police network radio, which allegedly formed probable cause to warrantless arrest me, thereby compounded its extrinsic fraud misconduct to my prejudice and unduly denied my constitutional right to cross-examine, confront, and offer the testimony of witnesses, and/or compel their attendance if necessary, is, in plain terms, the right to present a defense, the right to present my version of the facts as well as the prosecutions to the jury, so it may decide where the truth lies, amounts to arbitrary and capricious deprivation of a fundamentally fair trial before and an impartial judge and jury, denied equal protection and due process of the law in violation of Amendment 14 of the US Constitution.

If the reader be so inclined, they are invited to lookup the Supreme Court of Virginia's decision in the case of *State Farm Mutual Auto INS. Co.* V *Remely* citing *Owens-Corning Fiberglass Corp.* V *Watson*, more Supreme Court of Virginia law that support my above trial court made rulings throughout my 1976 trial it could not legally adopt amounted to improper misconduct, extrinsic fraud violation.

Moreover, the other scenario with respect to the aforementioned claim regarding, the trial court made rulings not supported by established law involved the trial court's above prohibiting defense from questioning the alleged male victim about the probable cause description information he gave the first officials. Plus, restricting defense from questioning state's primary witness Trooper Fow, about the nature of the conversation he had had with the aforesaid first officials (i.e., twin black sheriffs) who talk to the alleged male victim after he was let out of the alleged abductor's car, constituted the suppression of materially relevant exculpatory defense impeachment testimony evidence that improperly relieved the commonwealth's attorney's duty to prove every element of my charged offenses beyond a reasonable doubt, as well as allowed the commonwealth's attorney to use known false pretrial rehearsed license plate number and black top probable cause description information testimony (i.e., uncorrected by trial court, commonwealth's attorney and appointed defense attorney) to convict me, thereby denied me due process of law and violated the Fourteenth Amendment of the US Constitution and is contrary to the Brady Rule, as determined by the United States Supreme Court's 1963 established law in the case of *Brady v. Maryland*. Also its decision in the case of *Giglio v. United States*.

The Supreme Court of Virginia 1970 established precedent in the case of *Powers v. Commonwealth* decided that "it is elementary that the burden is on the commonwealth to prove every essential element of the offense beyond a reasonable doubt."

Trial court's aforesaid rulings was improper as tending toward allowing the jury to believe Mor and Fow's perjured (i.e., North Carolina license plate and black top testimony; causally connected with the alleged male and female victims was in his automobile and said it was a yellow Mustang II with dark stripe pretrial rehearsed probable cause description information) pretrial rehearsed testimony was credible, and they could link by speculation both Deputy Mor and trooper Fow's perjured pretrial rehearsed probable cause testimony evidence to me, if they wish, which was introduced at trial against me, may have influenced the jury to adopt the court's judgment rather than its own views of said evidence was also improper as tending to intimate the bias of the court with respect to the character of the weight of Mor and Fow's pretrial rehearsed probable cause perjured testimony evidence, constituted extrinsic fraud, compounded by trial court's over ruling defense motion to suppress alleged procured evidence on grounds of illegal search (preserved in May 26, 1976, Tr. Ex. 50, and id. Tr. Ex. 50-B, pp. 283–84), to my prejudice, thereby arbitrarily denied me due process, in violation of Amendment 14.

Further, the May 26, 1976, Tr. Ex. 50-B, p. 284, reveals that the trial court recalled Shf (i.e., my Caucasian coworker) my character and departure from Lexington, North Carolina, time factor witness, and disqualified him in jurors' presence.

As portrays, the above extrinsic fraud misconduct by the trial court have been compounded by its failure to instruct the jurors regard principles of law in evaluating facts surrounding noncontradicted evidence of impeached witness credibility so holds the Supreme Court of Virginia in the case cited *Hankerson v. Moody* quoted by the Virginia Court of Appeal's case, cited as *Commonwealth v. Flaneary*: Therewith, prejudiced and discriminated against me by arbitrarily and capriciously preventing a fair submission of my alibi defense fact/witnesses to the jury, thereby deprived me of my constitutionally guaranteed right to a fundamentally fair trial before an impartial judge and jury, in violation of Supreme Court of Virginia Rules of Judicial Conduct and denied equal protection and the due process in violation of Amendment 14 of the US Constitution.

Reader, the aforesaid rules of Judicial Conduct Canons may be viewed in the Virginia Codes Annotated via your local law library or perhaps your Google search per your cell or smart phone. Now with regard to above Court's failure to instruct the jury matter the Supreme Court of Virginia in the case of *Dowdy v. Commonwealth* determined that

> It is always the duty of the Court at the proper time to instruct the jury on all principles of law applicable to the pleading and the evidence.

But see the Supreme Court of Virginia Ruling in the case of *Taylor v. Commonwealth* that held, "A correct statement of the law applicable to the case, which the law is stated [is one of the] essentials of a fair trial."

In the case of such above improper comments of a judge connected with its capricious rulings causally connected with appointed defense attorney McLau's collusion efforts with the commonwealth's attorney to wrongfully convict me. The Supreme Court of Virginia in the case of Jones *v. Willard* in pertinent part held courts have long-held that the judgment of a court, procured by extrinsic fraud (i.e., "by conduct which prevents a fair submission of the controversy to the court, is void and subject to attack, direct or collateral at any time").

Means such a case cannot be time barred by rules of the Supreme Court of Virginia Rule 1.1's 21 day rule, neither by Code of Virginia statute of limitations, when filed in any State Circuit Court, specifically under Code of Virginia Sec. 8.01-428(D).

Additionally, for your edification, Code of Virginia provides in pertinent part:

> Upon Motion of the plaintiff or judgment debtor and after reasonable notice to the opposite party, the court may set aside a judgment by default or a decree pro confesso [i.e., a term applied to a bill in equity and the decree founded upon it, where no answer is made to it by the defendant. Under Rules practice, this has been replaced by a default for want of prosecution. Fed. R. Civil. Procedure 55(a)]. Upon the following grounds: (1) a judgment which ought not, in equity and good conscience, to enforced; (2) a good defense to the alleged cause of action on which the judgment is founded; (3) fraud, accident, or mistake which prevented the defendant in the judgment from obtaining the benefit of his

defense; (4) The absence of fault or negligence on the part of the defendant; and (5) The absence of any adequate remedy at law.

Section (D) provides,

> This section does not limit the power of the Court to entertain at any time an independent action to relieve a party from judgment or proceeding, or to set aside a judgment or decree for fraud upon the court.

Now may I influence the reader to look at the Supreme Court of Virginia determination in the case cited in *Powell v. Commonwealth*, quoting from the 1878 established law had by the Supreme Court of the United States of America in the case entitled *United States v. Throckmorton*, defining extrinsic or collateral fraud, held in pertinent part that:

> Keeping the adversary's witness from court; secreting or purloining his testimony; or any conduct of the kind mentioned (which) would tend to prevent a fair trial on the merits, and thus to deprive the innocent party of his rights. So if a Judge sits when disqualified from interest or consanguinity; if the litigation or collusive. This definition is in substance approved by the holding of the Supreme Court in the case, as set forth in the learned and instructive opinion delivered by Mr. Justice Miller.

Moreover, in matters of forbidding cross-examination along with being allowed to make one's defense, I insist that you make every effort to view or revisit the Supreme Court of the United States' decision in the case of *Gordon v. United States* (decided 1953), especially if you are an African American or person of color with very little money, because I personally believe you should be knowledgeable about the rights which the constitution of the United States declare to be yours and mine as citizens. Not to say or assume you aren't already aware of such. Otherwise, you could so easily discover yourself in my position, seventy eight, having endured forty-six-plus years of unlawfully incarceration with no lawyer or support organization, news media, or program to take on the commonwealth of Virginia.

Chapter 8

Hitherto, the preserved recorded facts demonstrates that I have not been given a chance, much less a fair trial or impartial jury one, nor the one in the Circuit Court of Halifax County State Court, which the due process clause of the Fourteenth Amendment of the US Constitution require. Notwithstanding that I am to be presumed innocent until proven guilty beyond a reasonable doubt. According to the established law narrated by the Supreme Court of Virginia in the case of *Powers v. Commonwealth*, **"It is elementary that the burden is on the commonwealth to prove every essential element of the offense beyond a reasonable doubt."** Also, check out the case entitled *Hankerson v. Moody*, quoted in *Commonwealth v. Flaneary*, indicating the commonwealth's attorney's duty was to seek justice and prove every essential element of my charged offenses beyond a shadow of doubt. Not with conjecture, speculation, or extrinsic fraud misconduct as has been demonstrated herein.

Importantly, during the abovesaid time, neither did I know nor understand that the trial court judge had equally breached its Judicial duty to safeguard my federal constitutional rights—a nondiscretionary duty as prescribed in the language of Section 1 Amendment 14 US Constitution, as declared by the Supreme Court of the United States in the case of *Hawk v. Olson* held, in pertinent part, **"In the exercise of the duty which lies on us as well as the Nebraska Courts to safeguard the federal constitutional rights of petitioner"** (*Lisenba v. California; White v. Ragen*).

My interpretation of that holding, is that Judges in the United States are required to protect the constitutional rights of any citizen (i.e., person) from risk of loss, who come before its bench charged with breaking written or posted laws.

Reader, it should be observed that in the 1960s and 1970s, the presumption of innocence when a Caucasian or person with political ties and money came before a court of proper jurisdiction was very strong! For example, during the trial of such aforesaid cases, if the law enforcement officials did not follow the constitutional law to the letter, the case would be dismissed or over turned and reversed on appeal. To the contrary, when it pertained to me, a lone black man with no political connection or adequate financial substance to defray the expense of a competent attorney with integrity, the presumption of innocence never came into the court officials mind, or among the appointed defense attorney's arsenals. History attests to the fact that the same mindset was the mode of procedure for any person of color with no finances whether teenager or ninety-nine years of age. Same as today, 2020, the courts have adopted the trap thing, entitled harmless error doctrine—that is, if the law enforcement officials do not make any effort to follow the letter of "constitutionally" required law, the Justices by n large do not dismiss the case because the judge (i.e., not the facts) alleged vested discretion determines that the error was harmless.

On a similar note today (1976), I received a response from one of the Liberty Baptist college instructors regard my put forth earnest query that ask, Which day—Saturday or Sunday—do we acknowledge as the day my King James Version of the Bible in the book entitled Exodus 20:8–11 command believers who have repented of their sins and accepted Jesus Christ to be our Lord and Savior keep/observe? I am talking about the Fourth Commandment, which Holy inspired Writ declares! was etched in stone tablets with the ONLY

TRUE LIVING GOD's finger while Father Moses looked on (check it out in the Old Testament book entitled Exodus 31:12–18, but specifically verse 18 or the book entitled Deuteronomy 9:10), which says in pertinent part,

> You shall keep the Sabbath, to observe the Sabbath throughout your generations, for a perpetual covenant. It is a sign between me and the children of Israel for ever: **For in six days the LORD made heaven and earth, and on the Seventh day He rested, and was refreshed.**

The liberty Baptist College minister's response interjected that "because Jesus was raised from the dead on Sunday the first day of the week, we worship on Sunday to celebrate that. I hope this help to answer your question."

Although said response did not adequately justify me to be disobedient to God's express command to keep holy the Seventh Day—Saturday, particularly in light of God's admonishment to His believing flock by the inspired words spoken by the Prophet Samuel, in the Old Testament book entitled 1 Samuel 15:22, saying,

> **Have the LORD as great delight in burnt offerings and sacrifices, as in obeying the voice of the LORD? Behold, to obey is better than sacrifice, and to hearken than the fat of rams.**

As occasion would have it, I continued with my search of the scriptures as I begun consciously to encounter numerous new mountains to climb consisting of unrelenting challenges to my new unveiled faith, which is grounded in the ONLY TRUE LIVING GOD Son's death and resurrection from death's grip. So it was for the second time in life, my submission and mental spiritual comprehension permitted God to give me up close and personal inventory views, regarding the vacillation of human compassion in daily sustenance.

That is to say I recognized that so many (i.e., including myself), far too many people are love starved and spiritually scarred, one of many reasons why various youngsters take their own lives at times, be it drug overdose or self-annihilation. Also, in the above named Court system and jail, there existed hourly trouble and dejection, teetering on the brink of irreversible disaster. Calamities existed of such magnitude that they can only be corrected by the outstretched hand of Jesus (i.e., my humble inspired view, of course).

Reader, often times I have reflected over the past wasted opportunities and years as the tiny small voice of God urged me to attempt to engage the fellows there in the Halifax County jail cell block in a positive spiritual manner. Also, during those communicative interactions, it appeared at times that those engaged were somnambulating through this temporal earth tainted by the stench of complacency and apathy, compounded by what I coined the "I syndrome" (please view the Old Testament book entitled Isaiah 14:12–15), pausing only to dispute as to why "I" should not have this or that.

In my resolve within, this "I" syndrome mirrored my pass, after being honorable discharged from the army at Fort Hamilton located in New York in that I was taught by the daily covetous practices observed of my peers, practices I seemingly accepted unquestionably. Importantly, this "I" syndrome had bred and will yet breed selfishness in both adolescent young and in the JESUS, unbelieving aged adult folk minds.

A typical example is had in the judge presiding over my criminal case, also its commonwealth's attorney, court-appointed attorney, and their state sworn witnesses, and aged nonregenerated jurors' mind resulted in them learning or retaining little or nothing of integrity value. Instead, many such bore not the invisible, but real wounds caused by weaponized words, which they wrongly wheeled at me during my trial. Here, I've made abstract reference to the New Testament Holy Spirit-inspired book entitled James who understood the potential danger of our words to cause destructive and long-lasting harm when he called the tongue an unruly evil, full of deadly poison (i.e., James 3:8 KJV). By employing this strong comparison,

James emphasized the urgent need for believers in Christ to recognize the immense power of their words. Even more, he highlights the inconsistency of praising the ONLY TRUE LIVING GOD (Jesus) with one phrase and then injuring others who are made in God's image with the next word (James 3:9–10). Such were the inconsistent pretrial rehearsed testimony verbal attacks during my mock trial to my detriment, so all thought.

Furthermore, the *I* syndrome, relative to my past, does not cause conjuncture in that as earlier unveiled herein my LORD found me there in prison, and there showed me the detestable state I'd been cunningly led into. There, I abhorred the position I was in and earnestly made pleas to the ONLY TRUE LIVING GOD [Jesus] to give me the guidance and courage that I would need to become fruitful to HIM, both at that present time during my mock trial and future in other areas of God's dominion to which He would, from time to time, according to the counsel of His own Divine will, plan and purpose, appoint me.

Then and there arose the question "What is anything without love?" I discovered that this did not mean that there was/is something wrong in caring about oneself. But quite the contrary, it is my belief that it is necessary to maintain wholesome self-esteem in order to become fruitful and be productive. Also, in contrast to my previous nonregenerated years bound by sin, I discovered, by obeying the instructions I began to receive from the Holy Ghost. I was yet learning that my fellow mankind: should have uppermost in our souls and conscience or love for others as one's self! However, while gleaning this and other invaluable insights from the above named experiences, it is evident that the trend of action/interaction among most people whether behind bars or in society is not to be altruistic or compassionate and loving. Why? Television and news media dramatically reveal that so many are rich in carnal, academic, scientific, social knowledge, and material possessions, yet their souls and humanity appears impoverished. I've resolved in my inner man that while it can be difficult to make the efforts and/or expressions to show compassion and TRUE love for one's fellow human being. It can be done with God's guidance.

Additionally, in contrast to my previous non regenerated years in sin (i.e., disobedience to God's revealed will) prior to Jesus—the WORD of the ONLY TRUE LIVING GOD transforming work within my inner man. I believed that "love" had to be discerned and/or found in some kind of tangible action/or material thing or love's presence remained concealed. Now I believe and have concluded as a result of further instructions provided from God the creator: that the ability to love others comes (ONLY) through and from God, our Creator, my strength and buckler, and rock of my salvation. John one of the initial Apostles of Jesus was moved by the Holy Spirit to penned this reality in the King James version of the Bible New Testament book entitled John 15:9–13. Albeit, it seems to be an acceptable concept among the masses of scholarly folk that good manners, good breeding, developed culture, and/or degrees of social refinement are morally good. However, by comparison to mature God fostered love. I have determined the aforesaid are all secondary to lasting genuine love.

During this time while attempting to digest and apply the creator's love directives in my association with others, many of who did not embrace inspired biblical formulas, especially those in the Circuit Court of Halifax County Court room. Notwithstanding, God's ever present love and compassion, compelled! me to reach out via United States Postal Service's snail mailing system to those that I may have offended in the North Carolina neighborhoods (from which I was taken captive on November 10, 1975) to seek forgiveness from: Gene Perry Kindle, Vernom Holmes (a.k.a. Pete), LaTonya M. (Princess) Smith, and Tony J. Matthews for not being the father to them as I learned, I should've been. Also forgiveness from my children's mothers namely Patricia Kindle, Virginia Ann (Holmes) Duke, Mae Ruth (Norman) Edwards, Daphine J. Matthews, and Rosylin, plus others. My mood was wow! I had not yet felt compelled to reach out by God's empowered instructions with earnest care, as I made attempts again and again, to touch and make understandable difference in everyone, as the ONLY TRUE LIVING GOD (Jesus) caused me to inhabit the circle of interaction influence among same.

Meanwhile, my pretrial rehearsed "farce of a trial" in the Circuit Court of Halifax County Virginia continued, with the presence on the bench a judge who was not impartial, coupled with the absence of defense counsel due and/in part to said counsel's loyalty to the pretrial rehearsed collusion/covenant he'd made with the commonwealth's attorney and trial judge.

Further, the record show that commonwealth's circumstantial case depended almost entirely on speculative/suggestive matter and the testimony of Trooper Fow, without it, there could've been no indictment and no evidence to carry my case to the grand jury. Fow's credibility as a State witness was therefore an important legal issue in my case, and any evidence of fraud or perjury on Fow's part was relevant, and the jury was entitled to know about it. Fraud on the court that centers around the said pretrial rehearsed time factor probable cause and credibility issues that was/is in sharp dispute, which presented serious questions for determination by my jury and not the judge.

For example, during my March 3, 1976, trial segment, upon defense cross-examination of state's star witness Fow, the below exchanges occurred:

> Q: Trooper Fow, in your direct exam testimony on February, do you remember the following, "I saw, observed this car getting [sic] on Route 58 answering the description of the one given to me as being used in the crime I opened the right front door, and took the flashlight, as I looked between the corner of the right front seat was a blond Caucasian hair. I retained that and labeled it. I was shining the flashlight around in the glass in the back, and I could see some smudges or whatever (id. 03/03/76 Tr. Ex. 47, p.

84, & Tr. Ex. 47-B, p. 85, also preserved in 12/12/75 Juv. Tr. Ex. 54-S, p. 113).

A: Let me stop you right there. I saw through the glass what I thought were finger prints on the right front glass. I never did get in the car. I closed it up and locked the car.

Q: Was that your testimony? (preserved in 03/03/76, 1976, Tr. Ex. 47-B, p. 85)

A: I believe so, this occurred after the arrest was made (id. Tr. Ex. 54-T, p. 86).

Q: But Trooper, do you understand that your testimony in the (i.e., indictment) preliminary hearing was clearly that you used your flashlight and looked and saw finger prints? You then opened the door and went inside the car. Isn't that what happened?

A: I don't know, you are getting me confused. What was my testimony? (id. March 3, 1976, Tr. Ex. 54-T, p. 86).

Q: Well, are you saying that the testimony was mistaken?

A: No, sir, I am not denying anything in that testimony.

Q: Now, Trooper, would you read your testimony?

A: No, sir. I don't think it would be necessary.

Q: All right, let me read it to you again (id. March 3, 1976, Tr. Ex. 54-V-2, p. 95).

These contrasting statements was critical of the accuracy of Fow's prior testimony and tended to discredit Fow's credibility and affected the weight of his testimony said the United States Supreme Court justice's decision in id. *Davis v. Alaska*, which held in pertinent part,

> The sixth amendment right of confrontation of witnesses requires that a defendant in a

State criminal case be allowed to impeach the credibility of a prosecution witness's by cross-examination directed at possible bias deriving from the witness's probationary status as a juvenile delinquent not withstanding that such impeachment would conflict with the State's policy of preserving the confidentiality of juvenile delinquency adjudication.

Some of the language of the US Supreme Court's opinion appears particularly applicable here, in my case, where that court interjected,

> That one way to discredit a witness is to introduce evidenced of a prior criminal conviction of that witness to afford the jury a basis to infer that the witness's character is such that he would be less likely than the average trustworthy citizen to be truthful in his testimony.

That court then added that,

> A more particular attack on the witness's credibility is effected by means of cross-examination directed toward revealing possible bias, prejudices, or ulterior motives of the witnesses as they may relate directly to issues or personalities. The partiality of a witness is subject to exploration at trial, and is "always relevant as discrediting the witness and affecting the weight of his testimony."

Similarly, the Virginia Appeals Court in the case of *Garnett v. Com.*, citing the Supreme Court of Virginia decision in *McGhee v. Perkins*. **"He cannot escape the consequences by saying he does**

not recall what he said on the prior occasion." A similar holding can be viewed in the Virginia Appeals Court decision in *Curie v. Commonwealth*.

Perhaps it would interest you to know that contrary to the aforementioned Supreme Court of the United States' established precedent law in the *Davis* case and precedent held by the Virginia Appeals Court in the *Garnett* case, the trial court intervened by interjecting, **"Mr. McLau, he has testified and in his best recollection of what he is saying today is right. But contrary to that he is not denying it. It will be up to the Court to determine which is correct. I do not wish for you to read it to him again"** (preserved in id. March 3, 1976, Tr. Ex. 54-U-2, p. 95) was improper.

In that the aforesaid trial court's intervention-interjection, wrongfully prohibited my defense from attacking states star witness Fow's credibility. Secondly, the trial court's intervention interjection remarks ruling of (extraneous matter) was improper misconduct and evinces a legitimate inference which indicated Court official's deliberately suppressed evidence that may have impeached Fow's credibility, as well as presents a possible knowing use of perjured testimony to support the State's case, which conflicts with the Supreme Court of the United States clearly established precedent law in the case of *Napue v. Illinois* holding, "The prosecution may not knowingly present false testimony and has a duty to correct testimony that he or she know to be false." Similarly echoed in Its 1935 decision in the case of *Money v. Holohan*. Plus, a plausible inference can be drawn here that the Trial Court aforesaid remarks was [vouching]for the credibility of State's star witness Fow's perjured testimony, which may've influenced the jurors to trust the Court's judgment Ruling rather than its own views of said evidence, thereby prejudiced my defense by preventing me from offering the said perjured testimony evidence to a fair and an impartial judge and jury of my peers, denied due process, in addition, regarding the aforementioned matters of the trial court's improper remarks upon state's star witness's perjured testimony evidence tending toward intimating the bias of the court with respect to the character or weight of the testimony evidence, constituted extrinsic fraud misconduct, denied me the due process of law, in violation of Amendment 14 of the US Constitution in contravention of the juror's prerogative, thereby prejudiced my defense: as penned in the previous chapter, supported by the Virginia Court of Appeals established law in the case *Henshaw v. Commonwealth*, citing *Mazer v. Commonwealth* held the following:

> The high official position of the trial judge in a criminal case gives great weight with the jury to his words and conduct, and it is incumbent upon him to guard against any manifestation of his opinion either upon the weight of the evidence or the credibility of the witnesses. All expressions of opinion, or comments, or remarks upon the evidence which have a tendency to intimate the bias of the Court with respect to the character or weight of the testimony, particularly in criminal cases, are watched with extreme jealousy, and generally considered as invasions of the province of the jury.

Particularly, when clearly established law as determined by the Supreme Court of Virginia Justices in the case of *Diggs v. Lail* said, "It is the jury's duty to determined witnesses [Fow's] credibility, accorded testimony, and inferences to be drawn from proven facts". As was applied by the Virginia Court of Appeals in the case of id. *Barsdale v. Commonwealth*. Same is/was applicable in my case, where the commonwealth's case relied primarily on circumstantial pretrial rehearsed evidence and defense attorney's collusion; meaning the credibility of the commonwealth's attorney's star witness, was therefore relevant.

Thitherto, the above court officials' extrinsic fraud misconduct was compounded by the trial court's failure to instruct my jury regarding principles of law in evaluating disputed facts in issue, weight of the evidence and credibility of witnesses involving contradicted evidence of impeached witness, as determined by the Supreme

Court of Virginia's 1979 established law in the case of *Dowdy v. Commonwealth*. Particularly, egregious conduct when appointed trial counsel (via pretrial rehearsed collusion/covenant with the trial court and commonwealth's attorney) elected to remain speechless, tantamount to improperly relieving the commonwealth's attorney of his duty to prove every essential element of my charged offenses beyond a reasonable doubt, as the 1970 established precedent law by the Supreme Court of Virginia Justices determined in the case of id. *Powers v. Commonwealth* requires, as was applied in the case of *Hankerson v. Moody*, quoting *Commonwealth v. Flaneary*.

Tended toward allowing my jurors to believe Fow's perjured testimony was credible, and they could link by speculation Fow's purported information evidence regard probable cause, also alleged found blond hair strand (i.e., that could not be scientifically connected to alleged victims), bodily fluids and print(s) testimony to me, which was introduced at trial against me, if they wish. Plus, this may've conveyed the impression that state's star witness Fow and the commonwealth's attorney were in a special position to influence the judge, was improper as tending to intimate the bias of the court with respect to the character of the weight of Fow's perjured testimony, constituted extrinsic fraud, which was double compounded by the court overruling defense motion to suppress alleged procured evidence on grounds of illegal search (preserved in May 26, 1976, Tr. Ex. 50 & Tr. Ex. 50-B, pp. 283–84), particularly since Mic the alleged male victim testified that he never saw or talk to Fow the night of the alleged crime, at his home until after the officials had found his sister (preserved in March 3, 1976, Tr. Ex. 25, p. 18). So where did Fow's probable cause information emanate?)

Reader, if your interest has been stimulated, even a little, consider visiting your local tax payer sustained law library to heighten your constitutional rights knowledge and view how the judges reached their precedent setting laws in the Virginia Court of Appeals decision in the case of *Henshaw v. Commonwealth*, quoting id. *Mazer v. Commonwealth*, a Supreme Court of Virginia case decided in 1925. Plus the Supreme Court of Virginia case cited *Powell v.*

Commonwealth (decided 1922 yet is still precedent) at p. 754, quoting from *United States v. Throckmorton* (precedent decided 1878) by justices in the United States Supreme Court, precedent that corroborates the favorable legal position penned above. But the credibility matter has more…

In other words, the aforementioned pretrial rehearsed covenant/collusion acts of appointed defense attorney, commonwealth's attorney Bled/Benn together with the trial court, effectively foreclosed my defense from any inquiry regarding state's star witness Fow's December 12, 1975, indictment conflicting testimony that said, "I used my flashlight and looked and saw fingerprints? Then I opened the door and went inside the car," contrasts Fow's March 3, 1976, trial testimony interjections, "Let me stop you right there. I saw through the glass what I thought were finger prints on the right front glass. I never did go in the car, I closed it up and locked the car" credibility of commonwealth's alleged probable cause contrived information by virtue of the trial court's judgment ruling prohibiting defense cross-examination probe on Fow's credibility, thereby prejudiced and discriminated against me, by virtue of its impeding my constitutionally protected right to cross-examine, confront and offer the defense theories, is in plain terms, the right to present a defense, the right to present my version of the proven facts as well the prosecutions to the jury, so it can decide where the truth lies was improper misconduct and constituted extrinsic fraud misconduct.

For further clarification, the trial court's above ruling is in direct conflict with the clearly established (precedent) controlling law set forth above held by the Virginia Court of Appeals, the Supreme Court of Virginia, and the United States Supreme Court in the case of id. *Davis v. Alaska* holding the following:

> If the right to effective cross-examination, embodied in the Constitution's sixth amendment, is denied, constitutional error exists without the need to show actual prejudice; because, the jurors were entitled to have the benefit of the

defense theory before them so that they could make an informed judgment as to the weight to place on [their] testimony.

Similarly held by Its decision in the 1953 case of *Gordan v. United States*. My court-appointed defense attorney McLau, was unable to commit to making such a typical required defense on account of his pretrial rehearsed agreement made with the trial court and commonwealth's attorneys, was improper, constituting extrinsic fraud misconduct, as tended to prevent me from obtaining the benefit of my defense before a fair and impartial judge and jury of my peers, thereby arbitrarily and capriciously deprived me of a fundamentally fair trial in violation of Section 11 of the Constitution of Virginia, as well as violated plaintiff's equal protection and due process of law rights under Section 1 Amendment 14 of the US Constitution.

There is another established precedent you may find of interest that should've been applied which was decided by the Virginia Appeals Court the case of *Rose v. Com.*, holding that

> **An Order is void Ab initio [i.e., Lat, and means: from the beginning; from the first act], if the mode of the procedure used by the Court was one that the Court could "not lawfully adopt the lack of jurisdiction to enter an order under any of those circumstances renders the order a complete nullity and it may be impeached directly or collaterally by all persons, anywhere, at any time, or in any manner."**

Also the Supreme Court of Virginia in the case of *Jones v. Willard* said,

> **Courts have long-held that the judgment of a Court, procured by extrinsic fraud [i.e.,**

"by conduct which prevents a fair submission of the controversy to the Court, is void and subject to attack, direct or collateral at any time"].

At this early stage of this mock trial, I was completely unaware of the devastating jury damage already done, including commonwealth's attorney's several usages of extraneous term "boy" matter during his direct exam of Deputy Mor testimony concerning his (pretrial rehearsed) modified 11:51 p.m. time factor probable cause theory and radio transmission with Deputy Tay where Mor interjected, "I said that this boy [referencing me] might be armed and to hold him until I get there" (preserved in March 3, 1976, Tr. Ex. 61-B, p. 112), causally connected with commonwealth's attorney's direct exam of its Star witness Troop Fow, regard question of the validity of his second warrantless search of my impounded car—during grand jury indictment hearing where Fow's testimony interjected, "It is hard for me to tell you what I found in South Boston before I tell you what I found in South Hill and went back with this boy [reference is to me] now that I've had time to think about it, it's racist as well as an extraneous matter" (preserved in December 12, 1975, Juv. Tr. Ex. 61, p. 111), inserted into what was already a racially sensitive prosecution, an issue I may commit to exploring before this issue of the book close. Meanwhile, In 1974, the Supreme Court of the United States clearly established precedent in the case of *Davis v. Alaska* determined that a defendant (i.e., me) in a criminal trial has the right "to seek out the truth in the process of defending himself." Also held in the case of *Chambers v. Mississippi* held that "few rights are more fundamental than that of an accused to present witnesses in his own defense."

CHAPTER 9

Now we are getting into the thick of things at my 1975 indictment 1976 criminal trial where we must move backward to the biological evidence and its chain of custody, which the commonwealth's attorney, trial court, and appointed defense attorney (i.e., acts in collusion) purposely failed to ascertain the validity and the proper chain of custody thereof said (alleged) illegally seized biological evidence and/or the premises of state's star witness Trooper Fow's home to ascertain the security of said home and book case where said biological evidence was placed on-top, unsecured, neither sought summons or Court Order for State Trooper headquarters (located at Appomattox) /or for the Halifax County Sheriff Department to produce established policy/protocol in-place at the time of alleged offense occurred that govern the disposition of such seizures to ascertain whether or not Fow was required to commit said alleged biological evidence to a (law enforcement agency evidence room/safe, to be properly processed)/

Nor did aforesaid named officers of the court conduct interviews with Fow's sixteen- and twenty-year-old daughters who Fow testified had unfettered access and frequented the book case room; and/or failed to investigate Fow's poodle dog's whereabouts

J.D.

Relative to said alleged biological evidence failed to ascertain the validity of Trooper Fow's testimony, which is preserved on December 12, 1975, Juv. Tr. Ex. 58-F, pp. 147–153, respectively. The evidence of this witness—when commonwealth's attorney Bled asked, "Trooper Fow, did you obtain samples of saliva from the defendant?" Fow's answer was, "Yes, sir."

> Q: What did you do with the wet cotton swabs?
> A: They were taken to my home, laid out in the air to dry.
> Q: Then what did you do with them?
> A: They were labeled along with three taken from the female victim, mailed by certified mail to the laboratory in Richmond.
> Q: A report thereon was later returned to you?
> A: Swabs also. I have the swabs.

Thereafter, appointed defense attorney McLau upon cross-examining Fow, asked, "You say you took it home to air dry, the saliva?" Fow answered, "Yes, sir."

> Q: Where did you put it at your home?
> A: In my bookcase in my den.
> Q: Was it locked up inside something?
> A: No, sir.
> Q: And it was placed where it was no books, I take it, for the purpose of drying?
> A: They were placed in front of the encyclopedias, on the shelf.
> Q: Did members of your family have access to that room?
> A: Yes, sir. They were there when I placed them there.
> Q: How many people live in your house?
> A: I have two daughters, age twenty and sixteen.

Q: And they would frequent this room?
A: Yes, sir.
Q: How long was this material laid out in your den before you took them to Richmond?
A: This was just one night.
Q: And then they were taken the next day by you?
A: No, sir, I didn't take those. I mailed them by certified mail.
Q: Where did you seal them?
A: At my home. You see there was just three. This is the sample taken from the defendant here, and I have the ones in another envelope here, and the three envelopes were placed in a larger envelope, you see, and mailed by certified mail to the consolidated laboratories in Richmond.
Q: At what time did you lay out these swabs to be air dried, about what time of the day?
A: It was after six. I don't know exactly what time I got home that evening, around eight, I believe.
Q: Did you have any guest at your home that night?
A: No.
Q: Are there any pets at your home?
A: Yes.
Q: What kind?
A: One dog, poodle.
Q: As to the other items which have been submitted over objection, I am talking about the hair and the other matters that you testified about, which were received from the car. These were sealed at the time you received them?

A: Yes, sir.
Q: Where were these envelopes kept?
A: With me, in my vehicle.

Also preserved on May 26, 1976, Tr. Ex. 58-G, p. 129, and Tr. Ex. 58-H, p. 134, was same above issue

> Q. Okay…What did you do to preserve the items that you had taken…the gun, the clothing and the hair sample?
> A. Well, it was only the one hair sample at that time, and her clothes, and the gun. After we got to the sheriff's office, I, the defendant, was made to change clothes, and I took the clothing of the female victim and the clothing of the defendant, John David Simpson, and hair [i.e., which could not be connected to this offense], and clothing that I found the semen specimens on, and I personally transported same and gave them to Mr. Bob, the finger print expert in Richmond: was improper misconduct.

This tends toward the defense attorney's bias with respect to the weight of state's star witness Fow's testimony, which allowed the jurors to link by speculation—non verified, unsecured, and noncontested, noncumulative alleged biological evidence and Fow's speculative conclusory—purported information/illegally seized alleged evidence to me, my car, clothing, the alleged female victim and her clothing, if they wish, which was highly prejudicial to my defense.

In addition, there is no proven fact or indication that said above alleged evidence was ever properly committed to a legitimate law enforcement agencies' evidence room/safe per established policy/protocols. To wit, my alleged biological evidence was obtained from the fruit of the poisonous tree doctrine (i.e., as was detailed in chapter 4 by reference to commonwealth's attorney's structured invalid probable cause saliva affidavit—that Fow used to illegally seize my saliva, constituted fraud on the court false positive identification matter that was placed in question by indictment Judge Carm, yet illegally ruled to establish probable cause. Also, chapter 6 above, regarding commonwealth's attorney, trial court and appointed defense attorney's pretrial rehearsed theatrics probable cause description garnered from Deputy Mor about me, my car, and North Carolina license plate number that Mor had observed and noted results of his initial alleged routine license check stop, which the alleged victims and twin black sheriff's testimony did not support, including Deputy Tay's search and gun seizure without a search warrant versus perjured testimony: As well as demonstrated above, in chapter 8, where the trial court judge's improper remarks and intervention prevented me from presenting state's star witness Trooper Fow's December 12, 1975, illegal search and seizure indictment testimony, compare to his March 3, 1976, trial warrantless search perjured testimony evidence to a fair and impartial judge and jury of my peers that was suppressed and knowingly used by the commonwealth's attorney, trial court, and appointed defense attorney to obtain my grand jury indictment and July 26, 1976.

Conviction, thereby amounted to extrinsic fraud misconduct as tending to intimate the bias of the trial court with respect to the character of the weight of the commonwealth's attorney's pretrial rehearsed embellished 11:23 to 11:50 p.m. time factor probable cause testimony evidence, thus improperly relieved commonwealth's attorney's duty to prove every element of my charged offenses beyond a reasonable doubt, to my prejudice, thereby denied my constitutionally protected due process rights, in violation of Section 11 of the Constitution of Virginia, as well as violated Section 1 Amendment 14.

Noting that the Justices in the United States Supreme Court in the case of *Wong Sun v. US*, determined that "evidence which is spawned by or directly derived from an illegal search or illegal interrogation is generally inadmissible against the defendant because of Its original taint." Also it held that "knowledge garnered from copies of illegally seized documents could not be used to frame an indictment or secure a subpoena for the originals," as decided by aforesaid Court in the case entitled *Silverthorne-Lumber Co. v. US*.

Moreover, an examination of the abovesaid material facts together with cited Supreme Court of the United States and Virginia's controlling law evinces that the trial court breached its duty to safeguard my federal and State constitutional rights, likewise did the commonwealth's attorney breach his fiduciary duty to seek justice, as established precedent set forth respectively in *Hawks v. Olson*, and *Berger v. US*. Also, please view *US v. Young*.

It would be remiss of me, not to at least provide the citizens of the US of America, a measure of understanding (i.e., such as I've been able to glean) about the substance whereby they may determine whether valid probable cause exists for an official to arrest or search him/her/them without a warrant, depends on the following.

Whether at the moment of arrest or search, the *facts* and circumstances within the police officer's knowledge, and of which he had reasonably trust worthy information, were sufficient to convince a prudent person that the person arrested had committed or was committing an offense or that there was contraband, weapons, or other illegal materials on the premises. To this explanation, the Supreme Court of the United States in the case of *Terry v. Ohio* held in part, **"In articulable hunches cannot justify Fourth Amendment intrusions, suspicion, hunches, or guest work of the police officer, even if based in good faith, are simply insufficient to establish probable cause, unless that officer could support that conclusion with fact"** as said in the case of ***United States v. Cortez***. **"The totality of circumstances—the whole picture—must be taken into account."**

The cases and various holdings are numerous, therefore from the research I've done. There are two major questions or principles related to the requirement that the police have probable cause to act without a warrant. First, prior to the arrest or search did the police officer have in his possession the facts upon which probable cause was based. The reader should try to review the case of *Henry v. United States*. Second, should the courts strictly enforce the "probable cause" requirement when the police have acted without a warrant in public areas? See the Supreme Court of the United States established precedent in *United States v. Watson*. Powell J., concurring, said, "Warrantless arrest should receive careful judicial scrutiny if challenged."

Thus, the above set forth facts regarding my case and controlling law raises significant questions, plus evinces a legitimate inference that show the trial court's extrinsic fraud set out several paragraphs earlier was compounded when that court neglected to issue jury instructions on the integrity of the chain of custody evidence evaluation, solving credibleness questions of fact with respect to the integrity and chain of custody question, determining weight of the evidence and/or credibility of state's star witness Fow, which evinced serious credibility issues throughout, from beginning of indictment onto this point. Also there is no indication in record facts of the appointed trial attorney McLau's demand for any jury instructions nor fact base formalized argument against the several illegal search/seizures, why? The Supreme Court of Virginia in the case referenced above, *Diggs v. Lail* held that **"it is reversible error not to so instruct the jury. This applies to all evidence in the case, including evidence introduce during the sentencing phase."** As was determined in the Supreme Court of Virginia case of *Saunders v. Commonwealth*.

By the way, at this stage in my mob rule trial, the commonwealth's attorney, trial court, and my court-appointed defense attorney's pretrial rehearsed collusion efforts have gone unimpeded, leaving the lot of them fairly confident with the addition of state's primary witness Fow's introduction of clothing that he—a nonexpert determined contained semen specimen thereon: were confident they'd convinced the jury that this was the smoking gun, so to speak.

Therewith the commonwealth attorney proceeded and called Dr. J. J. Bat, commonwealth's alleged expert medical witness, who testified about the medical treatment he performed on the alleged female victim, the night this alleged rape offense occurred. Commonwealth's attorney ask Dr. Bat, "Did you give her any treatment? How did you treat her?" Dr. Bat's answer was, "Yes, I gave her penicillin CR, which is a long acting penicillin…2.4 million units, and I prescribed ten five-hundred milligrams of oxacillin, which is a broad spectrum penicillin. This was done as preventive therapy, to prevent gonorrhea."

> Q: Why did you prescribe that?
> A: It is considered to be adequate treatment because a female required more than a male...2.4 million units ordinarily would be enough to cure a male. Then you talk in terms of 94–96 percent cure, and I like to be 100 percent.
> Q: Doctor, you said you gave her medication to prevent gonorrhea. Is this done in all cases, or did you find some cause here to administer this? (preserved on May 26, 1976, Tr. Ex. 44, p. 48)

Mr. McLau, court-appointed defense attorney intervened and vehemently objected, interjecting: "Your Honor, I would like to be heard on this, in the absence of the jury." The trial court uttered a pretrial rehearsed signal. "Do you insist on the question?" (i.e., operative inside phrase). Defense attorney McLau's answer was, "Yes, sir." The trial court, out of jurors' presence, ordered Dr. Bat to answer commonwealth's attorney's question, "Why did he administer penicillin for prevention of gonorrhea?" Dr. Bat intimated motive for the alleged rape. Thereafter, commonwealth's attorney asked Dr. Bat, "Did you find a gonorrhea germ there?" The answer was, "We found gram negative diplococci. Now they are usually the only kind found in the genital region are gonorrhea organism." commonwealth's attorney asked, "With reasonable medical certainty, are you able to say that came from the man?" Dr. Bat answered, "With a general amount of certainty, I would say so...Yes, because it was taken from the solution that was removed from the vagina, and, we feel reasonably certain that it was expressed at the time the sperm were expressed" (id. May 26, 1976, Tr. Ex. 44-B, p. 49).

Reader, are you ministering questions about what just happened? No marvel! It took me thirty-five years before I could truly understand what the tiny small voice of the Holy Spirit (1 Kings 19:12 KJV) had been telling me what had transpired. Please remember that the covenant/collusion court officials not only extended my trial to total above eight hundred typed recorded records for the purpose of disguising probable cause time factor, plus to discourage anyone, especially those within an integrable attorney arena—from supporting or accepting my case. But after marrying Joyce Y. Blount Simpson on June 7, 1998, both she, Ricky (a black brother who I embraced as my Christian brother), and I invested years of perusing every page thereof while making and retaining notes for comparison. Now…the above along with the following are the results.

Please forgive me, but it has become necessary to reiterate the aforementioned occurrences in lay terms the aforesaid Tr. Ex. 44, p. 48, shows commonwealth's attorney's alleged expert witness Dr. J. J. Bat under sworn oath, testified in the hearing of my jurors that he treated the alleged female victim with penicillin to prevent gonorrhea (Tr. Ex. 44-B, p. 49) shows court-appointed attorney vehemently objecting and made request to be heard out-of-my jurors presence.

In chamber, out of the jury's presence, Dr. J. J. Bat explained, they had removed gonorrhea disease germ specimen from the alleged female victim's vagina. Also interjected that he was fairly certain that the alleged rape perpetrator deposited it in the alleged female victim during alleged rape (preserved in id. May 26, 1976, Tr. Ex. 44-B, p. 49 and, id. Tr. Ex. 44-B-1, p. 50). Now at Tr. Ex. 44-B-1, p. 50, the judge asked McLau, appointed defense attorney, "What is your objection?" The answer was "Well, Your Honor, to start with it doesn't have a thing to do with the charge. It doesn't have a thing to do with the case, and not linked up in any way, and the doctor's speculation as to motive is entirely irrelevant and improper and inadmissible. And secondly, the question of whether or not there is some gonorrhea in that sperm that were found has absolutely no bearing whatever, on whether or not this defendant is guilty of this crime. It is not linked up in any evidence!" The judge asked the commonwealth's attorney, "Whether or not the said alleged gonorrhea germ specimen can be connected to me?" The commonwealth's attorney reply was, "No, sir," (i.e., would've created reasonable doubt in my jurors' mind).

Listen, the aforesaid fact evidence alone clearly demonstrates that my court-appointed attorney was in pretrial rehearsed covenant/collusion with said above named court officials, and he made the objection to keep my jury from knowing the gonorrhea germ specimen (testimony) evidence, allegedly removed from the alleged female victim, could not be tied to me.

According to the aforementioned record (i.e., Tr. Ex. 44-B-1, p. 50) the trial court Judge is still in chamber out of jurors' presence and chose to prohibit any further discussion and/or question about said alleged gonorrhea disease germ specimen and when court resumed with jurors present, no further testimony was presented nor questions developed regarding gonorrhea testimony, per judge's in-chamber directive, amounted to improper misconduct, as tending toward suggesting to my jurors that they may be allowed to link prior penicillin treatment to prevent gonorrhea in alleged female victim testimony evidence (i.e., extraneous matter) by speculation to me, my car, motive, and the alleged rape, if they wish, was highly prejudicial to me. Also, the trial court compounded its extrinsic fraud misconduct when it failed to issue required jury instructions "to disregard the gonorrhea and penicillin treatment testimony they had previously heard," thereby improperly relieved the commonwealth's attorney's duty to prove every essential element of my charged offenses beyond a reasonable doubt, therewith improperly shifted the burden of proof to me, thus arbitrarily prevented me from a fair submission of my defense to a fair and impartial judge and jury of my peers, constituted extrinsic fraud misconduct. That was further compounded when the trial judge refused my request to be examined by a mutual/impartial physician (preserved in id. May 26, 1976, Tr. Ex. 50-B, p. 284), so I could submit surrebuttal evidence to rebut the prejudicial gonorrhea and penicillin treatment testimony evidence given against me. Plus show my jurors that I didn't have gonorrhea before or after that alleged November 10, 1975 crime denied my Sixth Amendment constitutional right to compulsory, or confrontation process, thereby violated my due process rights under Section 1 Amendment 14 of the US Constitution and Section 11 of the Constitution of Virginia.

Importantly, the aforesaid issues, raises major questions of paramount interest to the United States Judicial System and the tax-paying public at large whose dollars pay the lavish lifetime salary of both the State Supreme Court, Circuit Court, United States Supreme Court and United States District Court politically appointed judges who also, from time to time, travel from one destination to another, whether inter or out of their respective states or commonwealth: "Why didn't the judge and my court-appointed attorney McLau want my aged all Caucasian/one lone token African American jury to know, the commonwealth's attorney and trial judge Merid had determined in chambers out of jurors' presence that the aforesaid alleged gonorrhea sperm evidence could not be connected to me?" and "Why did not my court-appointed attorney McLau proclaim the above defense argument that he so eloquently uttered in chambers, concerning said gonorrhea germ specimen in the presence of my jury, before he vehemently objected, requesting to be heard out-of-jurors' presence?" Neither did my court-appointed attorney make any motion demanding the judge to issue my jury follow-up instructions to disregard prior purported gonorrhea and penicillin treatment testimony placed before my jurors by commonwealth's attorney's alleged medical expert witness—Dr. J. J. Bat nor did my court-appointed attorney preserve or raise the above stated (extrinsic fraud) issues for my first appeal as of right and United States Supreme Court Appeal that I never knew existed until appointed attorney sent me a denied copy thereof a year after it was due.

In addition, the aforementioned recorded fact information raises a plausible inference which positively demonstrates that the commonwealth's attorney, trial court and my appointed defense lawyer McLau conjointly partook in a pretrial rehearsed scheme/collusion to scam convict me, which is evident when those court officials made the decision to knowingly withhold materially relevant gonorrhea sperm testimony evidence helpful to determinate of innocence or guilt from my jurors, evidence that could've created a reasonable doubt in the mind of my jury, was improper misconduct, as tending to show the bias of the trial court with regard to the weight of materially relevant testimony evidence helpful to defense, amounted to improper misconduct.

That is to say the exclusion of the in chamber commonwealth's attorney, trial court, and appointed attorney's decision: determining that the aforesaid alleged gonorrhea sperm testimony evidence could not be connected to me, prejudiced me severely, thereby denied me due process of law in violation of the federal constitution's Amendment 14. The exclusion made it virtually impossible for the jury (the trier of facts) to reach a fair conclusion as to my guilt or innocence. It therefore directly prejudiced me. The state should be ordered to release me unless a new trial is held immediately, at which time the excluded in chamber testimony evidence can be weighed by the jury before a new verdict is reached that, in all likelihood, would have been the decision of the trial court had I not been a person (alone) of color or had possessed sufficient funds to defray the cost of an attorney with legal integrity, then the trial court may not have been at liberty to outright egregiously breach its sworn oath of office which encompass the exercise of duty to protect my federal constitutional rights, as determined by the below set forth United States Supreme Court established precedents.

Brady v. Maryland held the following:

> **Both the withholding of exculpatory evidence from a criminal defendant by a prosecution and the known use of false testimony, violates the due process clause of the fourteenth amendment to the United States constitution.** [See also *Giglio v. United States*.]

Additionally, the reader is encouraged to view the United States Supreme Court's 1945 established law in the case of *Hawk v. Olson* whose opinion in pertinent part held that

> **Petitioner was in the penitentiary after conviction for murder. The writ was granted because a substantial federal question as to restraint without due process of law under the fourteenth [273] Amendment seemed to be presented by the petition for Certiorari and the response. In the exercise of the duty which lies on us as well as the Nebraska Courts [i.e., State Courts] to safeguard the federal constitutional rights of petitioner, examine for ourselves whether under the facts stated the petitioner is now entitle to a hearing on the claimed violation of the due process clause in his conviction for murder in the first degree.**

The court cited *Lisenba v. California* and *White v. Ragen* to support its above decision.

Then again, if we think about it, had my court-appointed attorney not been in pretrial rehearsed time factor covenant/collusion with the commonwealth's attorney and trial court to wrongfully convict me, he would've sought a Ruling in the presence of the jury with regard to this aforementioned materially relevant gonorrhea sperm exculpatory in chamber testimony evidence on grounds that the trial court's in chamber ruling forbidding further discussion or questions about said gonorrhea sperm testimony evidence, constituted suppression of helpful exculpatory evidence favorable to defense and improperly relieved the commonwealth's attorney obligation to prove every essential element of my charged offense beyond a reasonable doubt to my prejudice as has been determined by the Supreme Court of Virginia's 1976 legal precedent in the following cases, deciding that said above questions were for the jury *McGhee v. Commonwealth* after its pronouncement in the case of *Hodge v. Commonwealth* and the case of *Delp v. Commonwealth*.

Now hear this. Neither did the court-appointed attorney seek a continuance for the purpose of a renewed effort to obtain an independent medical examination of me, with respect to the alleged gonorrhea disease testimony. This would have enabled him to develop the probability that an unknown infected assailant, rather than I had committed the alleged offense. At the very least, such a motion would have established in the minds of the jury fact information that the trial court had denied me the benefit of my medical examination defense for surrebuttal evidence fact, to show the jury I didn't have gonorrhea disease before or after said alleged November 10, 1975, crime.

To wit, McLau was acutely aware a conviction was highly probable if the defense did not produce any evidence or witnesses against the alleged material medical and/or other speculative forensic testimony; nor did counselor enlist a single professional witness during my trial (i.e., secret evidence hearings) or sentencing phases. Further, my older sister Lucile S. Loppe, Sallie Clodfelter, George Fortune, General Wayne Talbert, Jr., JD Shf, Wonda Goins, or James, George, and/or Mr. Barks were available to defense counsel as my time factor and whereabouts alibi witnesses but appointed defense counsel denied my defense an opportunity to strengthen the question of the time factor offered against me by the commonwealth's attorney. Had McLau conducted a bare bones discussion with the aforesaid requested witnesses—they would have supplied him with sufficient fact information to mount the defense that the law enforcement officials (i.e., pretrial rehearsed time factor theory) were mistaken about my whereabouts, in opposition to the conflicting times of the alleged crime beginning and ending. Rather, counsel opted to remain silent—in covenant/collusion with trial court judge and commonwealth's attorney's pretrial rehearsed scheme and did not make sufficient effort to interview or subpoena these most important witnesses, thus failed to make appropriate investigation based on discovery.

Furthermore, my appointed attorney McLau knew during the identification one-on-one parade lineup, I was not identified by any alleged victim as their assailant, that the person who allegedly raped the female victim had gonorrhea, that the gonorrhea could not be connected to me, that I had advised him that I did not rape or commit the alleged crimes, that I had no prior felony convictions or criminal record, that I was an honorably discharged Army veteran who was gainfully employed at time of said alleged offenses. Notwithstanding, Attorney McLau, never discussed a plan of defense with me, plus never offered a stitch of evidence to defend against speculative scientific and medical testimony evidence as presented before my jury during the extended trial in light of the fact that the United States Supreme Court in the case of *Strickland v. Washington* has held, "An attorney must bring such skill and knowledge as will render the trial a reliable adversarial testing process."

Although the Supreme Court avoided a specific guideline for attorney conduct above in *Strickland*, it did affirm that reasonably effective assistance of counsel require undivided respect for the "duty of loyalty, a duty to avoid conflicts of interest." The aforesaid court rendered a similar opinion in the earlier case involving *Wood v. Georgia*. But so does the Supreme Court of Virginia Rules of Judicial conduct found in the Virginia Code Annotated 2004 Edition under Ethical Conduct (EC 2-39), provides in part that:

> **Employment should not be accepted by a lawyer when he is unable to render competent service. Likewise, a lawyer should decline employment if the intensity of his personal feelings, as distinguished from a community attitude, may impair his effective representation of a prospective client; or other such Ethical conduct Rules.**

Reader! Why don't you decide whether or not my court-appointed attorney and trial court above detailed conduct, amount to misconduct that went outside the perimeters of its discretionary duties outlined in the above quoted established duty provisions, as determined by the Supreme Court of the United States and precedent setting Court law in the commonwealth of Virginia or whether the commonwealth's attorney acts of vouching for state star witness Fow's false probable cause deficiently vague invalid affidavit is a "false positive car identification statement information," which the commonwealth's attorney structured (detailed above in chapter 4). Then commonwealth's attorney used the false invalid affidavit to secure my indictment and trial conviction, plus during trial against me also knowingly withheld exculpatory gonorrhea sperm impeachment testimony evidence from my jury and used said erroneous gonorrhea and penicillin treatment testimony information against me during trial, knowing that same could not be scientifically connected to me, which conflicts with the following US Supreme Court precedents, violate constitutionally protected due process rights, as in the below cases.

For instance *US v. Young* held, "The prosecutor's vouching for the credibility of witnesses…carries with it the imprimatur of the government and may induce the jury to trust the government's judgment rather than Its own view of the evidence." *Brady v. Maryland* held, "Both the withholding of exculpatory evidence from criminal defendant by a prosecutor and the known use of false testimony, violates the due process clause of Amendment 14, USC." *Napue v. Illinois* held, "The prosecutor may not knowingly present false testimony and has a duty to correct testimony that he or she knows to be false" amounted to improper misconduct, in contravention of commonwealth's attorney's duty to seek justice in all criminal cases, says the aforesaid court in the case of Berger *v. US*, constituted extrinsic fraud, which was compounded by the trial court overruling defense motion to suppress saliva seized evidence, violated Section 11 of the Constitution of Virginia, plus Amendment 4 and my guaranteed right to due process of law under Amendment 14.

With regard to the aforesaid invalid affidavit, the Supreme Court of Virginia in the case of *Drumhellor v. Commonwealth* determined "where the Affidavit fails to uphold a determination as probable cause, then such failure renders the warrant void and the search illegal and any evidence secured through illegal search becomes inadmissible at trial."

Also said the above Court in the case of *Wiles v. Commonwealth*. Perhaps you are wondering why I have attached the phrase "extrinsic fraud" misconduct to specific improper behavior herein the pages of this book? May I permit the Courts of proper jurisdiction to explain! The essence of when extrinsic fraud misconduct occurs during a specific trial.

Okay! First, the Supreme Court of Virginia as early as 1982 in the case of *Powell v. Commonwealth*, citing the Supreme Court of the United States 1878 decision in the case of *United States v. Throckmorton*, defining fraud extrinsic or collateral, held in pertinent part that

> **Keeping the adversary's witness from court; secreting or purloining his testimony; or any conduct of the kind mentioned (which) would tend to prevent a fair trial on the merits, and thus to deprive the innocent party of his rights. So if a judge sits when disqualified from interest or consanguinity; if the litigation is collusive; if the parties be fictitious; if real parties effected are falsely stated to be before the court." The latter character of proof tends to show that no fair trial on the merits has been had. It's matter not suspected to have existed, and so impossible to have been considered or to have been "matter tried by the first court" which the Courts have in mind which adhere to the intrinsic and extrinsic fraud doctrine. [See opinions of chief justice Shaw in the leading case on the latter subject of *Greene v. Greene*, 2 Gray (Mass), 361, 61 Am. Dec.**

> 454.] Hence, the granting of a new trial on the ground of proof of perjury or mistake, where the evidence of it has come into existence since the former trial, and appears to be true not to be collusive, and ought, if true, to produce a different verdict on a new trial, does not violate the doctrine just mentioned.

Afterward, the Supreme Court of Virginia in the case of *Jones v. Willard* in 1983, in pertinent part held the following:

> Courts have long-held that the judgment of a Court, procured by extrinsic fraud [i.e., "by conduct which prevents a fair submission of the controversy to the court, is void and subject to attack, direct or collateral at any time"].

Other examples of fraud upon the court (i.e., extrinsic fraud) includes the assertion of improper influence over the court, said the Fourth Circuit Court Appeals for the Fourth Circuit in case of *Bright v. Norshipco*, citing id. *Mazer v. Commonwealth*, holding the following:

> The high official position of the trial judge in a criminal case gives great weight with the jury to his words and conduct, and it is incumbent upon him to guard against any manifestation of his opinion either upon the weight of the evidence or the credibility of the witnesses, all expressions of opinion, or comments, or remark upon the evidence which have a tendency to intimate the bias of the court with respect to the character or weight of the testimony particularly in criminal cases, are watched with extreme jealousy, and gener-

ally considered as invasions of the province of the jury. Such expressions have been uniformly held to constitute reversible error.

Moreover, the Supreme Court of Virginia in the case of *State Farm Mutual Auto INS. Co. v. Remely,* citing, *Owens-Corning Fiberglass Corp., v. Watson* determined:

When deciding whether a fraud has been committed upon a court, a controlling factor is "whether the [claimed] misconduct tampers with the judicial machinery and subverts the integrity of the court itself."

Thitherto (i.e., up until this point), in summary, the cited precedent setting court case law decisions have made the following findings of fact regarding the abovesaid court official's conduct at my 1975–1976 trial case.

a) Trial court improperly denied defense motion to suppress alleged evidence allegedly obtained resulting of the initial and subsequent warrantless searches of my car as the searches of my car denied my Fourth Amendment constitutional rights, in a case where the recorded facts show that Deputy Sheriff Tay, State Trooper Fow, commonwealth's attorney, trial court, and appointed trial attorney covenant/collusion contrived pretrial rehearsed 11:23 to 11:50 p.m. time factor probable cause information (i.e., yellow Mustang II, with black top and North Carolina license plate number description) spawn from Deputy Mor's initial routine license check stop of my car, plus description of my physical anatomy, when Mor testified that he radio communicated same information to Deputy Tay, who, warrantless, stopped, handcuffed me, and proceeded to warrantless search my 1975 automobile from which Tay allegedly found an unloaded pistol on bases of aforesaid pretrial rehearsed source: conflicts with the alleged male and female victims' story who testified they never saw the top or license plate number of their assailant's car. Plus, the alleged male victim testified that he only talk to Fow one time the night of the alleged crime, around 2:00 or 2:30 a.m., after the officials had found his sister. Although, both alleged victims and commonwealth's witnesses partook in said pretrial rehearsed time factor scheme, violated my constitutionally guaranteed right to due process of law under Amendment 14.

b) Trial Court improperly denied defense Motion to Suppress illegally seized evidence as Deputy Sheriff Tay did not have probable cause to arrest me, and thus Tay's subsequent warrantless search of my car which allegedly revealed an unloaded pistol in my car and was not supported by the necessary probable cause, denied Fourth Amendment protection and violated my due process rights, under Amendment 14.

c) The remarks of the trial court tantamount to vouching for the credibility of state witness Sheriff Tay in the midst of prohibiting defense to cross-examine Tay regarding possible impeachment testimony responses to defense queries about trash or no trash in my car plus legality of Tay's warrantless searches, where the judge with disdain demeanor emphatically interjected, "Yes, he said exactly what he knows about it. He said he can't remember particularly, and he knows there wasn't anything over the bulge. You can't make him say anything, so I don't see any point in pursuing it." This was improper as tending to intimate the bias of the court with respect to the weight of Tay's impeached testimony and carried with it the official approval of the government, which may well have influenced the jury to trust the court's judgment rather than its own view of the evidence, thereby amounted to deliberate suppression of helpful defense impeachment evidence evinces extrinsic fraud misconduct, that was compounded by trial court's failure to instruct my jury about the principles of law in evaluating facts surrounding non contradicted evidence of impeach witness credibility, thus severely prejudiced and discriminated against me by arbitrarily and capriciously obstructed me from a fair submission of my defense to a fair and an impartial judge and jury, thereby denied due process of law, in violation of Section 11 of the Constitution of Virginia, as pertaining to Amendment 14 of the US Constitution.

d) commonwealth's attorney vouching for state's star witness trooper Fow's false probable cause identification invalid sworn affidavit statement information—alluding to his own personal/oath of office to bolster the government's case, in that the recorded facts show Trooper Fow was not certified to be a forensic science expert, neither was commonwealth's attorney the invalid affidavit's author, thereby abrogated the benefit of my defense, and denied my constitutionally protected due process rights, in violation of Section 1 of Amendment 14 of the US Constitution.

e) The action of the trial court and commonwealth's attorney under color of state and constitutional law, unduly prohibited defense probe cross-examination of the alleged male victim about the initial probable cause description information he gave the first law enforcement officers (e.g., defense alibi witnesses)—that is, twin black Sheriff C. J. and C. W.—causally connected with said Court officials prohibiting defense probe cross-examination of state's star witness Trooper Fow, regarding the conversation description information had with twin black sheriffs prejudiced and discriminated against me, thereby denied Sixth Amendment confrontation/compulsory process, in violation of my due process rights embodied in Amendment 14 of US Constitution.

f) Trial court's ruling prohibiting defense from questioning alleged male victim about anything he might have told anyone other than state's star witness Fow regard probable cause description information he gave the first law enforcement officers (i.e., twin black sheriffs) contravened my Sixth Amendment cross-examination/confrontation rights was improper and constituted extrinsic fraud, which was compounded by trial court's improper comments on the weight of defense impeachment evidence by its interjected rulings. That defense was not allowed to question the alleged male victim about anything he might have told anyone other than Trooper Fow unless it develops to be relevant, but the probable cause is based on what this young man might have told the officer and he has testified on this, was certainly improper—as tending to intimate the court's bias toward defense impeachment probable cause evidence and carried with it the official disapproval of the government, which might've influenced my jury to trust the court's judgment instead of its own view of the prohibited impeached probable cause evidence, also constituted deliberate suppression of helpful defense probable cause impeachment evidence, and amounted to extrinsic fraud with the court's improper relief of commonwealth's attorney's duty to prove every element of my charged offenses beyond a reasonable doubt, double compounded by trial court's failure to instruct the jury regard principles of law in evaluating facts surrounding contradicted evidence of impeached witness credibility, thereby prejudiced and discriminated against me by arbitrarily and capriciously obstructed me from obtaining the benefit of my defense and a fair submission of my defense to a fair and an impartial judge and jury, deprived me of due process under Section 1 Amendment 14 of the US Constitution and Section 11 Constitution of Virginia.

g) The trial court's ruling prohibiting defense probe cross-examination of state's star witness Trooper Fow, regard the conversation he had had with twin black sheriffs, regarding probable cause description information the alleged male victim provided them (i.e., information that allegedly provided state's asserted probable cause to warrantless arrest me), denied me Sixth Amendment cross-examination/confrontation rights, constituted extrinsic fraud misconduct that was compounded by trial court's improper comments on the weight of defense impeachment evidence, when the court interjected, *"What kind of difference does the conversation make? Well, ask him any relevant things. You are just imposing on the court's time with a matter that I cannot believe had anything to do with this thing. Just tell me what difference does it make!"* This was improper as tending to intimate the trial court's bias toward defense probable cause impeachment testimony evidence, which carried with it the official disapproval of the government which might well have adversely influence the jury to trust the court's judgment rather than its own view of the testimony evidence, and constituted deliberate suppression of helpful defense probable cause impeachment evidence. Plus, improperly relieved commonwealth's attorneys' duty of having to prove every element of my charged offenses beyond a reasonable doubt, constituted extrinsic fraud misconduct, which was compounded by trial court's failure to instruct the jury about the principles of law in evaluating facts surrounding contradicted testimony evidence of impeached witness credibility, therewith prejudiced and discriminated against me by arbitrarily and capriciously prevented me from obtaining the benefit of my defense, and a fair submission of my defense to a fair and an impartial judge and jury of my peers, denied me equal protection and due process of the law, in violation of Section 11 of the Constitution of Virginia and Section 1 of Amendment 14 of the US Constitution.

h) Trial court's ruling prohibiting defense probe cross-examination of state's star witness Fow's credibility, regarding impeachment testimony responses to queries about the validity and legality of Fow's initial, then subsequent warrantless search entries into my car, denied my Sixth Amendment cross-examination/confrontation rights, amounted to extrinsic fraud misconduct, which improperly relieved commonwealth's attorney's duty to prove every essential element of my charged offenses beyond a reasonable doubt, compounded by trial court's vouching—interjection remarks that he has testified and his best recollection of what he is saying today *is right*. But contrary to that he is not denying (i.e., that he entered the defendant's car) it. *It will be up to the court to determine which is correct. I do not wish for you to read it to him again*, was improper misconduct, as tending to intimate the court's bias toward the character or weight of State witness's perjured testimony evidence that carried with it, the official approval of the government, which in all likelihood influenced the jury to trust the court's judgment rather than its own views of said impeached testimony evidence, in contravention of juror's duty to evaluate facts, weigh evidence and witnesses credibility, constituted extrinsic fraud misconduct, thereby evinced a legitimate inference that also indicates court official deliberately suppressed testimony evidence that would have impeached Fow's credibility, as well as presents a possible knowing use of perjured testimony to support the state's case, therewith discriminated and severely prejudiced me by arbitrarily and capriciously preventing me from obtaining the benefit of my defense and fair submission of His version of the facts to a fair and an impartial judge and jury of my peers, thus denied me equal protection and the due process of the law, in violation of Section 11 of the Constitution of Virginia and Section 1 of Amendment 14 of the US Constitution.

i) Appointed trial attorney McLau owed the duty of loyalty to me, a duty to avoid conflicts of interest, and to bring to bear skill and knowledge as would render my trial a reliable adversarial testing process but breached that duty throughout my trial by entering into pretrial rehearsed time factor probable cause collusion/covenant with commonwealth's attorney Bled/Ben and the trial court to scam convict me. Therefore, they made no effort to conduct an appropriate investigation based on discovery/subpoena of black (twin) sheriffs, inmate trustee at the jail, tended toward allowing the jury to link by speculation Deputy Sheriff Tay, State Trooper Fow, commonwealth's attorney, trial court and his covenant/collusion contrived pretrial rehearsed 11:23 to 11:50 p.m. time factor probable cause description information—yellow Mustang II, with black top and North Carolina, license plate number account that spawn from Deputy Mor's notes during routine license check (i.e., but not from the alleged male or female victims), speculative/conclusive testimony, if they wish, effectively denied my Sixth Amendment right to competent counsel, thereby severely discriminated against and prejudiced my defense, which improperly relieved commonwealth's attorney's duty to prove every essential element of my charged offenses beyond a reasonable doubt, constituted extrinsic fraud misconduct, prevented me from obtaining the benefit of his defense and a fair submission of his version of the facts to a fair and impartial judge and jury of my peers, thereby denied him equal protection and the due process of law, in violation of Section 11 of the Constitution of Virginia and Section 1 of Amendment 14 US Constitution.

j) The actions of commonwealth's attorney in failing to correct/clarify the state's medical expert witness's statement regarding gonorrhea and penicillin treatment after in chamber testimony determined gonorrhea sperm removed from alleged female victim could not be connected to me was improper misconduct, as tending toward suggesting to my jurors that they may be allowed to link by speculation. The gonorrhea and penicillin treatment testimony evidence to me, my car, motive and the alleged rape, if they wish, was highly prejudicial to me, amounted to knowing use of false testimony, thereby breached its oath of office (i.e., to seek justice), constituted extrinsic fraud acts that arbitrarily and capriciously prevented me from obtaining the benefit of my defense and from receiving a fundamentally fair trial before an impartial judge and jury of my peers, thus denied my due process rights, in violation of Section 11 of the Constitution of Virginia as well as Section 1 of Amendment 14 of the US Constitution.

The above findings constitute finding of facts up to this juncture of my trial and are presumed to be correct, said the Supreme Court of the United States in the case of *Sumner v. Mata* II.

Moreover, if a state court system arbitrarily withholds the benefit of a state rule of law from a criminal defendant, due process of law is denied. At the same time, if a state court system treats similarly situated criminal defendants differently, equal protection of the law is denied. See US Constitution, Amendment 14. Again you, the reader, is challenged to visit their federal or state law library, to review the aforesaid court's decision that supports my aforementioned conclusion in the case of *Hicks v. Oklahoma*. More on this topic will be discussed herein.

Chapter 10

Meanwhile, several months have rapidly gone headlong into the annals of history to the month of April, 1976, where I was found praying and musing within my soul about how my chances of being acquitted from these hideous trumped up abduction/rape charges appear to have grown slim to none, yet my maturing faith in Jesus's, the Only True Living God, WORD left me unconcerned with the manner—the commonwealth's attorney, trial court, appointed trial attorney and many of the commonwealth's witnesses had undertaken to cause me and my children's demise with this well contrived collusion/covenant pretrial rehearsed embellished 11:23 to 11:50 p.m. probable cause theatrically performed farce of a trial.

Also, amid my aforesaid mind reasoning came the fact that I had not yet fully put into complete focus for every day and night season practice, my creator and savior's principles (i.e., that is, my teacher) concerning love for one's neighbor like until love for self-preservation (i.e., found in the New Testament books entitled Matthew 19:19, Mark 12:31, and Old Testament book entitled Leviticus 19:18). Strange as it may appear, at this stage of my trial and me domiciling behind steel bars against my will. I felt compelled to reach out by God's Holy Spirit's inspired instructions with mature love (i.e., care), again and again to touch and make understandable/discernible difference in everyone there at the Halifax County Jail, and those who I was so very blessed to remain in contact with in Lexington, North Carolina, even as God the father of my Lord and Savior Jesus Christ had caused me to inherit such circle of influence.

Notice, the circumstances I became surrounded by were employed by my Creator (i.e., Sustainer) to both reveal and teach me other vitally important virtues, namely how to receive and help other people achieve an alike peace-filled spirits.

One such aspect that God's spirit (WORD) prompted me to adopt in route to promoting harmony among my children at large, teenagers, young adults, and aged folk is to learn to communicate with each other. I arrived at this viewpoint after I became empowered by the everlasting, merciful Word of God then! Thrust head on into the aforementioned nonphantom wilderness. Having so said, it is my humble opinion that words are the instruments, the necessary tools by which both children, teens, and grown people communicate, plus cultivate ideas, that my present and past experiences—that is, interaction with other human beings possessing unalike views—strongly suggests that too frequently we take this asset for granted, and I suppose I'll go so far to say that only those who are familiar with the logical and critical study of the source and nature of human knowledge mental phenomenon can be aware of the processing and amplification of one's ideas, in fixing them in the mind and retaining them for recall and regular contemplation, and/or usage.

To a greater extent, so far, I have learned while studying the Holy Writ (i.e., Bible) regarding the four New Testament books. First that is according to Matthew, whose credited author is named Levi. Second, Mark (i.e., real name is John) reference is made to the Gospel of Mark. Third, Luke, better known as the beloved physician. And the fourth book is called the Gospel of John. All testify facts that evinces that Jesus was and is still the master of the aforesaid application, for his Words though frequently spoken in every day simple child alike terms. Yet they (i.e., Jesus's Words) literally gripped young and mature people's mind and moved/stirs their hearts/soul, plus, compels us to listen. With emphasis, I say "to be sure," there were those (i.e., as it is today) who remained stubborn, adhering to the same every day concepts of nonyielding opinions notwithstanding Jesus's words still moved them in some manner, either to believe and follow/obey His instructive guidance and love Him unquestionably or hate Him without cause. As for me, I began anew to seize every available opportunity to communicate and discuss various subjects that Jesus taught with my children, Grands and others who become so inclined to interact with me.

With regard to my four children—Gene P. Kindle, Vernom Holmes (a.k.a. Pete), LaTonya (BOL Princess) N. Smith, and Tony J. Matthews—immediate launching me on a field trip...For instance, at the time of my abrupt 1976 physical separation from my biological family, Tony was three years old, very attentive to listen to instructions, but afterward, he would take to task driving his battery-motorized toy vehicle into our console TV. Vernom (Pete, age fourteen) with earnest regret, my former sin, unregenerated selfish agenda kept me from an intimate relationship with Pete during that time. LaTonya (BOL Princess) also age fourteen possessed decisive virtues, although encapsulated in a spirit of tranquility, reinforced by willingness to interact and learn, plus displayed a readiness to communicate with an exceptional behavior of a young mature adult. On the other hand, Gene P. (age fifteen) lived with me although privy to instructions, yet his forward outgoing calmness and desire for open communication took on command attributes...while the lot of them sought opened dialogue channels. It was my duty to set forth the truth, the absolute standard of how our decisions ought to be made in line with God's Holy Spirit inspired written revealed will and plans as set out in the King James Version of the Bible. Why? Because God says by the mouth of His Prophet Jeremiah: "I know the thoughts that I think toward you, thoughts of peace and not evil, to give you an expected end." Reader, please except this invitation. Look up the book entitled Jeremiah 29:11–15 located in the Old Testament, if you desire to verify this Godly view for all those who can believe. I simply want my family to be such as those who believe Jesus.

May this scribe have your ear for a little longer, please, because I'll have you to know that although the ONLY TRUE LIVING GOD, Jesus has not completed his plan or work in my life's journey. He have begun to bless my spiritual understanding, His Holy Spirit gave me wisdom sufficient to propel me to take a brief peek back over the various tools God has been able to implement into my life. God also permitted me to behold the forth coming multitude of trials which the enemy Satan, the arch enemy of the TRUTH, would employ, to purposely compel me to relent to an overwhelmed hopeless mindset. Yet God didn't leave me there rather God's tiny small voice, whispered, "Just put one foot before the other one and lean not to your own understanding, but trust my instructions." Here, before I could absorb everything by association, especially in the midst of attempting to explain my absence to my children.

I began anew to realize that I am one of God's messengers/tools (for the lack of an apt term moves out of range). This in itself by faith enables me to meet the needs of my offspring and everyone God's spirit of peace draws to the influence of God's spirit who live and abides in my decision making faculties. In the very same breath, I do not profess to be a prophet, priest (i.e., howbeit, God's living word in both the old and New Testament declares that "we are a holy priesthood"; see Exodus 19:6, 1 Peter 2:5 and 9) or rabbi, yet I have received the anointing from the ONLY TRUE LIVING GOD because I have earnestly repented for my sins and have both confessed Jesus Christ to be my LORD and Savior as I trust in Jesus's risen merits. Moreover, I rejoice in the fact that my thoughts momentarily raced back to the events of my children being conceived in their respective mom's womb, connected with my own conception in my mother Blanche Simpson's womb on February 28, 1942. Still, those memorable events prior to my redemption did not per se, raise any significant questions in my mind with respect to the known conception, or the new obvious miracle of God bringing forth human life, not as resulting from the monkey evolution or big bang explosion theories same compelled me to contemplate as my mind ministered the following questions:

1) What role did I play other than sexual intercourse gratification? What role did my children's mothers play other than sexual intercourse, then carrying them to the time determined God formula (i.e., as recorded in the Old Testament book entitled Genesis 18:10–14, then Genesis 21:1–2 KJV)?
2) Neither did my children's mother or I partake in our offspring's DNA genetic formula, nor did we offer assistance or provide any advice for the below creation.
3) Our children's nervous system—nerve cell axons, myelin sheaths, red or white corpuscles, brain nerve tissues, cerebellum, cerebrum, medulla oblongata, the heart or its rate/rhythm, liver, kidneys, cervix, clitoris, vagina, vulva, stomach/abdomen, gall bladder, scrotum, genital, penis, breast, chest, nose, nostrils, limbs, knees, joints, fingers, toes, ears, lips, tongue, tonsil, throat, neck, digestive tract, intestines, buttocks, thighs, vertebrate, shins, ankles, foot, arch, finger and toe nails, eyes, pupils, iris, eye brows, eyelids, eye color, melanin, arms, elbows, back, hair, hair texture and color, esophagus, thigh rod gland, breath, oxygen, race, sperm or life itself, not inclusive.

Reader, if the aforementioned God wrought birth of a single human is noncontradicted fact and cannot be denied, then they must be accepted as truth: facts that indicates mankind (i.e., womankind) plays such a meager role in child conception and/or the bringing forth of human life! The aforesaid conclusion was cause for a shifting of the knowledge I possessed before accepting Jesus Christ into my life (i.e., will) same prompted me to commence a more intense study of all that is written in the entire old and New Testaments, as set forth in the King James Version of the Holy Spirit inspired words, esteeming that it speaks directly to me (i.e., with the exception of the names). The above eluded too intense study, also convinced me that long before I was conceived by my parents my birth was in the mind of God, as attested to by the Old Testament prophet in the book entitled Jeremiah 1:5, where the LORD interjected, **"Before I formed you in the belly I knew you; and before you came forth out of the womb I sanctified you, and I ordained you a prophet unto the nation."**

The apostle Paul equally acknowledged the above facts while writing a group of churches in Galatia located in Asia Minor. Bible scholars claims Paul's letter was written between AD 49 or 52. See New Testament book entitled Galatians 1:15. Paul was speaking by inspiration of God when he said, **"But when it please God, who separated me from my mother's womb."**

Reader, it is my respectful opinion that the Bible (i.e., herein, my references to the Bible quotes are always taken from the King James Version KJV) contains volumes of support for my above asserted conclusion, yet here is one additional authority, discovered in the book entitled Psalms, Holy Spirit penned by former King David and other inspired men of God. By the way, scholars claims the date of those referenced here begun in the tenth century BC and later. Psalms 139:13 declares,

> **You have possessed my reins: you have covered me in my mother's womb. My substance was not hid from you, when I was made in secret, and curiously fashioned in the lowest parts of the earth. "Your eyes did see my substance, yet being unperfect; and in your book all my members were written, which in continuance were fashioned, when as yet there was none of them."**

The above is only revelatory knowledge and understanding that my Savior via the Holy Spirit has been able to enlarge my pilgrimage with, after I'd begun acknowledging the ONLY TRUE LIVING GOD via

Jesus Christ's risen merits and how God prescribed every single detail of my body. He deliberately chose my race, the color of my skin, every strand of hair and all other features. My God custom made, my and your body just the way He wanted it. He also determined the natural talents I possess, plus the uniqueness of my personality. God made me for a reason. He also decided when I would be born and the length of my life span. He even planned the days of my life in advance, choosing the exact time this book would be written. The KJV of the Bible says, "To everything there is a season and a time to every purpose under the heaven. A time to be born, and a time to die." See the entitled Ecclesiastes 3:1–2. Scholars claim its author to be King Solomon during the tenth century BC.

Having penned the above available fact standards, it is important to note that the ONLY TRUE LIVING GOD via Jesus's risen merits communicates with me (i.e., mankind, specifically Christ repented believers) in several ways. He speaks to us through the Holy inspired scriptures (KJV) by holy angels through the sanctuary of Old Testament times, by means of a chosen people; providential circumstances, prophets/prophetess, through His still small voice of the Holy Spirit, which multitudes mistakenly refer to as their "conscience" (please see Old Testament book entitled 1 Kings 19:11–13, KJV). But see the book entitled Isaiah 30:21, which says, **"Your ears shall hear a word behind you, saying, this is the way, walk you in it, when you turn to the right hand, and when you turn to the left."** It is not my desire to bore you, but may we peruse one more instructive text in the Old Testament book entitled Zechariah 4:6, where Prophet Zechariah is found saying, **"The angel answered and spake to me, saying—this is the word of the LORD unto Zerubbabel, saying not by might, not by power, but by my spirit, says the LORD of hosts."** Also through pastors, teachers, born again brothers, transformed sisters, and nature.

It is my most humble opinion that God climaxed His efforts to communicate with sin-filled fallen mankind by one Supreme, Magnificent stoke of love by sending His Son Jesus Christ to live with mankind. Might I add that in my estimation, this actually was the ONLY avenue God could have taken to reveal completely what HE is like. It was the only way light could enter darkness. Jesus Christ (the Bible says) was fully God and fully man whom have ever divided the times from BC to AD and who is, and was, and forever shall be, the ONLY and final, incarnation of God the ruler (i.e., over all the kingdoms of the heathen, in whose hands there is power and might, so that none is able to withstand Him), creator, possessor, and sustainer of everything that exists, does not exist, or shall exist! My Savior who identified Himself with us for time and eternity believest thou this! Reader?

More than this, if you the reader want to know more of who is like God, please study as I'm doing—the life and teaching of Jesus in the King James Version of the Bible's New Testament book entitled John 1:1–5, 14, which states,

> **In the beginning was the WORD, and the WORD was with God, and the WORD was God. The same was in the beginning with God. All things were made by Him; and without Him was not anything made that was made. In Him was life; and the life was the light of man, and the light shown in darkness; and the darkness comprehended it not. And the WORD was made flesh, and dwelt among us, [and we beheld His glory as of the ONLY begotten of the Father], full of grace and truth.**

The Old Testament book entitled Genesis 1 and 2 confirms the aforesaid facts. Also, the New Testament book above mentioned, at chapter 4 verse 9 (b) Jesus said to His disciple Philip: **"He that have seen me have seen the Father [God]."** If the abovesaid deity facts concerning Jesus, cannot be factually contradicted, then they must be accepted as TRUTH.

This carries us back to the saga that has been a commonwealth's attorney, trial court, and appointed defense attorney's pretrial rehearsed development, in the criminal case involving me, and a host of commonwealth of Virginia actors under the due process clause of the constitution of the United States. Reader, as you have read and rationalized at various stages herein, plus penned scenarios depicted by the trial court, commonwealth's attorney and appointed defense attorney's collusion. What section seems the most difficult to believe?

Chapter 11

I surmise that approximately six months have evaporated, and there is no apparent end to this farce of a trial: Now the month of May 1976 is here...The actors' dramatized theatrics in my absence regarding the burden of proof: where, the accused is entitled to a hearing outside the presence of the jury when the introduction of seized evidence are at issue, as determined by the Supreme Court of the United States, in the case entitled *Lego v. Twomey*. In such circumstances, my appointed defense attorney was required to file a suppression motion requesting said evidentiary hearing, in accordance with the Circuit Court of Halifax local rules. Ironically, I was never advised of said evidence hearing.

The trial and grand jury indictment hearing transcribed records are silent with respect to any evidentiary hearing's substance. Also in the case of *Wong Sun v. United States*. The Supreme Court, not only held that the evidence obtained through unconstitutional police conduct must be suppressed but also that the fruit of the illegally obtained (i.e., seized) evidence must be suppressed.

In addition, a typical example of law enforcement and trial court officials' unconstitutional misconduct in obtaining alleged circumstantial evidence, is clearly visible during the following March and May 1976 trial transcribed record exchanges during commonwealth's attorney direct examination of State Trooper Fow, as developed in pertinent part.

Commonwealth's attorney asked Fow, "Did you take the footprint of the victim?" The answer was, "I made footprints...of both victims, the female and male" (preserved on May 26, 1976, Tr. Ex. 58-I, p. 138).

> Q: In the preliminary hearing below, were those prints introduced as exhibits in the general district court?
> A: This was tried in the juvenile court.
> Q: Excuse me, that court?
> Appointed defense attorney: Objection.

The Court intervened and improperly interjected, "Here is the exhibit filed in that case...if you want to use it." Appointed defense attorney interjected, "Your Honor, I submit this, I would like to be heard on this." The court asked, "Heard on what?" Appointed defense attorney answered, "On the introduction of the exhibit." Defense attorney (i.e., out of the hearing of the jury) interjected, "May it please the court, I know this is a long and difficult case. I submit when the Court indicates anger toward the defendant's counsel for raising an objection to the exhibit, the jury laughs at that indicates the court's demeanor toward us." The court said, "I don't recall that laughing." Defense continued, "This is the second time the court has indicated some impatience with the objection I have made. The time before, the court said It would jump over the foundation...I think counsel is supposed to make sure the exhibits are properly filed. I would move the court to grant a mistrial on the grounds of this indication of impatience" (preserved on May 26, 1976, Tr. Ex. 60-C, p. 139).

Further, commonwealth's attorney direct examination asked Fow.

> Q: There is one picture I forgot to introduce yesterday. I believe you took a picture of a footprint. Do you have that?

A: Yes. I believe the Court has that.
Q. It was not introduced. I don't think.

The court intervened and interjected, "These will be commonwealth's exhibits 8 and 9. Did you take these pictures?" The answer was, "Yes, sir." The court asked, "Would you describe these to the jury, and where it was taken, and where it was located...refer to the number... There are two of them?" Fow answered, "Exhibits 8 and 9 are the same. Both of these photographs reveal the footprint and toe prints that were lifted from the inside rear glass of the automobile. The footprints and the toe prints are the white in the very middle of the photographs. The large part is ball of the foot, and you can see the toes around the front" (preserved on May 26, 1976, Tr. Ex. 56-B, p. 169).

Notice, Fow, commonwealth's (star witness) under sworn oath testified above that he took the footprint picture is contrary to his March 3, 1976, Tr. Ex. 47-F, p. 54 testimony, where commonwealth's attorney asked him, "Were the prints lifted the next afternoon on the eleventh?" The answer was, "Yes, sir. The prints were lifted off both the windows by Investigator Jack. In my presence, he lifted the prints, handed them to me, and I labeled the prints. I kept them in my possession until I took them to the laboratory in Richmond."

Q: And you did not have a search warrant?
A: Search warrant? No, sir.
Q: All right. In South Hill, you do not have an arrest warrant?
A. No, sir. (preserved in id. Tr. Ex. 47-G, p. 55)

Fow's above interjection under oath in response to the Court that he took the pictures (i.e., footprints) together with his sworn interjection here (id. Tr. Ex. 47-G, p. 55) that Investigator Jackson lifted the prints off the windows well deserves credibility and perjury critiquing: but let us first causally connect Fow's aforesaid May 26, 1976, footprint testimony with one other. The reader's attention is appropriately directed to Fow's previous testimony during the March 3, 1976, segment of my mocked trial, where the appointed defense attorney asked Fow:

> Q: Did the female victim describe the content of the car, or anything in it?
> A: She described that it was trashy. She said there were papers and trash in the car, and a lot of clothes on the backseat. I asked her where did the man put her in the car. She said he put her in the backseat of the car and made her take all of her clothes off with the exception of her shoes and socks. (preserved on March 3, 1976, Tr. Ex. 56-B-2, p. 73).

This is sufficient fact testimony evidence to both contradict Trooper Fow's subsequent May 26, 1976, Tr. Ex. 56-B, p. 169, pretrial rehearsed testimony evidence—that is, the alleged victim's foot and toe prints was lifted from the inside rear glass of my automobile as well as establishes a legitimate inference that the alleged female rape victim did not remove her shoes or socks raises substantial credibility questions regard Fow's ability to be truthful together with the above conflicting testimony evidence of whether Fow or Investigator Jack took said impossible to be there! Prints or whether the said prints are in fact, part of the commonwealth's attorney, trial court, and appointed defense attorney's pretrial rehearse creation? At any rate, this record clearly demonstrates that said court officials conjointly suppressed materially relevant beneficial defense—"He put her in the backseat of the car and made her take all of her clothes off with the exception of her shoes and socks"—testimony evidence, which would have discredited the commonwealth's attorney's theory—that is, foot and toe print testimony evidence exhibits given against me by state's star witness Trooper Fow, thereby presents a reasonable doubt in the jurors' mind, constituted court officials' deliberate suppression of fact testimony evidence which would've impeached and refuted foot and toe print evidence given against me, was improper misconduct, amounts to extrinsic fraud misconduct that deprived me of equal protection and liberty interest without the due process of law, in violation of Section 11 Constitution of Virginia as well as violated Section 1, Amendment 14 of the US Constitution.

That was compounded, when the trial court improperly remark introduced commonwealth's footprint exhibits evidence to petitioner's jury, which had the tendency to intimate the favor of the court with respect to the character of commonwealth's alleged foot and toe print (i.e., extraneous matter) alleged exhibit/testimony evidence tended toward suggesting to the jury that they may be allowed to link the alleged foot/toe print exhibit/testimony evidence by speculation to me, my car, the alleged female victim, the rape of alleged female victim, if they wish, which was highly prejudicial to me, and may have influenced the jury to trust the government gestures rather than its own views, constitutes double compound extrinsic fraud misconduct, contrary to the Virginia Court of Appeals holding in the case of *Henshaw v. Commonwealth*, citing the Supreme Court of Virginia's opinion in *Mazer v. Commonwealth*, together with the commonwealth's attorney's direct examination of Trooper Fow.

> Q: Now when was the arrest warrant first issued?
> A: When we returned from South Hill with the defendant.
> Q: All right. Now you made sworn testimony on which the magistrate issued a search warrant. What was the sworn testimony that you gave him at that time?
> A: That the charges to be in this warrant are true to the best of my knowledge.
> Q: You didn't give him any additional information?
> A. No, sir, I did not. (preserved on March 3, 1976, Tr. Ex. 47-E, p. 98)

This is causally linked with appointed defense attorney's cross-examination of Deputy Sheriff Tay the initial warrantless search arresting law enforcement official. Defense asked Tay.

> Q: All right, now. Then you put him [i.e., me] in the car and took him where? South Hill.
> A: South Hill Police department.
> Q: Did you have a magistrate at the police department in South Hill?
> A: Yes, sir.
> Q: What did you say to the magistrate?
> A: I told him I wanted a warrant for concealing a weapon.
> Q: And what testimony did you give him under oath, on which he issued that charge?
> A: I am not sure. (preserved on March 3, 1976, Tr. Ex. 46, p. 149).
> Q: Now do you remember what time Trooper Fow first got there?
> A: No, sir. I do not.
> Q. Do you remember that you told him about this pistol before he placed the man under arrest?
> A. I am sure I did because, when he got there, I had him charged with carrying a concealed weapon. (id. March 3, 1976, Tr. Ex. 46-B, p. 150).

Equal—causally linked is Fow' cross examination when appointed defense attorney ask:

> Q: Trooper Fow, isn't it true that you did base probable cause for your arrest on the weapon as well other matter?

> A: I told you that the patrolman Tay told me about the weapon before the arrest was made. But I didn't see the weapon until after the arrest was made.
>
> Q: All right. So it is your testimony that you considered the description of the car and the description of the man, but you also took into consideration the fact that he had been found with a weapon, isn't that right?
>
> A: Yes.
>
> Q: And when you testified that you took the weapon into consideration in placing probable cause, you were testifying truthfully in the preliminary hearing, isn't that right?
>
> A. So far as I know, yes, sir. (id Tr. Ex. 54-R, p. 81)

Reader, although I do not have any formal legal training in the science of law, my state-appointed attorney McLau, did as he supposedly practiced law in a family-operated McLau Law Firm locally located, yet as a result of his pretrial rehearsed time factor probable cause collusion/covenant relationship with the commonwealth's attorney and trial court to wrongfully convict me (i.e., throw me under the bus). McLau failed to zealously defend my Fourth Amendment and procedural due process constitutionally protected rights (i.e., as demonstrated above in chapter 6), with respect to the trial court's introduction of commonwealth's attorney's star witness Fow's alleged footprint evidence to the jury.

To wit, the trial court, commonwealth's, and appointed defense attorney, acting under color of state and constitutional law, denied me constitutionally-protected due process rights via trial court's outward demeanor/display of anger and impatience toward defense's objection to court's introduction of commonwealth's attorney's alleged footprint evidence (i.e. causing jury to laugh), amounted to extrinsic fraud misconduct that severely prejudiced my defense in contravention of the juror's impartiality, thereby preventing me from obtaining the benefit of my defense and a fair submission thereof to a fundamentally fair and impartial judge and jury of my peers and violating Section 1 Amendment 14 US Constitution and Section 11 of the Constitution of Virginia contrary to the Virginia Court of Appeals decision in the case of *Mazer vs. Commonwealth*. The trial court's aforesaid misconduct, in all likelihood, influenced the jury to trust the government's judgment rather than its own views.

Notwithstanding, instead of arguing the above in the presence of my jury, appointed trial attorney made a "token" objection and asked to be heard out of jurors' presence, therewith intentionally concealed the above as well as the trial court's continued egregious misconduct, as revealed at the bench out of jury's presence, where appointed defense attorney's pretrial rehearsed collusion/covenant said, "May it please the court, I know this is a long and difficult case. I submit when the Court indicates anger toward the defendant's counsel for raising an objection to the exhibit, the jury laughs at… that indicates the court's demeanor toward us."

The court said, "I don't recall that laughing [appointed attorney continued at the bench out of jurors' hearing]. This is the second time the Court has indicated some impatience with the objection I have made. The time before, the court said it would jump over the foundation. I think counsel is supposed to make sure the exhibits are properly filed. I would move the court to grant a mistrial, on the grounds of this indication of impatience" (preserved on May 26, 1976, Tr. Ex. 60-C, p. 139, and id. Tr. Ex. 60-D, p. 125). The court said, "I'll skip over the foundation, the officer said he found a gun, do you have the gun, Mr. Commonwealth's Attorney?" This was improper misconduct, which compounded the trial court, appointed trial attorney's extrinsic fraud acts of commission as determined by the Virginia Appeals court in the case of *Henshaw v. Commonwealth*, citing the Supreme Court of Virginia opinion in *Mazer v. Commonwealth*, **"All expressions of opinion or comments, or remarks upon the evidence which have a tendency to intimate the bias of the Court with respect to the character or weight of the testimony, partic-**

ularly in criminal cases, are watched with extreme jealousy, and generally considered an invasions of the province of the jury."

A reasonable inference can be had on bases of appointed defense attorney's motion to grant a mistrial on grounds of trial court's expressed anger toward defense: to show that appointed defense attorney knew about the Supreme Court of Virginia's aforementioned 1925 *Mazer* opinion yet did not make any reference to it above at the bench, neither preserved he said issues for appellate review.

Furthermore, the Virginia Court of Appeals in the case of *Garnett v. Com.* citing the Supreme Court of Virginia's 1948 established precedent in the case entitled *McGhee v. Perkins*, holding, **"He cannot escape the consequences by saying he does not recall what he said on the prior occasion."**

For your additional edification reader, the US Constitution Amendment 14 guarantees the tax paying or other citizens and me the right to fairness in his/her criminal (i.e., persecution) process, right to public trial, and the right to fairness in proceeding procedures concerning state government deprivation of life, liberty, and property said the United States Supreme Court in the case of *Goldberg v. Keely*. Therefore, the trial court introducing commonwealth's attorney's alleged foot print exhibits/alleged gun evidence, together with commonwealth's attorney and appointed defense attorney's pretrial rehearse covenant/collusion to conceal materially relevant defense's alleged "female victim did not remove her shoes or socks" impeachment testimony evidence, coupled with the trial court's illuminated influential remarks about the character of state's alleged footprint and gun exhibit testimony evidence unduly impaired this abovesaid right to fairness before an impartial judge and jury. I emphasize, to this end, the Supreme Court of the United States in the case of *Turner v. Louisiana* decided a decade prior to my 1975–1976 trial, held the following:

> **The requirement that a jury verdict must be based upon the evidence developed at the trial goes to the fundamental integrity of all**

> that is embraced in the constitutional concept of trial by the jury. In the constitutional sense, trial by jury in a criminal case necessarily implies at the very least that the evidence developed against a defendant shall come from the witness stand in a public court room where there is full judicial protection of the defendant's right of confrontation of cross-examination, and of counsel.

This is the third or fourth time, I've had the blessing to extend an invitation for you, reader, to visit the local law library to look up the Fourth Circuit Court of Appeals For the Fourth Circuit's established precedent in the case of *Aston v. Warden* concerning what *Aston*, my, your, and any citizen's right to a fair trial means, the *Aston* Court held the following:

> The impartiality of the jury must exist at the outset of the trial and it must be preserved throughout the entire trial. The device of voir dire and the right to strike prospective jurors, both peremptorily, and for cause, are the means by which and impartial jury is seated in the box. Thereafter, the law guarantees that every defendant may have his case decided strictly according to the evidence presented, not by extraneous matters or by the predilections of individual jurors.

It is important to note that when a commonwealth's attorney, trial court, and appointed trial attorney suppress or conceal testimony evidence during trial, at the bench or in chambers (i.e., out-of-jury presence) or withhold previous March 3, 1976, alleged victim's statement made to Fow that contradicts Fow's statement made at the later part of trial, and which would've been materially relevant to impeaching and/or refuting the footprint exhibit testimony evidence that Fow gave against me, nondisclosure must be considered prejudicial. Thus, equal protection and due process require that this reasoning be applied to me, as well as the commonwealth's attorney foot print theory because the fact of suppression and contradiction are synonymous and because the credibility question of commonwealth's star witness Trooper Fow was of equal importance to both the commonwealth's attorney and myself. Wherefore, nondisclosure must be considered prejudicial in that I was deprived of my liberty interest without due process of law, in violation of Amendment 14, of the United States Constitution, plus section 11 of the constitution of Virginia, supported by United States Supreme Court justices' 1973 decision in the case of *Wardius v. Oregon*.

I respectfully ask the readers, to at least consider (i.e., relevancy to my position) the below decision of the Supreme Court of Virginia, in the case of *Powell v. Commonwealth*, citing the United States Supreme Court's determination in the case entitled *United States v. Throckmorton* defining fraud extrinsic or collateral as follows:

> **Keeping the adversary's witness from Court; secreting or purloining his testimony; or any conduct of the kind mentioned (which) would tend to prevent a fair trial on the merits, and thus to deprive the innocent party of his rights. So if a Judge sits when disqualified from interest or consanguinity; if the litigation or collusive.**

This definition is in substance approved by the holding of the Supreme Court in the case, as set forth in the learned and instructive opinion delivered by Mr. Justice Miller.

Also, for the reader's future musing and contemplation (i.e., relevant to my disclosed position herein this book), go check out the Supreme Court of Virginia's decision in the case of *State Farm Mutual Auto INS. Co., v. Remely*, citing, its determination in the case of *Owens-Corning Fiberglass Corp. v. Watson* resolving an alike legal matter as set forth above—that is, law enforcement officials and appointed defense attorney preventing me from submitting Fow's testimony that interjected "the alleged female victim told him that her abductor made her take off all her clothes except her shoes and socks," in jurors' presence.

By the way, additional legal precedent support for the above issues can be gleaned from another decision had by the Supreme Court of Virginia in the case of *Jones v. Willard*, holding in pertinent part that:

> **Courts have long-held that the judgment of a Court, procured by extrinsic fraud [i.e., "by conduct which prevents a fair submission of the controversy to the Court, is void and subject to attack direct or collateral at any time"].**

At this stage, it would be negligent of me not to partially rehearse those matters of probable cause relative to Trooper Fow's warrantless searches and receiving a gun from Deputy Tay. First, it will be noticed that my court-appointed defense attorney failed to earnestly defend my Fourth Amendment constitutional rights, which require that "I be secure in my person, house, papers, and effects, against unreasonable searches and seizures," said provisions will not be violated, and no warrant issued, but upon showing probable cause, supported by oath or affirmation, and particularly describing the placed to be searched, and the persons or things to be seized. I assumed that abovesaid, the court-appointed defense attorney knew of the aforesaid Fourth Amendment rights.

Moreover, courts interpreting the Fourth Amendment specifies that searches conducted outside the judicial process (i.e., above set forth), without prior approval by [a] Judge or Magistrate are per se unreasonable under the Fourth Amendment subject only to a few specifically established and well-delineated exceptions, says the Supreme

Court of the United States in the case, entitled *Katz v. United States* (emphasis in original). Those exceptions are jealously and carefully drawn, and any law enforcement official who seek to employ the exception, and not the rule, must show that exigencies of the situation made their course of action imperative, held the aforesaid court in the case of *Coolidge v. New Hampshire*.

To be valid, a search warrant must specifically describe the property or things to be seized. A warrant which contains a very broad statement of the categories of property subject to seizure may be invalid since general exploratory searches are forbidden even if probable cause exists to seize the item not particularly described in the warrant says the aforesaid controlling court in the case entitled *Lo-Ji Sales v. New York* and *Stanford v. New York*, respectively.

To wit, a search warrant must be properly signed by an independent judicial officer, who is not biased in favor of the police or prosecution, as is determined by the highest court in the nation in the case of *Illinois v. Gates*, **"A warrant must contain facts, not conclusions, to establish probable cause."**

More importantly, the sworn affidavit attached to an application for a search warrant must contain facts that will enable the issuing authority to make an independent determination that illegal activity was afoot and that a search would be reasonable and supported by probable cause, is the standard set by the Supreme Court of the United States established in the case of *Jones v. United States*. The same court in the case of *Terry v. Ohio* in essence said,

> **To determine whether probable cause exists to arrest or search an individual without a warrant depends on: whether at the moment of arrest or search, the facts and circumstances within the police officer's knowledge, and of which he had reasonably trustworthy information, were sufficient to convince a prudent person that the person arrested had committed or was committing an offense, or that there was**

contraband, weapons, or other illegal materials on the premises.

After perusal of above established law if you, the reader were in travel as I was, from point A to B with your unloaded weapon aboard your automobile, truck, mobile home, bicycle, or motor cycle/moped, and per chance you and/or your mode of transportation get stopped on routine license/registration check and you endure search of your vehicle or personage without being shown a properly issued search warrant signed by a magistrate or judicial judge. The issue may well become whether or not that law enforcement official had probable cause to arrest, search and confiscate your weapon/property. This is to say, whether at the moment of arrest, search or confiscation, there were facts and circumstances within the police officer's knowledge, of which he had reasonable trust worthy information were sufficient to convince a prudent person (i.e., unbiased judge or magistrate) that you (i.e., the person) had committed or was committing an offense, or that there was contraband, weapons, or other illegal material on board your (their) car, or on your property.

Moreover, in the interest of further clarification regarding commonwealth's attorney's gun introduction, linked in retrospect to Fow's warrantless first and second searches, arrest, plus alleged receiving a gun from Deputy Tay. Both the December 12, 1975, Juvenile Domestic Court grand jury indictment trial record, together with subsequent March and May, 1976 trial records shows that the evidence testified by this State primary witness Trooper Fow, evinces when commonwealth's attorney Ben asked, "Who showed you the gun?" The answer was, "It was in the possession of patrolman Tay. I learned after I arrived at South Hill he had charged this man with carrying a concealed weapon" (preserved in id. December 12, 1975, Juv. Tr. Ex. 54-M, p. 125).

Q: Was the gun loaded?
A: Not at the time I received it, no.

> Q: Were you told that it was in the same condition in which it had been seized?
>
> A: I was told that it was not loaded when it was seized.
>
> Q: Anything else on which you based probable cause?
>
> A: I based probable cause the first time as answering the description given to me by both of them [i.e., female and alleged male victims] on description of the man and the weapon. (preserved on December 12, 1975, Juv. Tr. Ex. 54-N, p. 126)

Three months after, during the March 3, 1976, trial session Fow under defense cross exam, when asked, "Did you base this arrest on any information you received from anyone other than the two children?" The answer was, "Absolutely not" (preserved in id. March 3, 1976, Tr. Ex. 54-0, pp. 77). "No one gave him any evidence about the case that he based his opinion on the arrest other than the two children. Neither the search before the arrest was made" (id. March 3, 1976, Tr. Ex. 54-P, p. 78).

Earlier, this same record illustrates that Fow's aforesaid sworn probable cause testimony is acutely contradicted by the alleged male victim's testimony during defense cross-examination that asked the alleged male victim.

> Q: How many times did you talk to Trooper Fow that night? The same night this thing happened?
>
> A: Once.
>
> Q: Once. Now that was about ten minutes after you had been let out of the car?
>
> A: No.
>
> Q: About how long after you were let out of the car did you first speak to Trooper Fow?

> A. Don't remember. It was after they [i.e., law enforcement] found my sister.
> Q: And where was this when you had that conversation?
> A. At my home. (preserved on March 3, 1976, Tr. Ex. 25, p. 18)

Moreover, the alleged victim's mother established the exact time Fow came to her home and talked with the alleged male victim. During defense cross-examination of the alleged victim's mother.

> Q: When you got home what police did you see there?
> A: Mr. Fow came to the house.
> Q: What time?
> A: It must have been about 2:00 or 2:30.
> Q: In the morning?
> A: Yes.
> Q: Where were your children at that time?
> A: At home.
> Q: At home with you; were they in bed?
> A: Female was in bed. Allege male victim was still up. They got a report from the children. (December 12, 1975, Juv. Tr. Ex. 52-D, p. 45, and Juv. Tr. Ex. 52-E, p. 46)

The above referenced testimony completely obliterates all traces of Fow's above pretrial rehearsed sworn time factor probable cause testimony, which previously interjected that "I base probable cause the first time answering the description given to me by both of them [i.e., alleged male and female victims] on the description of the man and the weapon" (preserved in id. March 3, 1976, Tr. Ex. 54-O, p. 77 and Tr. Ex. 54-P, p. 78). It is clearly contradicted by the alleged male victim's testimony interjection that "He saw Fow one time at his home around 2:30 a.m. after officials had found his sister. Plus,

Fow's own pretrial rehearsed testimony—equally show that by the time Fow actually saw the alleged male victim, I had been transferred to him by Deputy Tay, as indicated in the March 3, 1976, Tr. Ex. 47-G, p. 55, where the commonwealth's attorney Ben asked Fow, "What time does the record show that you picked Mr. Simpson, the defendant up in South Hill?" Fow answered, "Defendant Simpson was picked up by officer Tay at 12:22 a.m." The attorney asked, "And handed to you?" Fow answered, "Handed to me."

Although said testimony be pretrial rehearsed, they inadvertently establishes that by the time Trooper Fow got the alleged probable cause information from the alleged victims at their home around 2:30 a.m., I was already several hours ahead being warrantless apprehended by officer Tay.

Even to a complete novice, the above transcribed recorded facts clearly high lights obvious habitual credibility issues in dispute and how deeply entrenched the said pretrial collusion/covenant between appointed defense attorney, trial court and commonwealth's attorney was so much!

The trial court totally breached its duty to safeguard my constitutional rights, contrarily the court vehemently interjected (extraneous matter) to the effect, the court said (i.e., I'll skip over the foundation, the officer said he found a gun, causing jury to laugh), manifesting the Court's vouching remarks upon the weight of commonwealth's illegally seized unloaded weapon evidence was improper misconduct as tending to intimate the favor of the court with respect to the character and weight of said evidence, in contravention of jurors' duty to evaluate facts, evidence, and witness credibility, thus carried with it the official approval of the government that may have influenced the jury to trust the court's judgment rather than its own view of the evidence suggested to the jury that they were free to believe Fow's pretrial rehearsed gun testimony evidence was credible, and they were free to link by speculation said gun information to me, my car, the alleged victims and removal of the alleged female victim's foot/toeprints from the rear window of my car, if they wish, and also may have unduly suggested to the jury to adopt an attitude of disbelief and prejudice against the defense, which was highly prejudicial to me, and improperly relieved the commonwealth's attorney's duty to prove every essential element of my charged offenses beyond a reasonable doubt, constituted extrinsic fraud compounded by the trial court's overruling defense attorney's (i.e., token) motion for mistrial, on the grounds of Court's display of anger and indication of impatient demeanor toward my defense (preserved in May 26, 1976, Tr. Ex. 60-D, p. 233 & Tr. Ex. 50-B, p. 284), thereby prevented a fair submission of my case to the court, which denied me a fundamentally fair trial before an impartial Judge and jury of my peers, in violation of Section 11 of the Constitution of Virginia as well as violated my constitutionally guaranteed right to due process, under Section 1 Amendment 14 of the US Constitution.

Secondly, the appointed defense attorney owed me the duty of loyalty therewith had the duty to bring to bear such skill and knowledge as would render my trial a reliable adversarial testing process but breached that duty on account of his pretrial rehearsed probable cause time factor collusion/covenant with commonwealth's attorney and trial court. Thitherto, he made no effort to present or vigorously argue the aforementioned facts such as commonwealth's attorney could not legally establish Fow's asserted probable cause, on the below bases:

    a. The information Fow allegedly got from the alleged victims at the home at 2:30 a.m. because the alleged male victim testified, he talk to Fow only one time the night he was let out of his alleged abductor's car; and that was after law enforcement officials found his sister, at his home around 2:30 a.m.

    b. Nor on the bases of Fow's sworn interjection statement that the charges to be in this warrant are true to the best of my knowledge.

    c. Fow's knowledge and usage of the gun information garnered from Deputy Tay's illegal arrest, search of my car and warrantless seizure of an alleged unloaded gun to secure an arrest warrant from the Halifax County Magistrate (preserved on March 3, 1976, Tr. Ex. 54-0, p. 80 & id. Tr. Ex. 54-R, p. 81) is contrary to the Supreme Court of the United States, decision in the case entitled *Wong Sun v. US* holding the following:

Evidence which is spawned by or directly, derived from an illegal search or illegal interrogation is generally inadmissible against the defendant because of Its original taint.

But see the Supreme Court of Virginia decision, in the case of *Hart v. Commonwealth*.

Neither could appointed defense attorney McLau, trial court and/or commonwealth's attorney lawfully conceal commonwealth's star witness Fow's testimony interjection that **"she [i.e., the alleged female victim] said he made her take all of her clothes off with the exception of her shoes and socks"** (id. Preserved on March 3, 1976, Tr. Ex. 56-B-2, p. 73), on account that appointed defense attorney objected and requested to be heard out of jury's presence, thereby concealed materially relevant beneficial defense testimony evidence that would've discredited the commonwealth's attorney's alleged female victim's footprint evidence used against me and presented a reasonable doubt in the minds of my jury:

Appointed defense attorney had no difficulty concealing this materially relevant matter; neither did appointed defense attorney McLau, argue the trial court's continued egregious (i.e., pattern of bias behavior) outward demeanor/display of anger with impatient (i.e., extraneous matter) remarks toward my defense for tendering proper objections, which established precedent law has determined: constitutes extrinsic fraud misconduct. See *Henshaw v. Commonwealth*, citing *Mazer v. Commonwealth* or the trial court at the bench—out of jurors presence—compounding its extrinsic fraud misconduct by overruling defense appointed attorney's token mistrial motion in my defense.

Instead, as shown by the aforementioned recorded facts, appointed defense attorney McLau breached his duty of loyalty owed me—his client, by willfully opting to honor his pretrial rehearsed collusion/covenant with the trial court and its law enforcement officials when he deliberately concealed the above facts. Plus the trial court's improper vouching remarks regarding its favor toward the weight of the commonwealth's attorney's alleged gun and footprint exhibit impeachment testimony evidence, thereby improperly interfered with the jury's determination of those above disputed facts and Fow's credibility, which was one of the critical aspects in my trial, tended to prejudice his client's defense: in that he left the jury free to believe Fow's testimony evidence was credible, and that they were free to link by speculation Fow's asserted probable cause—use of Tay's illegally seized gun to obtain his search warrant as well as Fow's lifting alleged female victim's foot/toe print from the rear window of my car, if they wish, was mutiny! At the helm of said improper misconduct, amounted to collusion extrinsic fraud (see the Fourth Circuit Court of Appeals decision in the case of *Bizzell v. Hemingway,* **"Collusion between plaintiff's attorney and opposing party"**), as tending to have prevented me from obtaining the benefit of my defense as well as a fundamentally fair submission of my defense to a fair and an impartial judge and jury of my peers, thereby prejudiced and discriminated against me by denying my Sixth Amendment constitutional right to effective assistance of counsel, violated my equal protection and due process rights, under Section 11 of the Constitution of Virginia also violated Section 1 of Amendment 14 USC.

Ladies, gentlemen, young ladies and young men, boys and girls for your information, there are other such established legal precedents to support the above stated truth, shall we look in the United States Supreme Court's decision in the case cited early on herein, namely *Strickland v. Washington,* holding,

> **An attorney must bring to bear such skill and knowledge as will render the trial a reliable adversarial testing process. Although the**

J.D.

Supreme Court avoided a specific guideline for attorney conduct in Strickland, It affirmed that reasonable effective assistance of counsel require undivided respect for the "duty of loyalty, a duty to avoid conflicts of interest."

Something McLau abandoned at the onset during those ten- to twenty-minute audience he gave me there in the Halifax County Jail, the morning of the Indictment hearing, where he discussed no plan of defense. A similar counsel discussion is had in the case of *Wood v. Georgia*. Besides, the US Constitution Amendment 2, ratified in 1791, provided me the right to bear arms, specifically my unloaded pistol that was maintained on the dashboard or in the passenger side front seat of my car.

Chapter 12

Generally, after this somewhat oppressive performance of theatrical trial court vouching for the credibility of state's primary witnesses's alleged footprint/gun introduced evidence, coupled with commonwealth's attorney and appointed defense trial attorney's collusion, concealment of testimony evidence interjection that the alleged female victim did not remove her shoes or socks. Helpful defense impeachment testimony evidence works. I admit, at that time, I was unaware of the extent and devastating jury damage being done. My spirit and physical man resorted to God, then! Then afterward, to the temporarily assigned cell, in the Halifax County Jail to take continual counsel from my risen LORD and Savior Jesus Christ: whom, my king James version of the Bible declares stands always ready to help His human creation with any monsters/demons we face, whether during the night or day season (see Old testament book entitled Isaiah 41:13, 42:2, and 49. Plus, the book entitled Psalms 103:6).

There, in that six-man jail block single-cell unit, I mused about a favorable trial outcome since I had committed nothing worthy of a conviction. And although God had not scratched the surface of completing His plan or work for my temporal earthly pilgrimage, yet I was blessed with holy inspired wisdom to take a sneak peek

J.D.

back over the various attitudes and character tools that God miraculously implemented into my overall view of life, family, friends, and associates. God, the Creator of heaven, earth, and everything that exists. God also allowed me to behold the multitude of trials/conflicts which were or would be employed by the enemies of TRUTH—for the express purpose of compelling me to relent. That is to say to bring me to a state with an overwhelming mindset, but God didn't leave me there! Rather, His tiny small voice began anew to whisper just put one foot before the other and trust my instructions. Thanks be to Jesus! For the ongoing corrective measures being wrought in my decision making process, thus provided a juncture…the place where questions crop up, and that still small voice via the Holy Spirit grants lasting resolve (please view 1 Kings 19:12 KJV) answers to lingering matters. For instance, God wonderfully blessed my personal involvement with those early on eluded too—four Muslims and one Caucasian detainees domiciling adjacent to me in the jail, including several sheriff jailers, whose communication interaction with me, in my estimation, raised important questions.

For instance, one of the ministering questions that arose, "What are our human rights, or do we possess such a thing?" Under my circumstances, it caused me to write the library of congress in Washington, DC, where, within one week, a reply containing documentary information came, proffered by one scholar whose name is Dr. Joseph Hopkins. He writes, "Human rights are those conditions of life that allow us fully to develop and use our human qualities of intelligence and conscience, and to satisfy our spiritual needs. We don't speak merely of biological needs when we talk about human rights. Human rights are based on mankind's increasing demand for a life in which the inherent dignity of each human being will receive respect and protection, an idea that reaches beyond the comforts and conveniences that science and technology can provide. Human rights are fundamental to our nature. Without them, we cannot live as human beings. Human rights have been called the world's best kept secret, yet it should influence the way every one of us around the world is able to live our lives. Few know what the thirty articles of the Universal Declaration of Human Rights (UDHR) contains, and even fewer have seen a copy, yet it is supposed to be made available around the globe."

Importantly reader, my King James Version of God's divinely inspired writ shows that Prophet Hosea declared the dire judgment: "My people are destroy for lack of knowledge"! See the Old Testament book entitled Hosea 4:6.

Dr. Hopkins went on to report, "The UDHR controls and supersedes government policies; world leaders are accountable to it, and corporations and financial institutions are supposed to promote it in their business dealings." Yet to many, especially those on the receiving end of human rights violations, it could be just some old document gathering dust on a shelf in New York its existence either forgotten or ignored. The UDHR, written, adopted, and proclaimed by the United Nations as a response to the atrocities committed during the Second World War will mark its fiftieth anniversary on December 10, 1998. By adopting the UDHR governments promised to work toward a world without cruelty and injustice and to guarantee the basic human rights of all citizens, but what has happened in reality?

Successive governments have failed to live up to that promise. Half the world's countries still jail people solely because of their beliefs, their race, gender, or ethnic origin, and a third of the world's governments torture their prisoners. Open a newspaper, turn on a television or radio and you are struck by the amount of cruelty that persists from the hundreds of thousands of innocent women and children targeted in armed conflicts to the individual cases of people rotting in jail for signing a petition.

The UDHR forbids this and by committing these atrocities governments are breaking international human rights standards, violating international law. Yet they are getting away with abusing the rights they are legally obligated to uphold. Why? Perhaps it is because governments have denied possession of the UDHR to the people of the world they have failed to distribute it as they were supposed to do, and at the same time, they have argued that it is not relevant to their own particular culture or situation. They have failed to make their people Aware of its content and said that the people are not interested in the rights it entitles them to.

In 1948, the United Nations called governments to use every means within their power to distribute the text among all peoples of the world and to ensure that the UDHR was displayed in schools and colleges everywhere in as many languages as possible. Have you seen it, reader?

To transform the UDHR into a living document with the power to change our lives, it is time we reclaimed it from those governments. It is time that we made government leaders aware that it is their job to protect and promote these rights, not to violate them. It is time that we showed governments that we claim the rights enshrined in the UDHR and that we claim these rights universally, no matter whether we live in Singapore, Spain, Saudi Arabia, or America, Article 22 of the UDHR provides, "Everyone, as member of society has the right to social security and is entitled to realization…of…economic, social and cultural rights," you have the right by virtue of being a human being to have your basic needs met. Everyone is entitled to live in economic, social, and cultural conditions that allow them dignity and let them develop as individuals. All countries should do everything they can to make this happen."

On a personal note, I possess a copy of the section of the Universal Declaration of Human Rights (UDHR) which contains a least thirty articles of human rights, it amazes me how that prior to my 1975 false arrest, relationship with Jesus or during trials of momentary experiences through several communicative exchanges with opinionated jail detainees; it never occurred to me that jailed/incarcerated people—especially those with mentoring age children—undergo such uphill battle for an opportunity to simply possess meaningful tools to achieve basic human rights. Reader, if your interest have been stimulated, then you should write or email the Library of Congress in Washington, DC and request your copy (i.e., or down load same via the Internet system) of the thirty articles of human rights, embodied in the Universal Declaration of Human rights (UDHR).

Keeping it real, try on my present interjection that it is not just what we hear that inevitably form what we believe, but oftentimes! It is what we don't hear (i.e., as the jurors above did) as well, which helps to mold our belief system. America has achieved its status through in "God we trust." Afterward, when greed, pride, and arrogance subtly crept in and replaced God (i.e., a graphic depiction of that very identical spirit is seen in the Old Testament book entitled Ezekiel 28:13–15 and Isaiah 14:12–15). Words I have coined (the I syndrome), then they removed prayer from schools and public arenas. Plus, child rearing from their parents (i.e., transgressing God's instructions found in the Old Testament book entitled Proverbs 14:24, also Proverbs 22:6 KJV), as well as attempted to legislate laws, with the mistaken premise to resolve sin's attributes. Being acted out in and through, for example, the child who disrupts a class room compacted with his fellow students when he randomly discharged his/her father's automatic weapon at whomsoever is found in the line of fire or acted out by a racist bigoted Judge who was not impartial but acted in sin's own self-righteousness, instead of obeying God's directives contained in the Old Testament book entitled Deuteronomy 16:18–19, also the book entitled Leviticus 19:15. Don't pervert judgment between the poor and the rich; protect and defend the US Constitution.

Furthermore, the aforementioned, unlike the King James version of the Bible, which confronts each individual (i.e., including the above reference unjust court judge) human being with forced (yet God blessed free will) option. To wit, Jesus who God raised from death's prison says in the New Testament book entitled Matthew 4:19 (follow me). He attracts us, but so do some of the other aforementioned forces, many maneuver pathetically to delay or to find both an answer. Jesus's tiny small voice comes back insisting that its *either* or *or*. Which of you by taking thought can add one inch to his/her size? And why take thought for material things. Please take time out to view Matthew 6:27–28. It is certain that if throughout the years we keep saying, let's think this over a little longer before doing

J.D.

something rash, one day they will awake, to realize that the vision master has kept moving, while the unconscious decisions of everyday life were moving them in the opposite direction. God is firmly securing (cleansing) this sole of mine (i.e., as I daily, minutely exercise my God ordained gift of choice). At the same time folk, God have also appointed me (PURPOSE) for my life, some of which have permitted me to begun charting with pen and paper.

Moreover, in my view, nothing matters more than knowing God's purpose for my life and absolutely nothing can compensate for not knowing them—not success, fleeing financial gain, wealth, fame, or fault—momentary pleasure. And to I believe that without God's purpose, life is just motion without meaning, activity without direction, and events without reason. Without TRUTH, the absolute (i.e., unchangeable) standard of how decisions are made in line with the ONLY TRUE LIVING GOD's revealed WILL and PLANS, one's directed path and life is trivial, petty, pointless and subject to change as one's circumstances and/or geographic assignment alters, proving no true peace or enduring fulfillment exist there.

Herewith, I must passionately state that the King James Version of the Bible says,

> **The law of the LORD is sure, making wise the simple. The Statutes of the LORD are right, rejoicing the heart; the Commandment of the LORD is pure, enlightening the eyes [i.e., understanding]; The fear [i.e., respect] of the LORD is clean, enduring forever; The judgments of the LORD are true and righteous altogether. More to be desired are they than gold, yes, than much fine gold: sweater also than honey and the honey comb. Moreover, by them is thy servant warned; and in keeping of them there is great reward—who can understand his [her] errors? Cleanse thou me from secret faults. Keep back your servant also from presumptuous sins; Let**

them not have dominion over me; Then shall I be upright, and I shall be innocent from the great transgression.

 The aforesaid quotes can be found in the Old Testament book entitled Psalms 19:7–13.
 Is it okay if I continue? All right! There came the time in my life, where I was stopped and granted the PAUSE I desperately needed on November 10, 1975, herein expounded upon earlier. Whereat I was compelled to *halt* long enough to read, practically the entire New Testament (KJV). This allowed me to take inventory of where I had been, was and would need to proceed with regard to my maturity and ability to confront the TRUTH (i.e., reality) to examine the purpose of this temporal life with respect to the purpose of Jesus versus the finite that is the significantly limited opinions of mankind.
 Perhaps, this is as good a time as will come, before trial resumes, to attempt to expound a little about the term (SIN) and that that I perceive to be the Bible definition of sin. The Bible says in the New Testament book entitled Romans 3:23 that "all have sinned, and come short of the glory of God." Sin originated with God's archenemy Lucifer who became Satan and was banished from heaven, along with a third of the angels that agreed with him. If you, reader, desire to look into that matter, use the King James version of the Bible, and turn to the Old Testament books entitled Isaiah 14:12–14, then Ezekiel 28:12–15 (i.e., message goes beyond the King of Tyre to Satan). Plus, New Testament book entitled Revelation 12:7–9, which, in my respectful opinion, shows that sin! Then the willful transgression of God's revealed will, the divine boundary between good and evil. Father David expressed this in the book entitled Psalms 51. After he committed adultery with Bathsheba, wife of Uriah, an act inherently wrong, whether expressly forbidden or not, as supported in the New Testament book entitled Romans 1:19–23. Another on point example of sin can be viewed in Adam, God's original human creation, as demonstrated in the old Testament book entitled Genesis

2:16–17 (i.e., God's revealed instructions for Adam), then Genesis 3:1–6, but specifically verse 6:16–19.

Closer to home, I reiterate that from the time Geor, the Halifax County Jail inmate cadre, provided me a small New Testament Bible. I made every attempt to read and apply same to my actions, motives and decision making abilities while interacting with others. God's word instantly served as light with which to understand the intent of my motives and force me to confront other day to day realities in light of God's revealed will written in stone with His Own finger, as declared in the Old Testament book entitled Exodus 20:1–17, 31:17–18, and 34:28, called the Ten Commandments, namely:

1. **Thou shall have no other gods before me.**
2. **You shall not make unto yourself any graven image (i.e., pictures, etc.) or any likeness of anything that is in heaven above, or that is in the earth.**
3. **You shall not bow down yourself to them, nor serve them because I the LORD your God am a Jealous God, visiting the iniquity of the Fathers upon their children unto the third and fourth generation of them that hate [i.e., disobey] me; but showing mercy unto thousands of them that love [i.e., believe/obey] me and keep my commandments;**
4. **You shall not take the name of the LORD your God in vain [i.e., Profane]; because the LORD will not hold you guiltless that takes His name in vain;**
5. **Remember the Sabbath [i.e., Saturday] day, to keep it holy. Six days shall you labor and do all your work; but the Seventh day is the Sabbath of the LORD your God: in it you shall not do any work, you, nor your cat-**

tle, nor your stranger that is within your gates: because in Six days the LORD made heaven and earth, the Sea, and all that in them is, and rested the Seventh day; wherefore the LORD blessed the Sabbath day and Hallowed it;

6. **Honor your father and your mother that your days may be long upon the land (property) which the LORD your God gives you;**
7. **You shall not kill; you shall not commit adultery;**
8. **You shall not steal;**
9. **You shall not bear false witness [i.e., lie] against your neighbor;**
10. **You shall not covet [i.e., desire to possess], your neighbor's house, you shall not covet your neighbors wife, nor his manservant, nor his maidservant, nor his ox, nor his mule, nor anything that is your neighbors.**

If you wish, you may review the above commandments in the Old Testament book throughout, but here specifically in Exodus 19:17–19, plus Jesus's embodiment in Matthew 5:17–48.

More importantly, God did not leave any of His human creation to become overly concerned about having or not possessing the ability to read and/or commit the above Ten Commandment guideline principles to memory—for in the New Testament book entitled Hebrews 8:9–12, the Holy Spirit caused the following to be penned that in essence says,

> **This is the covenant that I will make with the house of Israel after those days, says the LORD; I will put my laws into their mind, and write them in their hearts; and I will be to them a God, and they shall be to me a people:**

And they shall not teach every man his neighbor, and every man his brother, saying, know the LORD: for all shall know me, from the least to the greatest.

Many Bible scholars claim this text was penned around CAD 68 after Christ Rose from that stony grave.

It would be negligent of me, not to write a little about the cause and effect of my (or maybe your) willful disobedience to the aforesaid Holy principles in connection with sin. The King James version of the Bible says, "All sins (i.e., murder, robbery, adultery, fornication, covetous, rapists, liars, etc.) shall be forgiven unto the sons [daughters] of mankind, and blasphemies wherewith soever they shall blasphemes, but he that shall blaspheme against the holy Ghost will never be forgiven, but is in danger of eternal damnation," as recorded in the New Testament book entitled Mark 1:28–29. Therewith, on the bases of the aforementioned, it is my conviction that the greatest (worse) sin is not doing or verbalizing something wrong. Instead, it is not doing what we know (i.e., should/could know) is the right thing to do. Thus, in connection with sin, the New Testament book entitled 1 John 1:9, says,

If we confess our sins, He (God/Jesus) is faithful and justified to forgive us our sins, and to cleanse us from all unrighteousness.

The facts above appear to both illustrate that the Ten Commandments is the only applicable standard given to mankind to examine our direction in life, with respect to commitment to the plan of God/Jesus, as well as to evaluate our daily position, regarding our ability to confront reality and be at liberty to love God and our neighbor as oneself in the midst of the apparent global, state, city, or neighborhood situations and/or discomforting trials that accompany everyday life.

Presently, I'm musing about everything that is transpiring in my bogus trial, coupled with family matters and my nephew's junior year at A&T University, located in Greensboro, North Carolina. This is to say I am discovering that by faith I believe, accept, obey, and make every effort to apply the inspired text penned in the New Testament book entitled 2 Timothy 3:16, which purports,

> **All scripture is given by inspiration of God, and is profitable for doctrine, for reproof, for correction, for instruction in righteousness: that the man [woman] of God may be perfect, thoroughly furnished to do all good works.**

Furthermore, in my association with blood related family, and others alike: there exist in my inner man (i.e., soul), the power and ability to put myself/oneself in the other person's position. To wit, readily enter into their emotions, their difficulties, their disappoints, their joys, and into their sorrows (i.e., problems). With this significant reality, I began fixing the aforesaid abnormalities, with scripture in my mind for remembrance and regular contemplation, plus apply same to my day/night season decision prayer utterance ability, acts of commission, motives and self-discipline, in route to identifying myself with their particular state of affairs, as I would hope them to deal with me as if they were to exchange circumstances.

In addition, I'll be candid to admit that I was more and more empowered to willfully modify that former controlling, non-altruistic, lack of compassion, selfish, and none true loving attitude, which once ordered my path. I began to realize that anything I willingly yield my God created members to obey, to them I became captive/slave. The New Testament book entitled Romans 6:16–18, declares,

> **Know you not that to who [whatsoever] you yield yourselves servants to obey, his [its] servant you are, to who you obey; whether to**

> **sin unto death, or of obedience unto righteousness? But God be thanked that you were the servants of sin, but you have obeyed from the heart that form of doctrine which was delivered you. Being then made free from sin, you became the servants of righteousness.**

And I suppose, there be many folk who will argue that they are not servants to food, money, clothing, automobiles, or a host of other in animated material objects or things. Notwithstanding, I believe that I can say with authority that before my earlier eluded too personal ongoing chosen relationship with the jealous guardianship of God's Holy Spirit (i.e., New Testament book entitled John 14:26, **"The comforter, which is the Holy Ghost, who the Father will send in my name, He will teach you all things, and bring all things to your remembrance, whatsoever I have said to you."**). I was ignorantly a captive slave (i.e., Satan's puppet on string) to the fast pace life, other people, money, the approval of associates, opinions of finite disbelieving young aged boys' and girls' formulas, even to serving automobiles—that is, by polishing, washing, and valued it above the attention I rendered most people—who are made after the similitude of the ONLY TRUE LIVING GOD/Jesus. It's the reader's choice…

Yes! I exclaimed. But glory be to God and His abundant grace and mercy by faith in His Son Jesus Christ's risen merits from death, I have been set free from all such, especially from the opinions of finite mankind and gods. The King James version of the Bible says,

> **Faith is the substance of things hoped for, the evidence of things not seen. Through faith we understand that the worlds were framed by the WORD of God. So things which are seen were not made of things which do appear. (Hebrews 11:1 and 3)**

THE JOURNEY

There be many as I have aforesaid herein who have commenced the act of sexual intercourse, with the hope of bringing forth birth of a child, yet played no part therein, with exception of the act of sexual gratification. Still, these folk fostered hope (faith) in that which was not seen although they believed not God's revelations regarding His authorship over all that lives! Exist and have it or their being therein.

Moreover, I understand that deeply embedded in our emotional lives/opinions are symbols like democracy, equality, Christianity, love, and service conflicting with existing counter drives, such as ambition, prestige, comfort, financial security tearing said personalities apart in search of opinions, and/or instructions their soul favor. Further, in my humble estimation, the aforesaid represents lonely people, with aching hearts and innermost longings, with a guilt consciousness that never leaves them day or night. And as I once did, they too! Have equally sampled the opinions/standards of the unbelieving mass of people in this world and found them an empty sham. They are weary of the glitter and dashing motor cars, the flashing drive-in screens, and the pointed shadows of their night spots. I'm convinced they're hurt will never be healed by offering them more dosages of the same…They must be searching for something quite different, perhaps standards that will not flip-flop or vacillate in the face of unfavorable circumstances. They are looking for standards—a map with instructions worth living or dying for.

Men and women, boys and girls, you may know the old adage that in essence says, "How can you know what direction you are headed without understanding [i.e., knowing] where you came from." With this food for thought, the question of yesteryear rekindles in my thoughts the following analogy: What is your life and it's pilgrimage without asking God of creation for instructions? For instance, the King James version of the Bible says,

> **Go to now, you that say, today or tomorrow we will go into such a city, and continue there a year, and buy and sell, and get gain: where you do not know what shall be on**

> the morrow. For what is your life? It is even a vapor [i.e., human life is fragile at its best] that appears for a little time, and then vanishes away. For that you ought to say, if the LORD will, we shall live, and do this, or that.

To verify the fore stated truth, the reader should open its King James Version of the Bible to the New Testament book entitled James 4:13–15.

> From what place come wars and fights among you? Come they not hence, even of your lusts that war in your members? You lust, and have not: you kill, and desire to have, and cannot obtain: you fight and war [i.e., indecisiveness implied], yet you have not, because you ask not. You ask, and receive not [i.e., a peaceful spirit] because you ask amiss [i.e., in a wrong or for improper purpose] that you may consume it upon your lusts.

Therefore, God speaking via the Holy Spirit, through the pages of the aforementioned book, specifically counsels us to be doers of God's word, and not hearers only, deceiving your own selves. See James 1:22. For the reason that if the unbeliever would say so, they would readily admit they're discontented with that stagnated state. They would declare (i.e., as I did, and still do) that they desire to progress and achieve a more peaceful spirit with its enlargement of life; oppose to continuing in that vicious non apologetic daily cycle.

In fact, if those in such a state of indecisiveness would communicate with all their being that they want and need the Spirit of camaraderie shown in the lives of people that earnestly walk in the faith of Jesus during His/her brief physical tenure on planet earth, they won't choose to go on making excuses and/or justifying their stagnated posture that tend to run only in circles—often vicious—

being conscious of no lack, tainted by the feeling they have need of nothing.

What is anything without love? I don't mean to imply that there's something wrong in caring about oneself. To the contrary, I believe that it is necessary for human beings to possess sufficient esteem in order to be productive. Nonetheless, we should, as Holy Writ teaches, have uppermost in our hearts and conscience and love for our fellow man, woman, and children. Nowadays, it's not the trend or flow of things to be altruistic, to be compassionate, loving, or caring. So many too! Many are rich in knowledge and material possessions, yet their souls and human compassion appears impoverished.

Chapter 13

Lord willing, we shall communicate more on the aforesaid matter, but at the moment, the commonwealth's attorney at the Halifax County Circuit Court continued criminal persecution and summons our attention. We must remember that the trial court's duty to safeguard my federal constitutional rights remains in force throughout until the trial concludes, says the United States Supreme Court in the case of *Hawk v. Olson*.

Upon a brief recap of the foregone facts and controlling established State and Federal law, the below facts reveals that both the failure of the commonwealth's attorney to legally or lawfully establish probable cause for Deputy Tay's warrantless search, seizures, and arrest on bases of Deputy Mor's pretrial rehearsed yellow Mustang II, with North Carolina license plate number and black top, alleged probable cause information description of my car (i.e., extraneous matter), which did not emanate from either alleged victim whose interjected testimony said they never saw the license plate or top of their assailant's car nor from Fow's pretrial rehearsed yellow Mustang II with dark stripe at the bottom description information, which was not garnered from either alleged victim who testified that they only talked with Fow at their home hours after Deputy Tay's warrantless search, alleged gun seizure and arrest. Neither from Fow's alleged acquired search warrant after his several warrantless search and alleged seizures by employing Deputy Tay's illegal warrantless search and seized unloaded gun information evidence. Neither upon commonwealth's attorney's structured invalid notarized affidavit (i.e., yet was used by trial court, commonwealth's attorney, appointed defense attorney and Fow to obtain a search warrant for search and seizure for my saliva or body fluid) because said sworn affidavit contained (false probable cause personal car identification statement information) that was outside the four corners of title 19.2-54 Virginia Statute and/or commonwealth's attorney's usage of its own personal oath of office to vouch for state star witness Fow's credibility to bolster the government's case.

Trial Court's improper comments on weight of the evidence, causally connected to its improper prohibiting defense cross-examination of impeached witness's testimony in contravention of the jurors' prerogative, commonwealth's attorney, trial court, and appointed defense attorney's collusion/covenant, preventing my witnesses from appearing in court, together with their deliberate suppression of helpful in chamber disclosed exculpatory gonorrhea sperm testimony impeachment evidence favorable to me creating a reasonable doubt in the juror's mind. Trial court's failure to instruct jury on the principles of law applicable to the pleadings and evidence. Trial court's direct prejudice toward me by refusing to grant my request to be examined by a qualified mutual private physician to rebut the prior prejudicial gonorrhea treatment testimony given against me. commonwealth's attorney trial court and appointed trial attorney's collusion/covenant prohibiting both the alleged male victim from testifying about the initial description information he gave the first officers (twin black sheriffs) as well as prohibiting defense's cross-examination of state's witness Fow regarding conversation description he'd had with same above named twin black sheriffs (i.e., information that allegedly provided state's asserted probable cause). And trial courts overruling defense's mistrial motion on grounds of it being the court's second time display of anger and impatience toward my defense [causing jurors to laugh], for raising proper objection to the court's improper introduction of commonwealth's attorney's alleged foot print exhibit evidence; plus, the covenant/collusion acts of appointed defense attorney, trial court and commonwealth's attorney's deliberate concealment of state's star witness Fow's sworn testimony which said the alleged female victim told him that her assailant made her take all of her clothes off with the exception of her shoes and socks materially relevant beneficial defense foot print impeachment testimony evidence, creating genuine issues in dispute.

Facts that evinces a legitimate inference sufficient to show that the trial court, commonwealth's attorney and appointed defense was aware the commonwealth lacked factual basis to prove every essential element of my charged offenses beyond a reasonable doubt as required by the Supreme Court of Virginia's established precedent in the case of *Hankerson v. Moody* and *Powers v. Commonwealth*, "It is elementary that the burden is on the commonwealth to prove every essential element of the offense beyond a reasonable doubt." plus that the trial court's decision to uphold commonwealth's attorney's structured affidavit containing false probable cause personal identification information that did not comply with State law; as well as the trial court's own improper comments on the weight of commonwealth's attorney's evidence and its in-chamber suppression of gonorrhea sperm testimony evidence helpful to disclosing reasonable doubt and my professed innocence, which did not comply with state or constitutional law; together with trial court's improper prohibiting defense cross-examination of impeached witness testimony, in contravention of the juror's prerogative that did not comply with state or constitutional law. The trial court's failures to instruct the jury on the principles of law applicable to the controversy and evidence, which did not comply with state law, together with numerous other improper misconduct listed above that did not comply with state law, as required by the United States Supreme Court established precedent in the case of *Hicks v. Oklahoma* holding as follows:

> **The State defendant had a federal constitutional due process right not to be deprived of his liberty except in accordance with the laws of the State, and that federal right was violated**

THE JOURNEY

when State Rules applied to other criminal defendants were not applied to Hicks.

Including the fact that the trial court, commonwealth's attorney and appointed defense attorney McLau knew or should've known about. Below attached are March 31, 1978, Richmond News Leader and April 1978 Richmond Times dispatch Art. 1 and Art. 2.

Article from the "Richmond News Leader"

Suit to Allege Punishment

MAR 31, 1978

A former state crime laboratory serologist is expected to file a federal lawsuit today charging that four lab officials conspired to punish her for filing an earlier suit. The first, filed in October, alleged that she was denied a pay increase because she voiced concerns about "serious discrepancies" in lab procedures.

The new suit is expected to make claims similar to those in the earlier suit, which was dismissed when Regina K. Demas failed to file an answer to a motion by defendants. That action apparently was a maneuver to allow inclusion in the new suit of the allegation that four lab officials conspired to punish her.

Miss Demas, 25, claims that she learned of discrepancies in tests performed by Mary Jane Burton, her former boss, last May. Miss Demas took her concerns to officials and asked for corrective action, the earlier suit said.

However, no action was taken and steps were taken to conceal the discrepancies, the earlier suit said.

No Moves to Halt

The suit also contended that "nothing was done to preclude their recurrence."

Mrs. Burton, chief serologist; Robert E. Edwards, assistant director of the forensic science bureau; Warren G. Johnson, deputy director of the forensic science bureau; and Dr. A. W. Tiedemann Jr., director of consolidated laboratory services, are expected to be named as defendants. In the earlier suit all but Edwards were named as defendants.

Miss Demas is now working in the product testing bureau which performs work for the state Alcoholic Beverage Control Department. The new suit is expected to claim that she was transferred because of the earlier suit. She began work in February 1977 as a serologist.

If Miss Demas' claims are proved true, it would raise the chance that new criminal trials would result for dozens of and possibly many more, persons who have been convicted.

Serologists conduct scientific tests on blood and other bodily secretions submitted by police in criminal investigations. The results of those tests often are critical in establishing guilt or innocence.

The new suit is expected to ask the U.S. District Court to award Miss Demas the pay increase, declare that her constitutional rights were violated and award her $300,000 in damages.

195

J.D.

*Article from the —
"Richmond Times Dispatch"
DATE: SAT APR. 1,*

Merit Pay Denial Is Alleged

A state crime laboratory worker has filed a lawsuit in U.S. District Court here that alleges she was denied a merit pay increase and subjected to "baseless" personnel actions because she expressed concern about what she called "serious" discrepancies in laboratory procedures.

The plaintiff, Regina K. Demas, a serologist employed

(Reprinted from yesterday's late editions.)

by the Division of Consolidated Laboratory Services, filed a similar suit in federal court last October.

The earlier suit was dismissed when Miss Demas failed to file an answer to a motion filed by defendants named in the suit.

Miss Demas contended in Friday's complaint that she learned of discrepancies in tests performed by Mrs. Mary Jane Burton last May.

Mrs. Burton is chief serologist for the crime laboratory.

Mrs. Demas complained in Friday's suit that no action was taken to correct the alleged discrepancies and that steps were taken to conceal the discrepancies.

Defendants named in the suit filed Friday were Mrs. Burton; Robert E. Edwards, assistant director of the Forensic Science Bureau; Warren G. Johnson, deputy director of the Forensic Science Bureau, and A.W. Tiedemann Jr., director of the Division of Consolidated Laboratory Services.

Serologists employed by the division conduct scientific tests on blood and other body secretions submitted by police in connection with criminal investigations. The results of such tests often are used in establishing guilt or innocence of defendants in criminal cases.

Tiedemann, Johnson and Mrs. Burton also were named as defendants in the earlier law suit.

The suit filed Friday contends that the three original defendants and Edwards conspired to damage Miss Demas' professional reputation and to destroy her career, "with the express purpose of penalizing for seeking redress in federal court."

Miss Demas contends that the four defendants carried out "numerous, baseless actions" intended to damage or destroy the plaintiff in her chosen profession.

The suit seeks $300,000 in general, special and punitive damages and asks the court to vacate the personnel actions complained of and to grant the merit pay increase allegedly denied to Miss Demas.

#4/
i.e. Article 2
Ex. 5B-I-Art-2

Therefore, the trial court resorted to (interjected—extraneous matter) modes of procedure rulings that it could not legally adopt, as demonstrated by the established law represented throughout this book which conflict with trial court's adopted rulings was improper misconduct, as tending toward intimating the bias of the trial court with respect to the character and weight of the commonwealth's witnesses pretrial rehearsed testimony evidence and may've influenced the jury to trust the government's judgment rather than its own views of the evidence, as the Virginia Court of Appeals in the case of *Henshaw v. Commonwealth* citing; the Supreme Court of Virginia established precedent in the case of *Mazer v. Commonwealth* thereby prejudiced and discriminated (inter alia) against my defense, constituted extrinsic fraud misconduct, as also held by the Virginia Court of Appeals decision in the case of *Rose v. Commonwealth* that said,

> **An Order is void ab initio, if the mode of the procedure used by the Court was one that the Court could "not lawfully adopt." The lack of jurisdiction to enter an Order under any of those circumstances renders the Order a complete nullity and it may be "impeached directly or collaterally by all persons, anywhere, at any time, or in any manner."**

Supported by the Supreme Court of Virginia, established precedent in the case of id. *Jones v. Willard* holding,

> **Courts have long-held that the judgment of a court, procured by extrinsic fraud [i.e., "by conduct which prevents a fair submission of the controversy to the court, is void and subject to attack, direct or collateral at any time"].**

In addition, those aforesaid trial court rulings so infected my trial with unfairness as to deny me due process of law, in violation of

Supreme Court of Virginia Rules of Judicial Conduct and Section 11 of the Constitution of Virginia also violated my equal protection and due process rights under Section 1 US Constitution Amendment 14.

In a similar, herein narrated controversy, the Supreme Court of the United States in reaching its decision in a case involving *Arizona v. Fulminante*, relied on its established decision in *Tumey v. Ohio*, which determined,

> **There was a Judge who was not impartial. These are structural defects in the constitution of the trial mechanism, which defy analysis by "harmless error" standard, the entire conduct of the trial from beginning to end is obviously [499 US 310] affected by the presence on the bench a Judge who is not impartial. Each of these constitutional deprivations is a similar structural defect affecting the framework with which the trial proceeds, rather than simply an error in the trial process itself," without these basic protections, a criminal trial cannot reliably serve its function as a vehicle for determination of guilt or innocence, and no criminal punishment may be regarded as fundamentally fair.**

Here, at this point, I respectfully admonish the reader to go online or visit your local law library to verify the commonwealth of Virginia Highest State Court—the Supreme Court of Virginia's decision addressing similar judicial misconduct in the case of *State Farm Mutual Auto INS. Co. V Remely*: **"Whether the fraud misconduct tampers with the judicial machinery and subverts the integrity of the Court itself."**

Now then, peradventure you the reader become apprehended (God forbid!) while traveling in your automobile or cycling or out with friends or family site seeing in an unfamiliar neighborhood or street, where you are detained without a proper magistrate or judge issued warrant, plus, handcuffed and not at liberty to complete your outing, by virtue of being transported to lock up, then questioned by law enforcement officials at that time. It would behoove you to know that in 1791 US Constitution Amendment 5 was ratified, which in pertinent part provides,

> **No person shall be compelled in any criminal case to be a witness against himself [herself], nor be deprived of life, liberty, or property, without due process of law.**

Moreover, the Supreme Court of the United States—interpreting the intent of the above Fifth Amendment language—in the case of *Mirando v. Arizona* held the following:

> **Custodial interrogations have the potential to undermine the fifth amendment privilege against self-incrimination by possibly exposing a suspect to physical or psychological coercion; To guard against such coercion, the Court established a prophylactic procedural mechanism that requires a suspect to receive a warning before custodial interrogation begins.**

If your curiosity has been piqued, then you're invited to view the case cited *Berghuis v. Thompkins*: **"Substance of the Miranda warnings must still be given to suspect today,"** said the aforementioned Court.

Listen, in relation to the established required warning, please, before you respond to any law enforcement officials' questions during lockup (i.e., or any place), the Supreme Court of Virginia, in the case of *Dixion v. Common.* determined:

> **In resolving this issue, we review settled principles of constitutional law that govern**

J.D.

> **our inquiry, under Miranda, before a suspect in police custody may be questioned by law enforcement officers. The suspect must be warned that he has a right to remain silent that any statement he makes may be used as evidence against him and that he has the right to have an attorney, either retained or appointed, present to assist him.**

Furthermore, one reason I delayed mentioning the Miranda warning issue is that I hope if nothing else you've read herein stick in your mind for recall. Perhaps this important issue will, particularly, if you are an African American or person of color with limited financial resources as was the case with yours truly on November 10, 1975, en route to New York.

I was stopped once on routine license check, then after about ten to fifteen minutes passed was stopped a second time, handcuffed, and told I was being held for further investigation. My car was also searched, and I was interrogated without Miranda warnings or search warrant. Secondly, on account that generally the issues that are being highlighted herein—never entered my mind, having been reared in a middle class, Mom and Father home, a high school graduate, with six years of voluntary military service, plus gainfully employed three-quarters of the thirty-four years of my life. No one during my military service nor at my job site had occasion to talk about such warning. Neither did anyone in my social arena discuss the issues aforementioned that were oblivious to me.

In the same voice, nowhere does my December 12, 1975, Juvenile Domestic Court grand jury indictment hearing, neither March 3 or May 26, 1976, trial record show an occasion where my appointed defense counselor McLau, trial court, or commonwealth's attorney asked Deputy Tay whether or not he offered me the required Miranda rights warning or produced me or my jury a valid search/arrest warrant. Why? However, during Juvenile Domestic Court preliminary grand jury indictment trial hearing, the following took place.

During appointed defense attorney's pretrial rehearse theatrically performed cross-examination of state's star witness Fow regard what rights did he advise the defendant (me)? Answer was, "On the night/next morning of the alleged offense—during the course of interrogating the defendant Simpson at South Hill Police Department (preserved on December 12, 1975, Juv. Tr. Ex. 48, p. 104). He did not present or offer defendant a waiver to sign (Juv. Tr. Ex. 48-B, p. 105). Nor did he advise defendant whether or not he could stop answering if he so desired (id. Juv. Tr. Ex. 48-C, p., 106). Neither did he asked defendant to sign a statement (Juv. Tr. Ex. 48-D, p. 107). Then defense objected to any statement made as defendant was not advised that he could stop at any time, there exist no indication of that (Juv. Tr. Ex. 48-D, p. 107). When the court took no action on defense cursory objection motion; defense questioned whether if the court would rule on the admissibility of said motion (Juv. Tr. Ex. 48-D, p. 107). The grand jury indictment hearing court sarcastically interjected, "They have not sought to put it in yet [i.e., although the jury heard that line of testimony evidence], so I wouldn't attempt to Rule on it at this time" (Juv. Tr. Ex. 49, p. 108).

Not only does the record maintained in the December 12, 1975, indictment grand jury theater (proceeding) demonstrate I was not provided established Miranda precedent warning, but it also ought to be interesting to hear Fow's response to appointed defense attorney McLau's pretrial rehearsed continued performance during my March 3, 1976, mock trial proceeding—when he again asked Fow, "Whether or not he gave the defendant [me] his Miranda rights?" The answer was, "I did." Then another question was asked, "What rights did you advise him of?" The intervening commonwealth's attorney's interjected, "I do not see the relevancy of this questioning and I do not think it is fair." In the presence of my jury, defense attorney apologetically stated, "The only reason I ask that is because the commonwealth may argue in some fashion that the statement made by the defendant [me] gave probable cause for some sort of search. Now if that is so, then I think it is fair."

Quite interesting that the appointed attorney chose this line of objection rather than stating the established above stated Miranda warning precedent held by both the Highest Court in the commonwealth of Virginia and United States of America. Hence, the trial court intervened by interjecting, "I don't think it is relevant because the way I understand it, this defendant [me] never said anything incriminating at time, and for that reason I don't think it is necessary to go into it any further. I do not allow you to question him on the rights at this time" (preserved in March 3, 1976, Tr. Ex. 48-D, p. 102). This evinces that the trial court made improper "I don't think it is relevant [extraneous matter] interjected vouching remark on the weight of my Miranda rights testimony evidence, as tending, towards allowing the jury to believe Fow's 'I did'"—probably perjured testimony was credible, and that they could link by speculation; Fow's pretrial rehearsed time factor probable cause testimony evidence information as a proven fact as well as tended to improperly relieve commonwealth's attorney's duty to prove every essential element of my charged offenses beyond a reasonable doubt. Plus tended to indicate a reasonable inference in the juror's mind that defense Miranda query was frivolous was improper misconduct in contravention of juror's duty to evaluate facts, evidence, and witnesses credibility, as well as carried with it the official approved of the government and may have influenced the jury to trust the trial court's judgment, rather than its own view of the evidence. Also may have unduly suggested to the jury to adopt an attitude of disbelief and prejudice against me was improper as tending to intimate the favor of the court with respect to the character of the weight of commonwealth's noncited Miranda warning testimony evidence, thereby constituted compounded extrinsic fraud misconduct, under the aforesaid Virginia Court of Appeals decision in the case of *Henshaw v. Commonwealth*. The Supreme Court of Virginia established precedent in the case of *Mazer v. Commonwealth*.

Here, I wish to highlight the trial court's "I don't think it is relevant ruling" interjection, in light of the Supreme Court of Virginia determination in the case entitled *State Farm Mutual Auto INS. Co., v. Remely*. Its own decision in the case of *Owens-Corning Fiberglass Corp., v. Watson* holding that "We have recently 'defined as relevant' as every fact, however remote or insignificant that tends to establish the probability or improbability of a fact at issue," accorded id. In the case of *McMunn v. Tatum*.

At the same time, I believe that said question regarding the nature of the rights trooper Fow advised me of was materially relevant to the issue of probable cause. Reader, we hope your interest has been tweaked as mine certainly have—to have found out how other out of state court decisions treat the term relevant verses material evidence which seem to be practically synonymous terms. An excellent source with which to test such a comparison, is the *Black's Law Dictionary*, which describes the term material evidence as, **"Evidence which is material to question in controversy, and which must necessarily enter into the consideration of the controversy, and which by itself or in connection with other evidence is determinative of the case,"** citing the Tennessee Court of Appeals decision in the case of *Camurati v. Sutton*, employing aforesaid definition. A New York State Court held the same decision in the case of *Barr v. Dolphin Holding Corp.*, Sup. Volume 141 NYS Second 906 at p. 908. (See *Black's Law Dictionary* Fifth Edition at p. 881).

The trial court's above-stated ruling, interjecting, "I don't think it is relevant, I do not allow you to question him on the rights at this time," also conflicts with the Supreme Court of Virginia Decision Case of *Dixion v. Comm.*, where that court ruled **"The safeguards required by Miranda must be afforded to a suspect as soon as the police have restricted his freedom of action to 'degree associated with formal arrest."** Supported by *Berkemer v. McCarty*, quoting another Supreme Court of the United States' opinion in the case of *California v. Beholer* at your leisure reader, perhaps you will gain more understanding of whether the trial court's prohibiting cross-examination of my Miranda right warning violated Fourth Amendment protection, if you peruse the case of *Burket v. Commonwealth*. Therefore,

> **[I]f a motorist who has been detained pursuant to a traffic stop thereafter is subjected to treatment renders him in custody 'for [270 Virginia40] practical purposes', he will be entitled to the full panoply of protections prescribed by Miranda.**

The aforesaid decisions creates a legitimate inference that show, the trial court's interjection, "I do not allow you to question him on the rights at this time" improper ruling may constitute the deliberate suppression of evidence (i.e., helpful defense witness), which would have impeached Fow's credibility. At the very least, this would've presented a material issue in dispute, requiring jury determination, plus carries with it the official approval of the government and may've had the propensity to influence the jury to trust the trial court's judgment rather than its own view of the testimony evidence, therewith foreclosed my defense from any inquiry regarding state's star witness Fow's March 3, 1976, "I did" trial, conflicting Miranda right warning testimony evidence, thereby arbitrarily prejudiced and discriminated against my defense by, impairing my Sixth Amendment constitutional right to cross-examine, confront and offer the defense Miranda warning theories is, in plain terms, the right to present a defense—that is, the right to present my version of the facts as well as the commonwealth's to the jury, so they may decide where the truth lies, amounts to extrinsic fraud misconduct that so infected my trial with unfairness as to constitute arbitrary and capricious deprivation of a fundamentally fair trial before an impartial judge and jury, thereby denied me equal protection and due process of law, in violation of Section 11 of the constitution of Virginia and Section 1 of Amendment 14 of the US Constitution.

Reader, perhaps you may recall our discussion above in chapter 6 regarding the Supreme Court of the United States established precedent in the case of *Davis v. Alaska*, which interpreted the US citizen's Sixth Amendment right, as cross-examining, confronting, and compelling witnesses in his own defense well! The same is applicable above supported by its decision rendered in the case of *Gordan v. United States*. In the very midst, the law and facts above, provides a legitimate inference which indicates the trial court employed modes of procedural rulings it could not lawfully adopt to bolster commonwealth's attorney's case, as set out in the Virginia Court of Appeals determination in the case of *Rose v. Commonwealth*.

> **An Order is void ab initio** [i.e., Latin meaning, In or at the beginning; in the first stage of the suit], **if the mode of the procedure used by the Court was one that the Court could "not lawfully adopt." The lack of jurisdiction to enter an Order under any of these circumstances renders the Order a complete nullity and it may be "impeached directly or collaterally by all persons, anywhere, at any time, or in any manner."**

Also, this evinces a reasonable inference to demonstrate that the trial court, commonwealth's attorney and court-appointed defense attorney, became aware that the facts regarding state witness Fow's pretrial rehearsed time factor probable cause assertion in connection with aforesaid no Miranda rights warning would be a commonwealth's attorney problem. Therefore, the said court officials having already entered into pretrial rehearsed covenant determined to veil (i.e., deliberately suppress) my abovesaid Miranda right warning facts and, at the same, decided to keep my alibi twin African American sheriffs—law enforcement official witnesses's testimony evidence from the jurors.

The United States Supreme Court's 1963 established precedent law in the case of *Brady v. Maryland* **(the withholding of exculpatory evidence from a criminal defendant by a prosecutor and the**

J.D.

known use of false testimony, violates the due process clause of the Fourteenth Amendment to the United States Constitution) supported by its 1972 decision in the case of *Giglio v. United States*. Further, causally connected with the trial court, commonwealth's attorney and appointed trial attorney's knowledge that the Juvenile Domestic Court grand jury indictment court clerk's (stenographer) claim it misplaced portion of the December 12, 1975, grand jury indictment recorded testimony evidence, alleged to have been on Tape No. A 4 (preserved in December 12, 1975, Juv. Tr. Ex. 43, p. 87), which, I say, contained the initial sworn testimony of Sheriff Deputies C. J. and C. W., two African American Twins, the initial officers to respond to a missing persons call at the alleged victim's home on November 10, 1975, who testified they were dispatched to the alleged victim's home around 9:25 to 9:55 p.m. because he wrote it in his log book, whose time factor was corroborated by the alleged female victim's testimony (preserved in Tr. Ex.34, p. 9). Plus, by state truck driver witness Charlie's testimony (preserved id. Tr. Ex. 41, p. 59).

Reader, should you desire to know some of what the law says as additional defense support against the aforesaid law enforcement officials improper misconduct of suppressed evidence, then you ought to be on your computer or headed to your local law library to look for the petition for a writ of Mandamus case decided by the Supreme Court of Virginia in the case entitled *Commonwealth of Virginia*, In Re, 278 Va. 1, which determined in pertinent part.

On Aug. 6, 1997, the commonwealth's attorney and certain law enforcement personnel met with Jones and his attorney to prepare Jones for Atkin's capital murder trial. This session was recorded with an audio tape recorder. At some point during the three hour trial preparation session, the commonwealth's attorney turned the audio tape recorder off for sixteen minutes because the commonwealth's attorney thought Jones's testimony was not going to do [the commonwealth's case] any good! During the sixteen-minute interval that was not recorded, the commonwealth attorney, law enforcement officers, and Jones "acted out" the events related to the murder of Nesbitt. Jones's initial version of the facts changed after the rehearsed and coached unrecorded reenactment of the murder. The Circuit court stated in its final judgment order that the office of the commonwealth's attorney for York County and the City of Poqueson improperly suppressed exculpatory evidence from the August 6, 1997, interview of William Jones, in violation of *Brady v. Maryland.*

As previously admitted, I have no formal training in the science of law. Notwithstanding, when it was decided that this book would be written reflecting the psyche of the law enforcement officials who accused, then falsely convicted me, an innocent black man for the heinous crime of rape and abducting a Caucasian boy and girl, on November 10, 1975, while in route from Lexington, North Carolina, to New York. It was equally determined in light of the above unveiled facts and established law that you the public citizen have the right to grant me the opportunity to present the unalterable facts and law to you, for the public fair trial that I was denied in the Circuit Court of Halifax County Virginia, which the due process clause of the Fourteenth Amendment of the United States Constitution, requires.

On account of aforementioned beforehand, I accessed the meager tools offered in the prison law library, as well as those beyond my secure status, with the purpose of supplying the reader with a semblance of established controlling law, whereby you might make informed assessments while reaching a fair judgment as it apply to me and those law enforcement officials herein charged with the sworn constitutional duty to uphold and defend my guaranteed constitutional rights connected with the ONLY TRUE LIVING GOD's personal orders given to judges **"not to respect persons in judgment, but you must hear the small [i.e., poor] as well as the great [i.e., rich]; you must not be afraid of the face [i.e., opinions] of mankind [i.e., public]; because the judgment is God's."** Reader, you can view said instructions in the Old Testament book entitled Deuteronomy 1:17 and Leviticus 19:5.

The above authority given is the principles of the ONLY TRUE LIVING GOD etched in stone, therewith patrons! There be several other previously cited case law which might aid your ultimate decision.

One such case concerns suppression of the abovesaid Miranda Rights warning by the aforesaid law enforcement officials' pretrial rehearsed probable cause time factor collusion/covenant, is had by the Supreme Court of Virginia in the case of *Powell v. Commonwealth*, citing the United States Supreme Court's long-time enduring established precedent law, in the case entitled *United States v. Throckmorton* defining fraud extrinsic or collateral, in pertinent part, determined the following:

> **Keeping the adversary's witness from court; secreting or purloining his testimony; or any conduct of the kind mentioned (which) would tend to prevent a fair trial on the merits, and thus to deprive the innocent party of his rights. So if a judge sits when disqualified from interest or consanguinity; if the litigation be collusive; if the parties be fictitious; if real parties affected are falsely stated to be before the court: The later character of proof tends to show that no fair trial on the merits has been had. It is matter not suspected to have existed, and so impossible to have been considered or to have been "matter tried by the first court" which the courts have in mind which adhere to the intrinsic and extrinsic fraud doctrine. [See opinions of Chief Justice Shaw in the leading case on the latter subject of *Greene v. Greene*, 2 Gray 361, 61 Am. Dec. 454.] Hence, the granting of a new trial on the ground of proof of perjury or mistake, where the evidence of it come into existence since the former trial and appears to be true not to be collusive, and ought, if true, to produce a different verdict on a new trial, does not violate the doctrine just mentioned.**

Also, view if you become so prompted, the Supreme Court of Virginia decision in the case of *State Farm Mutual Auto INS. Co., v. Remely*, quoting from its earlier 1992 opinion in the case of *Owens-Corning Fiberglass Corp. v. Watson*, citing the United States Supreme Court's 1944 established precedent law in the case of *Hazel-Atlas Glass Company v. Hartford Empire Company*, where that Court vacated a prior judgment, holding the following:

> **Tampering with the administration of justice in the manner indisputably shown here involves far more than an injury to a single litigant, it is a wrong against the institution set up to protect and safeguard the public institutions in which fraud cannot complacently be tolerated consistently with the good order of society.**

But please view the Fourth Circuit Court of Appeals for the Fourth Circuit in Virginia opinion in the case of *Bizzell v. Hemingway*: **"Collusion between plaintiff's attorney and opposing party constitute extrinsic fraud."** Likewise, said the Supreme Court of Virginia in Its 1983 established precedent determined in the case of *Jones v. Willard*:

> **When party aggrieved by decision of commission alleges in petition for review that decision was procured by extrinsic fraud committed by successful party and submits with petition a proffer of proof, verified by affidavit of witnesses, Circuit Court shall remand cause to commission for hearing on issue if, upon review of proffer and argument by counsel, Court finds proffer sufficient as a matter of law to establish prima-facie case of such fraud. (*Ford Motor Co., v. Labor Board*)**

The court continued to hold in that the Judgment of a court, procured by fraud by conduct which prevents a fair submission of the controversy to the court, is void and subject to attack, direct or collateral, at any time. (*Rowe v. Coal Corp.*)

In this posture, it was the commonwealth's attorney's duty to seek justice says the Supreme Court of the United States in Its 1935 established precedent setting case entitled *Berger v. US*: **"Prosecutorial misconduct justifies declaring a mistrial where it so infect[s] the trial with unfairness as to make the resulting conviction a denial of due process."**

Supported by its 1986 decision in the case entitled *Donnelly v. Dechristoforo*. Also, commonwealth's attorney may not knowingly present false testimony to the court or jury and has a corresponding imperative duty to correct testimony that he knows to be false said the aforementioned highest court in this nation in the case of *Napue v. Illinois*. Please view the aforesaid court's 1935 established precedent decision in the case of *Mooney v. Holohan* and the Fifth Circuit Court of Appeals 2002 decision in the case of *US v. Mason*, holding that **"Prosecutor's failure to correct government witnesses' statement plea agreement improper and violated due process."**

Chapter 14

Here, the major fact narrative evidence written above appears sufficient to contest the integrity and validity of the Circuit Court of Halifax County's jurisdiction to enter its July 26, 1976, conviction order on the grounds that the mode of procedure (i.e., conduct) employed by the trial court, commonwealth's attorney, and appointed defense attorney McLau's pretrial rehearsed time factor probable cause acts of commission covenant/collusion, is conduct they could not legally adopt; because, said misconduct as it appears herein above may've unduly influenced the jury or some member thereof to trust the government's judgment rather than its own view of the fact and evidence to my prejudice. That is to say said misconduct prevented me from fully and fairly submitting my defense to a fair and impartial judge and jury in contravention of the trial court and jurors' duty to accord every person the right to be heard and offer a defense according to established law; together with the commonwealth's attorney, trial court and appointed defense lawyer's duty to seek justice, constituted extrinsic fraud misconduct, thereby prejudiced and discriminated against my defense throughout the above set forth trial, denied me equal protection and due process of law, in violation of section 1 of the United States Constitution Amendment 14. Plus, this could've contributed to the May 26, 1976, two life terms, twelve years jury verdict, and the trial court's July 26, 1976 final judgment running consecutive conviction order, particularly in light of the fact that I have no prior felony convictions and the Supreme Court of the United States in its 1971 precedent established in the case of *Mayer v. Chicago*.

Its 1984 later decision in the case entitled *Waler v. Georgia* holding that such defendant has the right to public trial, as well as the constitutionally protected right to fairness in the trial proceeding procedures concerning a state government deprivation of life, liberty, and property. Reader, during your leisure time, you can check all the cases set forth herein by visiting your local law library, where you can also view the aforesaid court's 1979 decision in the case of *Goldberg v. Keely*.

To this end, the Virginia Court of Appeals, resolving a claim of fundamental fairness in the case entitled *Powell v. Com.* held,

> **A fair trial on the merits and substantial justice are not achieved if an error at trial has affected the verdict. Consequently, under Code Section 8.01-678, a criminal conviction must be reversed unless it plainly appears from the record and the evidence given at trial that the error did not affect the verdict. An error does not affect a verdict if a reviewing court can conclude, without usurping the fact finding function that had the error not occurred, the verdict would have been the same. (*Neely v. Commonwealth*)**

In addition, the fact narrative evidenced above illustrates that the trial court, commonwealth's attorney and court-appointed defense attorney's pretrial rehearsed time factor probable cause collusion/covenant action under color of state law from beginning of my preliminary grand jury indictment hearing and up to this point of my trial, improperly relieved the commonwealth's attorney's duty to prove every element of my charged offenses beyond a reasonable doubt; as well as, indicts the trial court for its improper remarks/comments on the evidence, which had a tendency to intimate the bias of the court with respect to the character or weight of the testimony evidence. Plus, the trial court, commonwealth's attorney collusion with appointed defense attorney's knowing suppression of gonorrhea disease germ in chamber testimony evidence that could not be connected to me, helpful exculpatory defense testimony evidence, which amounted to improper misconduct that may've influenced the jurors to trust the government's judgment rather than its own view of the facts/evidence was to my prejudice, where the trial court took no action to remove the appearance of a reasonable (i.e., plausible) likelihood that an improper inference might be drawn by the jury from the said extraneous matter (i.e., commonwealth's expert medical witnesses' interjected, "I gave her penicillin CR to prevent gonorrhea") improper conduct which court officials clearly made. Together with the trial court's failure to grant defense several mistrial (i.e., token) motions, which inevitably influence the jury against my defense throughout the aforesaid fact narrative testimony evidence, constituted extrinsic fraud misconduct inter alia and could reasonably have contributed to the May 26, 1976, guilty verdict, which raises the question of significant importance, "Whether the said misconduct [extraneous matter] as a whole, tampered with the Circuit Court of Halifax County's judicial machinery and/or subverted the integrity of the court itself, and its July 26, 1976 two life terms, plus twelve years running consecutive final conviction order?"

In support of the above illegal extrinsic fraud court officials' misconduct without reciting the entire rulings of opinion. Here we will simply provide the reader the name of each case involved *Powell v. Commonwealth*, citing the United State Supreme Court's established precedent in the case of *United States v. Throckmorton*, defining fraud extrinsic or collateral, together with the Supreme Court of Virginia's 1992 opinion in the case of *Owens-Corning Fiberglass Corp. v. Watson*, citing the United States Supreme Court's 1944 established precedent in the case of *Hazel-Atlas Glass Company v. Harford*

Empire Company, where that court vacated a prior judgment. Plus, the Fourth Circuit Court of Appeals for the Fourth Circuit decision in *Bizzell v. Hemingway*: "Collusion between plaintiff's attorney and opposing party."

Causally connected with the aforesaid, the record transcribed in the Circuit Court of Halifax County Virginia, shows the appointed defense attorney made a motion to strike the evidence as the charges of rape on the ground, "There had been no proof/evidence of venue— the trial court lack jurisdiction" (please view the May 26, 1976, Tr. Ex. 60-D-2, p. 231, Tr. Ex. 60-D-3, p. 232, and id. Tr. Ex. 60 D-4, p. 233), as well suggested by the alleged female rape victim throughout direct examination, when commonwealth's attorney asked, "What direction did you go after the man picked you up?" The alleged rape victim answer was, "Well, we went through the stoplight right when we got to Hudson's Motel, he gave us these socks for blind folds, and told us to put them over our eyes, and we went up the road three or four miles, after he put Mike out. He told me to take my clothes off, a few minutes later he told me to get in the floor in front."

> Q: Had you made any turns, after you left Mike, before you were required to take your clothes off?
> A: No.
> Q: You left, going in the same direction as he had since you had left the stoplight?
> A: Yes.
> Q: Then what do you remember about where you went?
>
> [Reader, you may view this record in the id. May 26, 1976, preserved Tr. Ex. 56-B-3, p. 29.]
>
> A: I don't know. He just kept turning.
> Q: Turning around?

A: Backing up and going forward…trying to turn around.
Q: Was he doing this on a paved road or a dirt road?
A: A dirt road.
Q: He had gotten on a dirt road when he was doing this?
A: Yes.
Q: So that means he must have gotten off 58?
A: Yes, sir.
Q: Did he stop the car?
A: Yes, sir.
Q: Is that when you were on the dirt road?
A. Yes, sir.
Q: Did you get out of the floor board?
A: Yes.

(See above dated Tr. Ex. 56-B-4, p. 30).

The facts maintained in the aforementioned May 26, 1976, trial transcribed record Ex. 60-D-4, p. 233 with Tr. Ex. 50-B, p. 284-shows that the trial court overruled aforesaid appointed defense attorney's token motion to strike. Howbeit, the forestated (i.e., no proof of venue) matter of fact, must exist before the Circuit Court of Halifax County could properly claim jurisdiction over my case. This recorded fact also notes appointed defense attorney's noted token objection and exception to the court's ruling.

Please note that chapter 6 and 7 causal links hereto the state providing no fact or material evidence to establish the existence of venue indicates that a legitimate inference exists to show: the commonwealth's attorney, trial court, plus court-appointed defense attorney possessed knowledge that the commonwealth's attorney's alleged evidence (absent extraneous matter—that is, improper government officials' extrinsic fraud misconduct action), lacked fact base essence to establish state's key witness Fow's asserted pretrial rehearsed venue, and/or commonwealth's attorney's theory as to my actual physical whereabouts at the time of the alleged 1975 offenses, as premised upon Fow's asserted 10:30 time of alleged crime occurrence (preserved in March 3, 1976, Tr. Ex. 57, p. 75).

Causally connected with said court officials' knowledge that under direct examination, the alleged female victim testified that "she and her brother left home at approximately 9:30 to 10:00 p.m., going to the little orange market (this non contradicted established time factor, is extracted from the May 26, 1976, Tr. Ex. 15-A, id. Tr. Ex. 16 and Tr. Ex. 17, p. 27 and 42–43 respectively). Plus, the alleged male victim testified, "It took five minutes to get from their house to the little orange market; and, took a minute or so in there, then started back toward home. In just two or three minutes their perpetrator's car picked them up" (said statements can be viewed on May 26, 1976, Tr. Ex. 36, p. 17). Together with commonwealth's truck driver witness's testimony interjection that "he saw a small girl that evening on the highway as he was heading West, at approximately 10:15 to 10:30 p.m." (as transcribed in id. May 26, 1976, Tr. Ex. 41 and Tr. Ex. 41-B, pp. 59–60), ending the alleged crime at 10:15 or 10:30. However, after learning that I didn't depart from Lexington, North Carolina, some two and a half hours away until 9:00 to 9:10 p.m. (supported by defense alibi witnesses). JD Shf's testimony was, "The driving time from his home in Lexington, North Carolina, to the court's parking lot takes two and a half hours." (This testimony is also found in May 26, 1976, Tr. Ex. 13, and Tr. Ex. 14, pp. 244–245). Also Sallie testified, "She was at her mother's home in Lexington, North Carolina, at approximately 8:30 p.m. when I came by to see her brother May" (can be viewed in same above record at Tr. Ex. 9, p. 246). Geor testified, "On the night of the alleged offense, I came by his house in Lexington, North Carolina, around 9:00 p.m. and asked him to go with me to New York to pick up my wife, and approximately ten minutes after 9:10 p.m. I left" (record as above, Tr. Ex. 10 and Tr. Ex. 10-A, pp. 248–249). This evinces a reasonable inference exists that indicates the trial court, commonwealth's attorney and court-appointed defense attorney realized this unveiled two-and-a-half-hour time factor testimony evidence may well have established a reasonable doubt about my whereabouts on the night of the alleged offense. Also, this could've created in the jurors' mind a virtual improbability that I could be departing from Lexington, North Carolina, at 9:10 p.m., then be committing a crime at 10:00 to 10:30 p.m. in Halifax County, as attested above by commonwealth's witnesses. Also, in the same instance, the presented facts, if evaluated by the jury may've impeached and refuted the commonwealth's attorney, trial court, and court-appointed defense attorney's pretrial rehearsed collusion covenant's 10:30 p.m. time factor evidence, concerning my whereabouts and commonwealth's probable cause theory and present a reasonable doubt in the jury's mind.

Therein aforestated posture, a legitimate inference appears to show that the trial court, commonwealth's attorney and court-appointed defense attorney knew (i.e., or should've known) the fore stated facts, regarding my 9:10 p.m. departure from Lexington, North Carolina, connected with the alleged female victim's uncontradicted 9:30 to 10:00 p.m. leaving from home, together with the truck driver's 10:15 to 10:30 p.m. interjected, sighting of the alleged female victim: might be a commonwealth's attorney problem that may've impeached state's primary witness's above 10:30 p.m. time that crime occurred. Therefore, the trial court, commonwealth's attorney, and court-appointed trial attorney entered into a pretrial rehearsal collusion/covenant to veil (i.e., deliberately suppress) my aforementioned "alibi witnessed 9:10 p.m. departure from Lexington, North Carolina, fact evidence," from the jury, and at the same time, thought it important to establish before the jury a more suitable time frame for Fow's asserted occurrence of said crime. The testimony that he received the call at 11:23 p.m. and spoke with alleged male victim, and about seven to ten minutes later, around 11:30 to 11:35 p.m., he put out the APB entirely on the information he'd received from Mic (preserved in id. May 26, 1976, Tr. Ex. 54-G, p. 91), compatible with the time I was passing through that area on November 10, 1975, around 11:30 to 12:00 p.m.

J.D.

Facts that show the trial court employed modes of procedural rulings, it could not lawfully adopt to support commonwealth's attorney's case throughout my trial, from the beginning thereof unto conviction, as have been demonstrated above, and as follows, trial court's pretrial rehearsed misconduct that suggested to my jurors that they may link commonwealth's witness's penicillin treatment to prevent gonorrhea testimony evidence (i.e., extraneous matter) by speculation to me, my car, motive and alleged rape, if they want to, trial court, commonwealth's attorney and appointed defense attorney pretrial rehearsed collusion, covenant misconduct that intentionally withheld gonorrhea testimony evidence which the commonwealth's attorney admitted could not be connected to me from my jury, thereby prevented gonorrhea testimony defense witness's appearance in court (fact is preserved in id. May 26, 1976, Tr. Ex. 44, p. 48; Tr. Ex. 44-B, p. 49 and Tr. Ex. 44-B-1, p. 50). The trial court, commonwealth's attorney, and appointed trial attorney's pretrial rehearsed collusion/covenant's refusal to allow me to be examined by a mutual/impartial physician, so I could put on surrebuttal evidence to rebut the prejudicial gonorrhea and penicillin treatment testimony evidence given against me by commonwealth's attorney's alleged expert witness (fact is preserved id. Tr. Ex. 50-B, p. 284).

Trial court and commonwealth's attorney's recall of Shf (my Caucasian coworker and my character witness) and disqualified him (fact preserved id. Tr. Ex. 50-B, p. 284). They extended my trial from December 12, 1975, March 3, 1976, and July 26, 1976, beyond required speedy trial requisites to reestablish its key witness Trooper Fow's March 3, 1976, trial asserted 10:30 p.m. all points posted bulletin time (fact preserved id. Tr. Ex. 57), to 11:23 p.m. (fact preserved id. Tr. Ex. 44-F, p. 89 and Tr. Ex.44-G, p. 90), as well as Deputy Taylor's time to approximately 11:51 p.m. (fact preserved id. Tr. Ex. 45-A, p. 135), was improper misconduct, as tending to intimate the bias of the trial court with respect to the character of the weight of the commonwealth's witness's pretrial rehearsed 11:23 time factor theory, regarding the time Fow first posted his all-points bulletin and may've influenced the jury to trust the government's judgment rather than its own views of the facts and evidence. The aforesaid facts can be supported by the United States Supreme Court decision the case of *Brady v. Maryland* and Supreme Court of Virginia's decision in *Powell v. Commonwealth*, citing the Supreme Court of the United States opinion in the case entitled *United States v. Throckmorton*, defining fraud extrinsic or collateral.

The State Supreme Court in the case entitled *Powell* decided,

> **Newly discovered evidence which impeached a key prosecution witness justified ordering a new trial. Testimony of an eye witness to a murder was impeached by evidence that the day after the trial the witness described the homicide differently than she had described it at trial, indicating that the accused had acted in self-defense. Although another witness also described the homicide at trial and, therefore, Ordered a new trial.**

In my case, whose conviction rested primarily on commonwealth's attorney's star witness Trooper Fow, trial court, commonwealth's attorney, plus court-appointed attorney McLau's pretrial rehearsed collusion/covenant. Similarly, in *Powell*, the Supreme Court of Virginia at pp. 754–755 addressed fraud extrinsic or collateral as defined by the United States Supreme court in id. *Throckmorton*, holding,

> **Keeping the adversary's witness from court; secreting or purloining his testimony; or any conduct of the kind mentioned [which] would tend to prevent a fair trial on the merits, and thus to deprive the innocent party of his rights. So if a judge sits when disqualified from interest or consanguinity; if the litigation be collusive; if the parties be fictitious; if real**

> parties affected are falsely stated to be before the court; the latter character of proof tends to show that no fair trial on the merits has been had. It is matter not suspected to have existed, and so impossible to have been considered or to have been "matter tried by the first court" which the courts have in mind which adhere to the intrinsic and extrinsic fraud doctrine. [See opinions of Chief Justice Shaw in the leading case on the later subject of *Greene v. Greene*, 2 Gray 361, 61 Am. Dec. 454.] Hence, the granting of a new trial on the grounds of proof of perjury or mistake, where the evidence of it has come into existence since the former trial, and appears to be true not to be collusive, and ought, if true, to produce a different verdict on a new trial, does not violate the doctrine just mentioned.

Compared to the alleged male victim's interjection (i.e., who Fow claim to have gotten the information with which to form his abovesaid, 11:23 p.m. APB posted bulletin transmission) that "he talked to Fow one time, at home [around 2:00 a.m.] that night—after they found his sister." Said interjection is preserved on March 3, 1976, Tr. Ex. 25, p. 18 is contrary to Fow's interjected testimony (preserved on May 26, 1976, Tr. Ex. 54-G, p. 91) and Fow's December 12, 1975 (Juv. Tr. Ex. 54-D, p. 123). Same matter.

Here, no set forth fact above has established evidence sufficient for the jury to ascertain the location the alleged rape offense occurred. In that it was for the jury to determine which witness, they would believe and what testimony they will accept in deciding whether or not the commonwealth's attorney's evidence established requisite venue. Reader, if you are following these peculiar events; then you may be interested in finding out what the law and Supreme

Court of Virginia held, in its 1960 established precedent in the case entitled *Diggs v. Lail* determined,

> **It is reversible error not to so instruct the jury that deciding credibility of the witnesses, weight accorded testimony, and inferences to be drawn from proven facts, are matters to be determined by the fact finder.**

The above determination is equally recorded by the Virginia Court of Appeals cases entitled *Barksdale v. Commonwealth* and *Birtcherds Dairy v. Randell.*

What's more interesting, is that the trial court never so instructed the jury nor did appointed defense attorney ever request the court to instruct the jury on the principles of law regarding the establishment of the venue facts, thereby prejudiced and intentionally discriminated against my defense by the trial court, commonwealth's attorney and appointed defense attorney's pretrial rehearsed collusion/covenant misconduct that—improperly relieved the commonwealth's attorney of its duty to prove each element of my charged offenses beyond a reasonable doubt, which could reasonably have undermined the juror's impartiality, resulting in preventing me from obtaining the benefit of my defense, and right to fairly submit that defense to a fair and an impartial judge and jury, amounted to extrinsic fraud misconduct, thereby denied me the equal protection and due process of law, in violation of Section 1 Amendment 14 of the US Constitution as well as violated Section 11 of the Constitution of Virginia. leaving the jury free to link up by speculation, Fow's above baseless venue assertion; also commonwealth's attorney, trial court. and appointed defense attorney's pretrial rehearsed 11:23 p.m. extended, baseless asserted APB bulletin posted time to my traveling through Virginia in route to New York constituted extrinsic fraud misconduct that was compounded, when the trial court overruled the appointed defense attorney's (token) motion to strike the evidence to the charge of rape on the ground that there had been no proof of venue (i.e., motion, is preserved in trial extended May 26, 1976, Tr. Ex. 50-B, p. 284, Tr. Ex. 60-D-2, p. 231, and Tr. Ex. 60-D-4, p. 233).

Reader, you've probably stored in memory for instant recall, many of the issues discussed above as they relate to the Supreme Court of Virginia and United States Supreme Court case decisions, resolving the abovesaid travesty of justice meted out to this citizen of color, but how have you as the Supreme jury found!

As for me, through self-experience and, the ever transforming power of the Word of the ONLY TRUE LIVING GOD, via Jesus's risen merits. I believe that by and large folk hear ONLY what they listen for. For this reason, my jurors' impartial (i.e., assumed) ears was the critical aspect throughout my December 12, 1975, grand jury indictment hearing, and my March 3 through May 26, 1976 extended trial; but especially here, during this…causally connected narrative, wherein my eleven Caucasian jurors (i.e., one of which has been confirmed to be a close relative of the alleged victims namely, Mrs. Joy) with one aged token African American juror who may have been exposed to the commonwealth's attorney, trial court and appointed defense attorney's appeal to repeated racial prejudice.

Howbeit, the main thing was their psyche jurist Mrs. Joy having previously communicated to her son Deputy Sheriff Edmon at the Halifax County jail "sentiments of hanging me," according to a Caucasian trustee inmate there at Halifax County Jail where I was confined. An idea those jurors in all likelihood were taught at an early age to look down upon and to hate people of African descent—hatred buried deep, deep within the throes of every fabric and fiber of their beings. Just as a light weight object placed into a glass of water will float to the top, no matter how long racism has been fostering in those bodies confronted with this black man, who commonwealth's attorney's African American (i.e., aged) alleged Dr. Expert witness testified, "He gave the alleged Caucasian female girl victim broad spectrum penicillin treatment to prevent gonorrhea disease" (preserved id. May 26, 1976, Tr. Ex. 44, p. 48). Then the judge permitted this jury to speculate, it came from me. The covert racism arose to the top! All of the subliminal messages weighing them down for years since infancy now surfaced and unabashedly—that is, after hearing commonwealth's attorney ask Deputy Sheriff Mor, "Have you led any information yourself over dispatch at that time?" Mor's (i.e., pretrial rehearsed) answer was, "Yes. This is normal procedure for South Hill. I said that this [Boy] might be armed and to hold him until I get there" (preserved on March 3, 1976, Tr. Ex. 61-B, p. 112). Together with appointed defense attorney interjected, in pertinent part asked Fow, "Did you use your key to get into the car to inventory the content thereof?" Fow's answer was, "At the time we left the police department in South Hill and went back, with this [Boy] went back to the automobile" (preserved on December 12, 1975, Juv. Tr. Ex. 61, p. 111). The jurors mindset became inflamed and heard only what their innermost being had been trained for decades to believe.

Causally connected with commonwealth's attorney's summation suggestive interjected remarks, "That the jury should do as much as it can do, with the suggestion that there might be another day of probation" (same can be reviewed on May 26, 1976, Tr. Ex. 50-B, p. 284). The extraneous matter, coupled with state employment of the term *boy* pretrial rehearsed (i.e., extraneous matter) categorizing reference to me presents a reasonable inference, to conclude that the commonwealth's attorney was acting in concert with the judge and officer of the court-appointed trial attorney to appeal to racism was improper misconduct in that said i.e., "Boy together with commonwealth's attorney's improper closing parole/probation remark—summation, extraneous matter severely prejudiced my trial as to deny me due process of law as guaranteed by Amendment 14 USC, as well as violated Section 11 of the Constitution of Virginia.

First, I reason that the above record of facts evinces that the trial court, commonwealth's attorney and court-appointed defense attorney's pretrial rehearsed collusion/covenant, sanctioned (i.e., did not object or caution instruct the commonwealth's attorney/and or jurors) the commonwealth's attorney's "BOY" presentation of extraneous matter remarks—as a commonly known (utilized Southern) Caucasian slave owner's term employed to denote disposable property (i.e., valuing blacks as a third of a man) to inflame my jurors, stirring up their deep-seated racial prejudices against me. In effect, commonwealth's attorney, trial court, and appointed defense attorney summoned the thirteenth juror as occurred in the Fourth Circuit Court of Appeals decision in the case entitled *Miller v. State of* North Carolina, holding,

> **Nothing is more fundamental to the provision of a fair trial than the right to an impartial jury. See,** *Aston v. Warden***, 574 F. 2d. 1169, 1172 [4th Cir. 1998]. The impartiality of the jury must exist at the outset of the trial and it must be preserved throughout the entire trial. The device of voir dire and the right to strike prospective jurors, both peremptorily and for cause, are the means by which an impartial jury is seated in the box. Thereafter, the law guarantees that every defendant may have his case decided strictly according to the evidence presented, not by extraneous matter or by the predilections of individual jurors.**

Briefly, *Black's Law Dictionary* in pertinent part defines the phrase **"extraneous evidence" (i.e., matter), as "such as is not furnished by the document itself, but is derived from outside sources, the same as evidence allude."**

Moreover, causally connected with the trial court, commonwealth's attorney, and court-appointed defense attorney's pretrial rehearsed collusion/covenant's sanction of the commonwealth's attorney's improper, interjected closing summary remarks on parole and probation (i.e., suggestion to the jury to do as much as it can do, with emphatic urging that there might be another day of probation). The extraneous matter was improper as tending toward interference with the jurors' unbiased evaluations, connected with the trial court's failure to issue both jury instructions to restrict deliberation to probative and relevant evidence, not (boy) extraneous racist matter as established above by the Fourth Circuit Court of Appeals in the *Miller* case and the Supreme Court of Virginia in the *Dowdy* case, and trial court's failure to issue jury instructions to the effect that "in deciding sentence matter, not to consider questions of probation/parole (as determined by the Supreme Court of Virginia in the case entitled *Clark v. Commonwealth*).

Also, *Hinton v. Commonwealth* was improper misconduct as tending toward intimating the court's favor with respect to the character of weight of commonwealth's attorney's improper (boy racist)/probation and parole remarks testimony evidence that may've influenced the jury to adopt the court's views rather than its own evaluation of the probative and relevant facts and evidence, therewith left my jury free to consider race and questions of parole/probation (extraneous matter) during trial and sentencing phase, thus compelled jurors to sentence me, a first-time felon, to consecutive terms of life in prison for alleged rape, life in prison for alleged abduction, seven years in prison for second count of abduction (i.e., that allegedly occurred at the same time), plus five years in prison for use of alleged (i.e., unloaded gun) fire arm in commission of a felony, with no blood or dead body, amounted to extrinsic fraud misconduct that so prejudiced my trial with unfairness as to deny me the benefit of my defense, compounded by the trial court's failure to grant defense's (token) motion for mistrial on grounds that commonwealth's attorney mention or suggested that the jury should do as much as it can do, with suggestion that there might be another day of probation that might be implied by the jury. (Reader, you may view this action in id. May 26, 1976, Tr. Ex. 50-B, p. 284.)

This was improper misconduct that compounded the extrinsic fraud misconduct, thereby prejudiced and discriminated against me by arbitrarily and capriciously abrogating the right to present my defense to a fundamentally fair and an impartial judge and jury of my peers, violated the equal protection and due process of law clause, as required under Section 1 Amendment 14 of the US Constitution, as well as violated Section 11 of the Constitution of Virginia.

Listen, it must be again noted with emphasis that the Supreme Court of the United States, in its established precedent law, in the cases entitled *Mayer v. Chicago* and *Waller v. Georgia* determined that I and all other citizens of the United States of America "**have a right to a public trial; plus, the right to fairness in proceeding procedures concerning state government [i.e., State Courts] deprivation of life, liberty and property,**" says it's established precedent law in the case of *Goldberg v. Keely*.

Interestingly, my court-appointed defense attorney, together with commonwealth's attorney and trial court knew or should've known that the Supreme Court of Virginia's 1907 and 1909 established law in *Ward Lumber Co., v. Henderson—White Mfg. Co.* and *Commission of Fishers v. Hampton Rds. Oyster Packers & Planters Ass'n.* provides me similar constitutionally protected due process rights, as the above Supreme Court of the United States precedents provides that

> **All authorities agree that due process of law requires that a person shall have reasonable notice and reasonable opportunity to be heard before an impartial tribunal, before any binding decree can be passed affecting his rights to liberty or property.**

The appointed defense attorney, commonwealth's attorney and trial court, equally knew or should've known that the Juvenile Domestic Court grand jury indictment hearing and trial transcribed recorded facts adequately demonstrates that Deputy Mor's initial (BOL) be on the lookout for a yellow two-door Mustang (preserved in December 12, 1975, Juv. Tr. Ex. 51, p. 60) car dispatch information, changed after Mor's stopped me on routine license check, where he reached into the back seat of my car to check beneath neatly stacked clothes, afterward told me to proceed and not drink anymore. Circumstances did not give Mor the requisite belief that probable cause existed to search or arrest me; compare to Mor, commonwealth's attorney, trial court with appointed defense attorney's pretrial rehearsed time factor probable cause collusion/covenant BOL description, after Mor's aforesaid initial routine license check stop. The place Mor wrote down my car color, model, top color, North Carolina license plate, plus my description information: conflicted with the alleged victims testimony evidence of not seeing their assailants' car top or license plate, created dispute in issue.

Trooper Fow, trial court, commonwealth's attorney and appointed defense attorney's pretrial rehearsed probable cause collusion/covenant, sanctioned Fow's interjected, "He got the first call from alleged male victim at 11:23 p.m., and about seven to ten minutes later after talking to alleged male victim, he put out the [BOL] all-points bulletin for a yellow Mustang II, black stripe at the bottom" and relied on Deputy Tay finding a gun, illegal search information testimony evidence contrary to the alleged male victim's testimony evidence that interjected, "he only talked to Fow one time, at his home approximately 2:00 to 2:30 a.m. created genuine issue in dispute."

Commonwealth's attorney's structured invalid affidavit (i.e., sworn to by Fow and used to obtain a search warrant for search and seizure of my saliva body fluid) containing erroneous probable cause personal identification statement information, constituted extrinsic fraud, compounded by commonwealth's attorney alluding to his own personal integrity/oath of office to bolster the government's case, created genuine issues in dispute.

Trial court prohibiting defense cross-examination of Deputy Tay, regarding possible impeachment testimony evidence response to queries about the legality of his warrantless search, seizure, and my arrest. Connected with its improper vouching comments on the weight of Tay's testimony evidence credibility, constituted extrinsic fraud, plus, created issue in dispute.

Trial court unduly prohibiting defense probe cross-examination of both: the alleged male victim about the initial description he gave the first officers (i.e., African American twin sheriff deputies) that came to him first (e.g. defense time factor alibi witnesses), as well as defense probe cross-examination of state's star witness Trooper Fow, with regard conversation description he'd had with aforementioned twin sheriffs (i.e., information that allegedly provided probable cause BOL) constituted extrinsic fraud, plus, evince issues in dispute.

Trial court, commonwealth's attorney, and appointed trial attorney pretrial rehearsed collusion/covenant, preventing my defense witnesses from appearing in court via deliberate suppression of helpful exculpatory gonorrhea sperm impeachment testimony evidence favorable to my defense, constituted extrinsic fraud misconduct that was compounded by trial court's denial of my motion to be examined by a qualified private mutual physician, to enable me to put on surrebuttal evidence to show the jury I was not gonorrhea disease infected before or after alleged crime, compounded its extrinsic fraud misconduct and created issue in dispute.

Trial court prohibiting defense cross-examination of state's primary witness State Trooper Fow regarding possible impeachment testimony evidence responses to queries about the legality of Fow's warrantless searches, connected with trial court's improper vouching comment, on the weight of Fow's warrantless search testimony evidence, in contravention of juror's duty to evaluate facts/evidence and witness credibility, constituted extrinsic fraud misconduct, also created genuine issue in dispute.

Trial court overruling defense motion for mistrial on grounds of it being the court's second time emphatic display of anger and impatient demeanor toward my defense, causing jurors to laugh, on account of defense raising proper objection to the manner the court Itself submitted commonwealth's attorney's alleged footprint exhibits, was improper, and amounted to extrinsic fraud misconduct, created issue in dispute.

Trial court's failure to instruct the jury that they were the judges of the weight of the evidence and credibility of witnesses, and they should disregard any and all court manifested impatient demeanor, constituted extrinsic fraud misconduct, to my prejudice, created genuine issue in dispute.

Trial Court's hostile outburst remark that interjected, **"I'll skip over the foundation, the officer said he found a gun…Do you have the gun Mr. commonwealth's attorney, [i.e., causing jury to laugh]."** Court's reaction to defense objection, noting the commonwealth's attorney failed to lay proper legal foundation, was improper, in contravention of jurors' duty to evaluate facts/evidence and witness credibility, constituted extrinsic fraud misconduct, to my prejudice, created genuine issue in dispute.

Trial court prohibiting defense Miranda right cross-examination of state's primary witness Fow, regarding what Miranda rights did he give me." Commonwealth's attorney objected, while interjecting, "I don't see the relevancy of this question and I don't think it is fair." The trial court interjected, "I don't think it is relevant. I do not allow you to question him on the right at this time," in contravention of jurors' duty to evaluate facts, evidence, and witnesses credibility, constituted extrinsic fraud misconduct, to my prejudice, created issue in dispute.

Trial court, commonwealth's attorney, and court-appointed trial attorney McLau's pretrial rehearsed theatrics, prohibiting African American twin sheriff deputy's 9:30 p.m. time factor testimony (i.e., prevented appearance in court) regard answering a missing persons call at the alleged victim's home on the night of alleged November 10, 1975, crime, one of my alibi witnesses, as well as JD Shf, my former Caucasian coworker's two-and-a-half-hour time frame drive, from Lexington, North Carolina, to the Circuit Court of Halifax County parking lot. My alibi witness from appearing in court: trial court denied JD Shf's one- to two-year day-to-day association with me, then disqualified Shf from being a character witness for me, in contravention of jurors' duty to evaluate facts, evidence and witnesses credibility, constituted extrinsic fraud misconduct, to my prejudice, created issue in dispute.

Trial court overruling defense motion to strike the evidence as to charge of rape on the grounds, "There had been no proof of venue" when commonwealth's attorney questioned alleged female victim, and "What do you remember about where you went?" The alleged female victim answer was, "I don't know. He just kept turning." The question was, 'Turning around?'" The answer was, "Backing up and going forward, trying to turn around" lacked fact base evidence to establish state's key witness Fow's asserted venue testimony evidence, constituted extrinsic fraud misconduct to my prejudice, created issue in dispute.

Trial court, commonwealth's attorney, and appointed trial attorney's appeal to racial prejudice, where the state witnesses' unimpeded repeated "this boy" (referring to me) interjection, in hearing of my jury, causally connected with commonwealth's attorney's remarks in summation that "the jury should do as much as it can do with the suggestion that there might be another day of probation" (i.e., extraneous matter) to irrelevantly arouse the jurors' prejudices throughout the grand jury indictment hearing and trial proceedings (i.e., persecution), most likely influenced the jury to fix the maximum penalty was improper misconduct, constituted extrinsic fraud misconduct, compounded by trial court's failure to restrict jury deliberation from considering extraneous "boy" matter. Plus, failure to issue cautionary jury instructions not to consider questions of parole/probation, to my prejudice, together with the court's refusal to grant defense's mistrial motion, amounted to extrinsic fraud misconduct, to my prejudice, created genuine material issues in dispute.

Improperly relieved commonwealth's attorney's duty to prove every essential element of my charged offenses beyond a reasonable doubt, constituted extrinsic fraud misconduct, which denied me the benefit of my defense, simply is not the kind of fundamentally fair trial in a State Circuit Court, which the due process clause of the Fourteenth Amendment to the USC require which, raises significant question regarding the integrity and validity of the Circuit Court of Halifax County's July 26, 1976, final conviction/sentencing Order, to my prejudice, creates genuine material issues in dispute:

Reader, you may desire to rereview the above mentioned Supreme Court of Virginia's 1983 established precedent in the case of *Jones v. Willard*, holding,

When party aggrieved by decision of commission alleges in petition for review that

> **decision was procured by extrinsic fraud committed by successful party and submits with petition a proffer of proof, verified by affidavits of witnesses, circuit court shall remand cause to commission for hearing on issue if, upon review of proffer and argument by counsel, Court finds proffer sufficient as matter of law to establish prima facie case of such fraud.**

At the very same time, reader, the court above in *Jones* determined,

> **The judgment of a court, procured by fraud [i.e., "by conduct which prevents a fair submission of the controversy to the court, is void and subject to attack, direct or collateral, at any time"].**

Necessitating a hearing on abovesaid extrinsic fraud issues that clearly violated my constitutionally protected due process rights. Yet the May 26, 1976, Tr. Ex. 50, p. 283, shows my appointed defense attorney McLau—without my knowledge or knowing consent—requested by motion a hearing, then afterward petitioned for a writ of error on same grounds unbeknown to me he had previously made at another hearing on grounds "of systematic discrimination on account of age in selection of the grand juror" and on grounds "of systematic discrimination on account of age in the selection of the venire from which would be chosen the petit jury which would try me." On April 27, 1977, the Supreme Court of Virginia denied the writ of error (i.e., record no. 761548).

Moreover, appointed defense attorney, commonwealth's attorney and trial court pretrial rehearsed collusion/covenant's aforementioned April 27, 1977, frivolous jury selection rhetoric writ of error, severely prejudiced me afterward thwarted any available constitutional and/or state remedies owed my defense by virtue of violating Supreme Court of Virginia's Rules, Rule 1:1, which in pertinent part provides,

> **All final judgments, orders, and decrees, irrespective of terms of court, shall remain under the control of the trial court and subject to be modified, vacated, or suspended for twenty-one days after the date of entry, and no longer.**

If the aforesaid improper abrogation of my constitutionally protected appellate due process rights, appear cruel and unusual, then appointed trial attorney McLau's loyalty to aforesaid pretrial rehearsed collusion/covenant with state court officials to convict me at any cost soared into an all time, new counsel client breach of loyalty when he, without my knowledge or knowing consent, filed my first appeal as of right by way of a petition for writ of certiorari on same jury selection grounds above stated that was denied by the United States Supreme Court on November 10, 1977, no written opinions rendered.

Chapter 15

Trying to recall the days following the Circuit Court of Halifax County, commonwealth's attorney, and its court-appointed trial attorneys' pretrial rehearsed collusion covenant's confluence of madness is hard work after being farther immersed into my most holy faith in Jesus Christ of Nazareth's risen merits. It seems so long ago that the Circuit court judge Merid on July 26, 1976, so eagerly and easily concurred with the jurors' fifty-six-minute deliberation guilty verdict, which recommended that I, a (would-be) first-time felon under the circumstances, be committed to the Virginia Department of Corrections (VADOC, hereinafter) prison system to serve a sentence of life in prison for alleged rape, life in prison for abduction, seven years in prison for second count of abduction (alleged to have occurred simultaneously), and five years for use of a (unloaded) firearm in the commission of a felony said sentences to run consecutively.

Therefore, between September and November 1976, I was transported to Powhatan Correctional Center Receiving/Reception Unit, where I was stripped of my clothes, shoes, social security card, driver's license, money, and newly purchased hygienic items. Then given a bar of soap, face towel and body towel, and directed to what appear to have been a community of showerheads. Upon completion thereof my shower, someone dumped a gallon or so vinegar over top my entire body, then gave me a pair of jeans, blue shirt, undergarments, boots, and a tiny tube of cheap toothpaste with toothbrush.

Afterward, I was led to a cell with a blanket, sheet, pillow case, and pillow beneath my arm pit. Upon entering said cell, I observed an iron spring loaded bunk, one aluminum chair and steel bar studded window with a view into the backyard and recreation room of Powhatan Correctional Center (PCC, hereinafter), located at State Farm, Virginia. During the following weeks/months, PCC receiving unit administration with its medical staff, cause me to be processed through various medical examinations, including dental, psychiatric testing and physical, including my private body members.

Breakfast, lunch, and last meals was accomplished down stairs on the first floor in a huge day room where metal tables, when unfolded, became tables with a bench that seated approximately six inmates on either side. A correctional official would bang several times while yelling chow time! Afterward the official would hand release and open the cells on one side to allow those prisoners to come out, proceed down stairs to the day room, then single-filed through the makeshift chow line with metal tray, cup, spoon, and fork in hand. During this course of activity, fellow prisoners behind the service counter proceeded to place food into our trays. We were compelled to file into the metal one way in, one way out dining tables where we ate but could not leave until the row on your side of the table finished eating. If you were not being processed, you could help fold the makeshift dining tables, push same to its storage area. Then watch TV or play other table games until headcount at 12:00 or 5:00 p.m. At those times, we were required to return to the cell assigned.

One incident, no, two occurrences sorta stuck in my head from the aforesaid 1976 inductee-type processing experience. The first occurred when two inmates while on lockdown and inside their respective assigned cells and house on opposite sides of second tier exchanged verbal comments. The morning after, during breakfast, when we'd just filed into the make shift (i.e., death trap) dining benches/table. I had consume one bite of scrambled eggs when this fellow ran up, jumped upon the top of the table amid our trays with shank/makeshift sharp object in hand, headed after a prisoner who was trapped in one of the middle seats, but still managed to climb atop the table as he knocked trays into the air until he got himself free and out of his knife slinging pursuer's path. There was several correctional official present in that respective dining area.

    The other involved five singing ladies and a preacher who I later learned was the minister from Norfolk, Virginia, named Earnest. He came to preach Jesus the word of God to those of us who chose to go to that in-house program. Minister Earnest and those five African American sisters sang as they taught scripture for more than an hour that day, which was the lift I needed to solidify my newly accepted faith in the gospel redemptive message of the unselfish work wrought by Jesus Christ of Nazareth for myself and the world, both known as well as the unknown.

    During the several months that I passed through the above named reception receiving processing unit, I was assigned 110023 as my state ID number, as well as saw the foundation of PCC's upcoming C-4, housing unit completed. Plus, I beheld the first floor thereof laid, before I was transported to the state penitentiary located at 500 Spring Street, Richmond, Virginia. Upon our arrival, the transporting van pulled up inside the penitentiary barb-wired fence's gate enclosure/tomb entitled Sally Port. I was ordered out of the van, strip-searched, then loaded back into that van, where a door rolled up and said van drove us into the prison. In addition, I was approached by a corrections official at the junction between B building, commissary, and (i.e., prison's control center) back office, then escorted to the clothing room located beneath data services shop and the prison infirmary, where I was issued three pairs of jeans, three blue denim long sleeve shirts, three pair of white socks, T-shirts and undergarments, and one pair state boots that were placed in a white laundry bag. Came up from there with said bag on shoulder, made a right turn, with a brief pause at the back office window to learn my temporarily assigned A building cell number commonly known as dead head, the place most new arrivals and unemployed prisoners were housed. Some of those very small cells, adorned double bunks.

Later, I learned that before my arrival, many young Caucasian and African American lightweight prisoners were made victims of a form of extortion and rape targeting scam. At that time, I weighed approximately 134 pounds, but such captivity never entered my thoughts. Some of the fellows took the liberty to share with me that as a result of a successful law suit submitted by the caring family of one wealthy (i.e., influential) Caucasian victim of rape in the United States District Court for the Eastern District of Virginia, Richmond, Virginia, who ordered the double bunking there at the state penitentiary to halt.

After a few days pass, I signed up for Saturday and Sunday church services in the one hundred, plus seat elaborately maintained spacious chapel under the guidance of a scrupulous minister name Pastor Tom. Also, this same day I placed a job application at the data service shop located at the rear of the back office adjacent to the infirmary. In the meantime, I took on a custodial job, maintaining two of the four tier floors in A building. But within two weeks, I was placed on data service shop's incentive pay role and assigned one of the lead computer verify/operator, positions. The said job consisted of typing paper recorded data—other information from cobalt documents, also extracting IBM financial card data, verifying and checking/correcting other operators' completed work, then preserved same on the 2400 key disk reel computer system provided by the corporation based in New York, yet operating within the penitentiary via Department of Corrections Division of Enterprises and Agriculture, data service shop...

I attribute acquiring the job with the data service shop so quickly to my favor with God, also as a result of having engaged and completed the business course offered during my junior and senior years at Dunbar High School, located in Lexington, North Carolina, under guidance of a superb teacher, Mrs. LG. Suddenly, it is 1977, when I became acutely aware that this was not a dream/nightmare.

I was in fact locked up away from family, my job, and friends. Therewith, I began domiciling at the state penitentiary under the auspices of Commonwealth of Virginia Title 53.1-Prison, Parole and Release Articles Code of Virginia Section 53-251, 53-252, 53-253, 53-238, 53-220, 53-213, 53.1-196, and 53.1-197 (as amended, 1950). Legislative Statutes which provided me opportunity beginning 1976 to participate in Virginia Department of Corrections (VADOC, hereinafter) good conduct time/extraordinary good time system to earn extra days off my sentences toward becoming parole eligible, as well as days off my maximum term of confinement, as a result my good behavior record.

Not many days after I began work in the VADOC Data Service Shop, I was summoned to the inmate treatment center by my assigned institutional counselor Ms. Ban, who advised me to move across the yard to cell 134 on second tier in B building, one of the units that housed its penitentiary workforce.

Meanwhile, I began to settle in at the state penitentiary on the street side of B building in (i.e., temporarily) assigned single cell 134 between inmate…the preacher in 135 and jazz musician in 133-a major saxophone player. Not without incident or being tested. However, during the course of arranging the cell, a young black prisoner appeared at my assigned cell door, asking whether or not I had any coffee.

Wow! I thought. Then I asked him where did I know him from or he, me? Because at the time, I had not yet fully put into practice (i.e., there in the actual prison setting, arena) my Creator's principles, concerning love thy penitentiary neighbor. Therefore, my reply was yes! But what made you think I should give you my coffee? An answer that was predicated upon various rumors and suspicions I had heard voiced by inmates housed in PCC Receiving Unit of how certain groups of scam artist deceptively trap the unsuspecting new arrivals into debt for the purpose of extorting. While the aforementioned was not the Redeemer's prescribed course of action. It thwarted that particular coffee seeker from approaching me again. However, that night, there in my prayer closet, I asked God to forgive me if I'd offended that prisoner or him.

J.D.

The following days, I made every effort to digest and apply Jesus's love directives in my association with others. In the data service shop, huge dining room, church congregation assembly, on the yard, commissary line, entering and exiting my temporal cell house unit, and with my four known, at liberty children, associates, and friends, many of who did not embrace the King James Version's biblical Holy Spirit formulas. Still, the love and compassion wherewith God's Spirit had begun instilling within my inner man compelled me to become father to my sixteen-year-old sons Gene Perry Kindle and Vernom, fifteen-year-old daughter Latonya, and youngest four-year-old son Tony J. Matthews, as well as a real caring younger brother to Robert Simpson Jr., my father's firstborn. Here, I must candidly admit that my older sister and I were always inseparable. Also, there in data service shop, I befriended Jerry, the data service shop architect and gospel song writer/singer musician, guitar player; John (a.k.a. Corn Bread); Mike; Eddie; Roy; Little Jim, the drummer/key board player; and a host of others who fellowship together daily during shop related work, also in the sleeping quarters, church services, plus during frequent weekly Bible studies conducted in my assigned cell as well as in other named brothers' quarters.

I made effort again and again while interacting with others to make distinct difference in all souls as the Spirit of the ONLY TRUE LIVING GOD, via Jesus's risen merits caused me to win confidence of staff members and those within the circle of Christ's influence through me. In that, I'm confident the circumstances I'd become surrounded by was employed by the Holy Spirit to both reveal and teach me other vitally important virtues, among which was also the "virtue" of how to accept and help other people achieve more peaceful spirits/attitudes. In addition, one particular aspect the WORD of God prompted me to adopt in route to promoting harmony among my own children, siblings, neighbors, young and aged people is to learn to communicate with each other. Furthermore, I claim to derive at the aforesaid view after I became more obedient to God's inspired written instructions (KJV) together with the practice of making my decision making faculties more sensitive and readily subjected to the still small voice of God (see the Old Testament book entitled 1 Kings 19:12; Exodus 30:21, which some others mistakenly refer to it as their conscience) instructing me (us) to thrust head-on into the aforementioned communicative adventure.

At the same time, it is my humble opinion that words are the instruments—the necessary tools by which both children, teenagers, and aged people communicate and cultivate ideas, and in my present and past experiences with associates having opposite views, there exist a strong inference which suggests that too frequently, we take this God-given asset for granted, and I suppose I can go so far as to say that only those who are familiar with the logical and critical study of the source and nature of human knowledge can be conversant of the mental phenomenon of the processing and amplification of one's ideas in fixing them in the mind and retaining them for regular contemplation and usage.

And I emphasis the fact that Jesus was and remains the grand master of the aforesaid application, as His words declare in every day simple childlike terms the TRUTH that is to say, biblical concepts so they in effect literally gripped young and aged persons' mind (i.e., stirred) stimulates their conscience and made them listen to be sure. There were those as it is today who remain stubborn, adhering to the same concepts of nonyielding opinions. Notwithstanding, Jesus's words still moved them in some manner either to follow his guidance and love unquestionably or to hate Him without a cause. Amen!

Further, I've tried to seize practically every available opportunity to communicate and discuss at length various everyday interests with my own children, other family, friends and prison neighbors, who, during the process, God used to grow me spiritually and developed my self-discipline…

In the midst, thanks be to my Lord and Savior Jesus Christ, I became a quick study among the nine, sometimes ten inmates assigned to work in the penitentiary data service shop. Six guys extracted and typed/entered the information into the computer system while others and myself followed up to verify and ensure the accuracy thereof. This work oftentimes contain admixture of word

J.D.

and numerical information. In no time at all, I was generating eight hundred thousand to one million plus accurate key strokes monthly. Moreover, the verified work netted me more than one hundred to two hundred dollars per pay period/monthly.

I join the choir of approximately eight to ten members, as well as the Babes in Christ National Ministries under the direction of the reverend James C., who also ran a theology seminar school class at the penitentiary the first! Oftentimes, he lived broadcast the Sabbath ongoing ministry held in the chapel after 5:00 p.m. every Saturday. Eight participating inmates signed up for extensive historical and Bible study in route to achieving certified minister and ordination license, with authority to teach and publicly proclaim the Gospel of Jesus Christ, my Lord and Redeemer's salvation message. I likewise enrolled, amen! As well as I involved myself in the Ephesus Seventh Day Adventist Church every other Sabbath/Saturday service and rejoiced to sing with Cecil's choir from 10:00 a.m. through 1:45 a.m. every Sunday morning—the first day of the week. This was a healthy and important environment, wherewith God more firmly established my future direction in Jesus Christ the Lord and Savior of my life. I was actually living out the inspired Words, which the Holy spirit gave the Apostle Paul to pen in the King James Bible version of the New Testament book entitled 1 Corinthians 1:26–29 that I quote verbatim:

> **For you see your calling, brethren, how that not many wise men after the flesh, not many mighty, not many noble, are called: But God have chosen the foolish things of the world to confound the wise; and God have chosen the weak things of the world to confound the things which are mighty; And base things of the world, and things which are despised, have God chosen, yes, and things which are not, to bring to naught things that are: That no flesh should glory in His presence.**

THE JOURNEY

With the aforesaid knowledge, from time to time I was given the usher's task during Bible studies conducted by Sister Gay, a twelve-string box guitar gospel player/singer and her husband brother Glass on Wednesday nights. While standing on this post, many scripture texts was repeatedly rehearsed in my mind. On one particular Wednesday night, quite a number of unbelievers adorn seats at the rear of the chapel. One inmate came forward to participate in the large prayer circle, where we kneel alone side sister Gay and her husband's hands joined to signify unity in our faith in Jesus's risen merits. Once we finished singing, praising and offering prayer to God, we stood for closing remarks. At that time, Sister Gay advised us that the unbeliever inmate in attendance had in appropriately touched her knee. There, being one of the on duty ushers, in my spirit, I asked God for the proper course of action to be taken under said circumstances.

The first thing came into my mind was the gospel of John 4, where Jesus interacted with the Samaritan woman, concerning Jews having no dealings with the Samaritans. Jesus unveiled the living water (i.e., the Word of God that will stand forever). Specifically, verse 24, says, "God is a spirit and they that worship Him must worship Him in spirit and in TRUTH." The revelation that adherence to this TRUTH, walking in it, then and there, thoughts rapidly raced through my mind as being essential to how the decision I'd make in line with God's reveal will and plans. Thus, I thought God would certainly have the violating man (who had now posted himself at the bottom of the two-tier descending exit chapel stair casing) to come to the knowledge of the truth (i.e., New Testament book entitle 1 Timothy 2:4 KJV).

At this junction, I walked to the top of the staircase and asked the violator for a moment of his time, then advised him that it was improper/wrong for him to physically inappropriately touch one of our fellowship outside guest, and that he needed to exit the chapel (i.e., perceiving he had paused to carry out yet another misdeed against our guest during their departure). Other ushers came to support this somewhat stout! Rebuke. The violator during his exit turned to vehemently invite me for an under the crying line (i.e., tunnel a.m. breakfast confrontation).

I being somewhat green (a novice prisoner), did not know the ill intent purposed by the unbelieving violator, kept it in my heart with God. The following morning, just after breakfast, in route to my assigned data processing job. I must need walk through the crying line tunnel. As I did, about forty feet away before me was the violator being wheel chair carried up the walkway, who upon espying me, bowed his head into his chest region. I immediately began to pray, asking God's forgiveness for the man who purposed to wrongfully harm me, not knowing from what or who said thoughts emanated (i.e., Satan). I call to mind the holy prophet David, speaking by inspiration in the Old Testament book entitled 1 Chronicles 16:22, recording that the ONLY TRUE LIVING GOD, said, "Touch not mine anointed, and do my prophets no harm." You might want also to review the New Testament book entitled John 2:13–16.

The aforementioned scenario provided me additional assurance that I was in the posture of those who make concerted effort to conduct themselves in conformity with God's word and the actual results of their course of action testify to the fact they are in God's reveal will, plan, and purpose.

What is more! Reader, wouldn't you agree that the Christ alike congregation, including ushers is supposed to serve as an example of the TRUTH wrap in human flesh, preserving the purity thereof as we parade Its bloodstain banner (i.e., please take a minute to take your KJV of the Bible in-hand and review the New Testament book entitled Acts 26:16–18 and 1 Timothy 3:5). For this reason, it becomes especially important that those entrusted with oversight in the congregation be able to apply "the WORD of TRUTH," a right.

In light of the fact that proper employment of God's Word enables said vessel to combat false teaching, both in the congregation as well as abroad, communicating with "those not favorably disposed." As perhaps God may give them repentance leading to an accurate understanding of that which is TRUTH. Now with the truth in heart, I began anew to distant myself from many secular activities, with exception to a few selective movies. Recalling well, I revisit the theater weekend, where movies were shown accompanied by "Corn Bread" Bro John. We entered the dining room, which was quite full with fellow convicts, and found seats directly in front of the huge screen that lowered down between the two entrance/exit dining room doors. But no sooner than we sat down, and the lights dimmed, a prisoner wearing a long dark coat came through the left entrance door. He walked past me, then turned himself about, and suddenly attacked the inmate sitting directly in front of John Red and I. With some sort of weapon, he started to repeat stab the fellow there in front us. Instantly, Corn Bread and I got up and departed the dining room, never to frequent the movie call again.

Other good news is that my counselor began awarding me ten days good time monthly, for every twenty days served without violating any posted written rule or regulation to be applied for the purpose of determining my eligibility for parole consideration. Plus, credit toward reducing my total term of confinement as provided by commonwealth of Virginia Title 53.1-Prison, Parole & Release, Articles Code of Virginia, Sections 53.1-196 & 97; plus 53-213, and 53-220 via 53.1-32(A)(as Amended 1950). Old law statutes in place, incident to my November 10, 1975, commitment to commonwealth of Virginia lock-up system, and July 26, 1976, commitment to VADOC, to govern my domiciling, under Virginia's first time felon statute.

John, Eddie, and a few others spent some leisure time on the ball park, and/or in the gymnasium atop of the chair factory on the fourth floor overlooking the interstate highway. Plus, we enjoyed percolated coffee from my eight cup coffee percolator during our Wednesday night Bible studies conducted in various cells. And with the data service monthly pay practically reaching a couple hundred dollars monthly, I became able to send my children monthly allowances.

Shortly thereafter, B building's security booth officer instructed me to report to the back office. Once there, a sergeant in a white shirt asked me to sign the legal mail log ledger for a parcel from

McLau and McLau, law firm, located in Halifax, Virginia, my former appointed less-than-loyal trial lawyer. Upon reading the brief letter's content, it was observed that McLau had struck another severe blow by having filed a petition for a writ of certiorari (without my knowledge or consent) on bases of systematic discrimination on account of age in selection of the grand jury and on grounds of systematic discrimination on account of age in the selection of the venire from which would be chosen the petit jury, which would try me. This, but not the abovesaid writ of error, constituted my first appeal as of right, (being frivolously) to use up the United States Supreme Court avenue of appeal whose November 10, 1977, denial order confirms. See Case No. 77-5152 cited *John David Simpson v. Virginia*. Why? I suppose the answer is to remain KKK loyal to his pretrial rehearsed collusion covenant relationship with the commonwealth's attorney and trial court to falsely convict me for a crime, I did not and could not have committed. Then and there, he completely abrogated any and all available appellate remedies, by which I had to challenge those officials' mock trial sham collusion scheme wrongful convictions was my thoughts at that time.

In addition to McLau's above cover letter correspondence was the glaring invitation which practically insisted on filing a petition for a writ of habeas corpus, and although I was unaware of the devastating damage done to me, and/or the future adjudication of my substantial due process and constitutionally protected liberty interest set out above, throughout this book. I politely declined McLau's offer, then ask him to send me all of the December 12, 1975, grand jury indictment transcribed records, plus any transcript involving my March 3 through May 26, 1976, extended trial.

Almost miraculously, within thirty days, I via US Postal Services received over eight hundred pages of the aforesaid transcribed records, some of which are highlighted above throughout this book. Howbeit, neither McLau, the appointed trial attorney, commonwealth's attorneys Bled and Ben, or trial court judge could've ever imagine, what is taking place today herein this book of full truth disclosure about that mock trial. The official acts of commission and omission of high court officials charged with the sworn duty to uphold my constitutional rights during trial and behind closed doors, as well as in the judge's chamber and/or at the bench out-of-jurors/and my hearing, in the Circuit Court of Halifax County, Virginia, being revealed to you the tax paying voter public, my jury today, some forty-six or so years after.

In light of the above scenario, my older (now) decease Sister Lucile and our god-fearing (also, deceased) Grandmother Janie L. Boone, hired attorney Tom Sur a prominent successful North Caroline lawyer, with home office located in Lexington. At that time, I was unable in knowledge and/or the science of law to recognize the additional inherent impairment that the aforesaid Virginia Court official's collusion/covenant practices had inserted into extending. To wit, enlarging of my indictment and trial records, in excess of eight hundred plus pages.

The said impairment intent became evident after I via postal services certified return receipt mailed the abovesaid court-documented records to Lucile, my sister for copying, who also conveyed copies thereof to lawyer Tom Sur upon his request. Sur's silence for almost one year necessarily piqued my sister Lucile's concern regard progress, sufficient enough to prompt her to contact lawyer Sur with progress update queries.

After several exchange communications with my sister Lucile, who conveyed to me that counselor Sur's answers became seasoned with a flare of rage eluding to suggestions that she (we) oughta be more thankful that he took on her brother's case. Thereafter, my sister reaffirmed her business points of discussion regard progress inquiry…When an impasse seemed to develop, I was informed via telephone. At which time I decided that prudence counseled to provide lawyer Sur additional perusal space, particularly considering the volume of the court documents relied on to provide resolution to my false incarceration…

Meanwhile, as a result of regular participation in the Seventh Day Adventists' Saturday Services, plus attending the Reverend James C. Sabbath Bible seminar classes. My spiritual and mental understanding became broadened as I begun to learn that those precious Holy Spirit inspired words embodied throughout both the Old and New Testament King James Version of the Bible are not simply standards to be obtained by one's own striving, but the description of a life conformed to the character of my Lord and Savior Jesus Christ. The life must become doctrine in work clothes. Its TRUTH becomes actual reality.

What's is more I was learning that the church assembly congregational body is supposed to serve as a pillar and support of the TRUTH of the good news expressed in redemption; preserving the purity of the Truth, defending and upholding it (see New Testament book entitled 1 Timothy 3:15 KJV). For this reason, reader, it is especially important that those entrusted with oversight in the congregation, be able to handle the word of TRUTH all right in that the proper use of God's Word enables everyone to combat false teaching in the congregation. Plus instructs "those not favorably disposed," as perhaps God may give same, repentance, leading to an accurate knowledge of TRUTH and salvation.

Listen, both the abovesaid 1978 seminar course, plus experience taught that not everyone is qualified to do the above type of instructing or teaching in the congregation. Men who have bitter jealousy and/are contentious have no bases for bragging about their being qualified to teach. Their claim would be false. As the disciple James wrote in chapter 3, verse 13–14,

> **Who is a wise man and endued with knowledge among you? Let him show out of a good conversation his works with meekness of wisdom. But if you have bitter envying and strife in your hearts, glory not, and lie not against the Truth.**

For members of the Christian congregation to be "a pillar and a supporter of the Truth," the members thereof must, through good conduct manifest the truth in its personal lives, says Father Paul in the

New Testament book entitled Ephesians 5:9–10. Our personal lives must be consistent and undeviating in right conduct, as if "girded about with TRUTH."

Besides, when emphasizing the need to keep the Christian congregation pure from lawless persons, the apostle Paul wrote as he was prompted by the Holy Spirit, purge out therefore the old leaven that you may be a new lump, as you are unleavened. For even Christ our pass over is sacrificed for us; therefore, let us keep the feast, not with old leaven, neither with leaven of malice and wickedness; but with unleavened bread of sincerity and truth. (See New Testament book entitled 1 Corinthians 5:7–8.) Consequently, reader, I'm learning that everything that a Christian does should be grounded in TRUTH. But not to earn or deserve Christ's salvation because that is by the ONLY TRUE LIVING GOD's grace. Yet I so chasten my flesh because I love God and desire to bring smiles on His face as he bless my later end more than before I came to the knowledge of the Truth. As I reflect back to the leadership of the first Baptist church I attended at age seven to eight, plus looking at the multiple of denominations established in Christendom (so-called) today. The preservation of Truth's purity is not the case. Falsehoods, illicit modern paganism celebrations, sun worship, immorality, involvement in command politics, the military and other gross conducts permeates almost the whole of Christendom.

Not long after eight other inmates and I were licensed to preach and teach Christ's good news, John (a.k.a. Corn Bread) filed a one page pleading upon yellow long paper to the United States District Court For the Eastern District of Virginia, alleging he was denied the effective assistance of counsel because the jury found him guilty of strong-arm robbery but made such finding in ignorance of the withheld evidence. If the jury had known that his six-foot tall codefendant had been identified as the robber. They might well have doubted the testimony of the by-standing witness who said it was John. Trial counselor did not make the height distinction difference given by the alleged victim. The excluded testimony tended to show John's innocence, plus trial counselor's ineffectiveness, violated his right to effective assistance of counsel and the due process of law. Judge Robert issued an order directing the State Court to grant John a new trial within thirty days, or release him. Corn Bread was released from the State Penitentiary because Judge Robert, obeyed the Supreme Court of the United States 1945 established precedent's determined in the case of *Hawk v. Olson* that in pertinent part, held,

> **As no response was filed or evidence received in the district court, we accept as true all well-pleaded allegations of the petition and, in the exercise of the duty which lies on us as well as the Nebraska courts to safeguard the federal constitutional rights of petitioner, examine for ourselves whether under the facts stated the petitioner is now entitled to a hearing on the claim violation of the due process clause in his conviction for murder in the first degree, citing cases.**

It was difficult seeing Brother John pack and depart as the officials there at times referred to us as the clergy, because the term delegates was rendered ineffective, due to the, shall we say, the uniform purpose that is the "target" for lack of a better term moves out of range. But on the other hand, when the minister can't be recognized because of a black suit and reversed collar, he is able to get on *on* target and sow the seed and present Jesus in every day simple terms, in His unpretentious, saving fashion. Thank you, Jesus! That had become the work for God had established us as undercover Agents, so to speak, in that he "slipped" us in unawares and before it was noticed there had been an effective ministry on the premises.

Brother John rejoined his wife and children in Gloucester and stayed in touch via US Postal Services. About that time, a young man named Michael joined our gospel singing group. Michael had a twenty-two-year sentence with a loving wife and several children, who he reveal! As he held down the tenor section in the group, and sorta longed to be physically connected with his wife and children. We became friends and he was found to be a man of integrity.

Then arose a unified work stoppage regard, then Warden Zarad. As best memory serves, I ventured out on the television and commissary yard, where other prisoners had resorted. And within approximately ten minutes, State Troopers had accessed and covered the entire fourteen feet or so high cat walk wall's over the ball park entrance, clad in shields, masks and what appear to have been automatic weapons aimed at those of us standing on the television/commissary yard. But suddenly, dark clouds appeared to instantly cover the entire area we occupied as God loosed such volumes of rain—as to literally drive the State Troopers off the wall and us inmates from the television yard. I have thanked God as I considered that merciful action to have been ordained by our Creator in accordance with his own divine will, plan, and purpose for all of our lives. Thank you, Jesus!

Near the end of 1978, I communicated my innocence plea to my Christian brothers, specifically Roy and Jerry. They suggested that I make a visit to the prison law library, located behind the chapel, whose entrance was accessible from the television yard. Upon entering the law library, an inmate named Bail listened intently to my complaint, although at that time, I knew nothing about the suppressed gonorrhea sperm that the commonwealth's attorney, trial court, and appointed trial lawyer admitted in chamber could not be connected to me. All I knew was that I did not commit said crime. Therefore, law library clerk Bail took a book from the shelves, escorted me to a room, and suggested that I read that book thoroughly. Also suggested that if questions arise, not to hesitate to ask him or the other clerk for assistance.

Quite frankly, this was not what I had envision. Nevertheless, I began reading said law book. Nothing made any cognizance impression on me, and after several hours passed, I returned the book with much thanks, then departed to my assigned cell, perked some coffee, pour some into my cup, added cream and a teaspoon of real sugar, and sat upon the bunk therein. I reached atop the locker and took my King James Version Bible in hand as I prayed asking God to bless my understanding, at the same time I put God in remembrance that He'd said, "I will never leave thee, or forsake thee." (See New Testament book entitled Hebrews 13:6 and Old Testament book entitled Deuteronomy 31:8). During that setting, I read above three hours until almost midnight, then fell asleep in peace. That week, inmate Al, a Caucasian printshop worker, accused of a sex crime against a minor girl, was brutally stabbed to death while showering. I do not recall whether or not anyone was ever found culpable for said crime.

Sometime between October and December 1978, my sister met again with the North Carolina attorney Tom Sum and determined that he should return the initial fee, plus all court documents without further delay: As a result, I received a brief letter from attorney Sum, which stated, "How could the alleged female victim's footprint be imprinted on my car rear window, when she testified she never removed her shoes or socks?" This fact alone indicated that lawyer Sum had done some fairly extensive reading of my March 3, 1976, trial records because the aforesaid footprint revelation was recorded on page 73 of that trial record, which shows that the eight hundred plus pages of indictment and trial court embolden transcribed records served to discourage any organization and Sum's firm from attempting to assist my unjust plight.

In the interim, a fellow prisoner whose name was Tyrone who was sometime found in attendance at the Seventh-Day Adventist Saturday evening Sabbath religious services. He struck up a communication chord with me and agreed to scan through my trial/indictment transcript in search of viable issues with which to form a criminal challenge to my false incarceration, brandishing glimmers of temporal hope for possibly getting my case overturned.

Ultimately, the still small voice of God put me in remembrance to not become anxious, instead to love my Lord without reservation as I make prayer requests for each situation throughout each day and night season. About this time, both Jerry, Jim, Mich, our pianist Rob (a.k.a. Ray Bob), and I were scheduled to sing in the Sabbath evening, plus First Day of the week Sunday morning services. But when I was preparing for work that Wednesday morning, my next door fellow prisoners were talking about someone had escaped who was housed in A building's work force side. Later, I learned that that inmate was Mic. The chapel services was canceled, and I resorted to my favorite thing to do—study the Holy Writ. For during this time, I, by choice, did not own a television or radio, as part of setting myself aside for the ONLY TRUE LIVING GOD via Jesus Christ's work of fishing for lost souls.

At the turn of the year, the prison employees in the data service shop heard that VADOC Enterprises had hired an ex-convict to its shops management staff by the name of Spirnk (i.e., Caucasian) who during the month of July 1979 entered the data service Shop and was introduced to those of us present. Mr. Spirnk plainly explained that there would be no more incentive pay bonuses. That everyone would be place on fifty to fifty-five cents an hour pay scales, with opportunity to gradually work upward to eighty cents. Everyone became enraged because Mr. Sprink's refused to answer questions as to why we was losing the long-standing incentive pay?

After Mr. Sprink exited the data service shop, the prisoners explained to the shop manager that they would petition him to permit us to begin a peaceful, brief work-stoppage, hopefully to cause Mr. Sprink's supervisor to grant an audience, in an effort to discover the reason for the abrupt incentive pay abrogation. The data service manager gave the nod to commence said work stoppage, although collectively everyone continue to report to work.

Over the weekend, I addressed a letter to the United States District Court For the Eastern District, Richmond Division, asking whether or not there exist any legal course of action under the grandfather clause, whereby the long standing incentive pay might be salvaged. This letter was deposited in the legal mail box sometime Sunday. When I came in from work Wednesday, the booth official instructed me to pack my property. Thursday morning, I was escorted to B basement, with no explanation, where I remained unable to summon my assigned counselor Ms. Ban or anyone with answers.

J.D.

Friday morning, one very hot day in July 1979, I was transported in a van and deposited at the Powhatan Correctional Center, State Farm, Virginia's front sally port outside holding cage with bag and baggage.

This epilogue is a descriptive note summary of the beginning or the work of full TRUTH disclosure above at the Halifax County Jail, Circuit Court of Halifax County, Powhatan Correctional Center reception and receiving unit, State Farm, Virginia, State Penitentiary, Richmond, Virginia. I've journeyed wheresoever the spirit of God directed my path with promised sequel detailing, commonwealth of Virginia Justice Court System's arbitrary withholding the benefit of Code of Virginia Section 8.01-428(D) State Rule and Federal Rule of Civil Procedure, Rule 60(b) law from me, denied equal protection of the law that it have applied to similarly situated criminal defendants after Virginia's twenty-one-day rule statute of limitations expired, in violation of the due process of law under United States Constitutional law embodied in Amendment 14, as well as Section 11 of the Constitution of Virginia and the reasons for my abrupt transfer to Powhatan Correctional Center State Farm, Virginia. Reader, stay connected…to the forthcoming sequel.

About the Author

JD Simpson (1942–to date) has forty-six-year long unlawful prison incarceration, together with being the only remaining third generation patriarch to four children (one deceased), sixteen grandchildren, eighteen great-grandchildren, and one great-great-grandchild. He does not want to die without revealing his earthly pilgrimage and God's transforming grace from within to them. The reader has been JD's, a novice writer, inspiration for writing The Journey, plus completing the coming sequel.